EASY HIKING
IN NORTHERN CALIFORNIA

FOGHORN OUTDOORS®

EASY HIKING
IN NORTHERN CALIFORNIA

Third Edition

Ann Marie Brown

AVALON
TRAVEL

FOGHORN OUTDOORS EASY HIKING IN NORTHERN CALIFORNIA

Third Edition

Ann Marie Brown

Text © 2004 by Ann Marie Brown.
All rights reserved.
Maps © 2004 by Avalon Travel Publishing.
All rights reserved.

Printing History
1st edition—1995
3rd edition—November 2004
5 4 3 2 1

Avalon Travel Publishing
An Imprint of
Avalon Publishing Group, Inc.

AVALON
publishing group incorporated

Some photos and illustrations are used by permission
and are the property of the original copyright owners.

ISBN: 1-56691-871-5
ISSN: 1085-4665

Editor: Grace Fujimoto
Series Manager: Marisa Solís
Acquisitions Editor: Rebecca K. Browning
Copy Editor: Kate Willis
Proofreader: Kay Elliott
Graphics Coordinator: Deborah Dutcher
Production Coordinator: Darren Alessi
Cover and Interior Designer: Darren Alessi
Map Editor: Olivia Solís
Cartographers: Mike Morgenfeld, Suzanne Service, Kat Kalamaras
Indexer: Laura Welcome

Front cover photo: McWay Creek, Big Sur © Lissa Funk/Alpine Aperture

Printed in the United States of America by Malloy

About the Author

© BILL RHOADES

The author of 12 outdoor guidebooks, Ann Marie Brown is a dedicated California outdoorswoman. She hikes, bikes, and camps more than 150 days each year in a committed effort to avoid routine, complacency, and getting a real job.

Ann Marie's work has appeared in *Sunset*, *VIA*, and *Backpacker* magazines. As a way of giving back a little of what she gets from her experiences in nature, she writes and edits for several environmental groups, including the Sierra Club and Natural Resources Defense Council. When not traipsing along a California trail, Ann Marie resides in her home near Yosemite National Park.

In addition to *Foghorn Outdoors Easy Hiking in Northern California*, Ann Marie's other guidebooks include:

Foghorn Outdoors 101 Great Hikes of the San Francisco Bay Area
Foghorn Outdoors 250 Great Hikes in California's National Parks
Foghorn Outdoors Bay Area Biking
Foghorn Outdoors California Hiking (with Tom Stienstra)
Foghorn Outdoors California Waterfalls
Foghorn Outdoors Easy Biking in Northern California
Foghorn Outdoors Easy Camping in Southern California
Foghorn Outdoors Easy Hiking in Southern California
Foghorn Outdoors Northern California Biking
Foghorn Outdoors Southern California Cabins & Cottages
Moon Handbooks Yosemite

For more information on these titles, visit Ann Marie's website at www.annmariebrown.com.

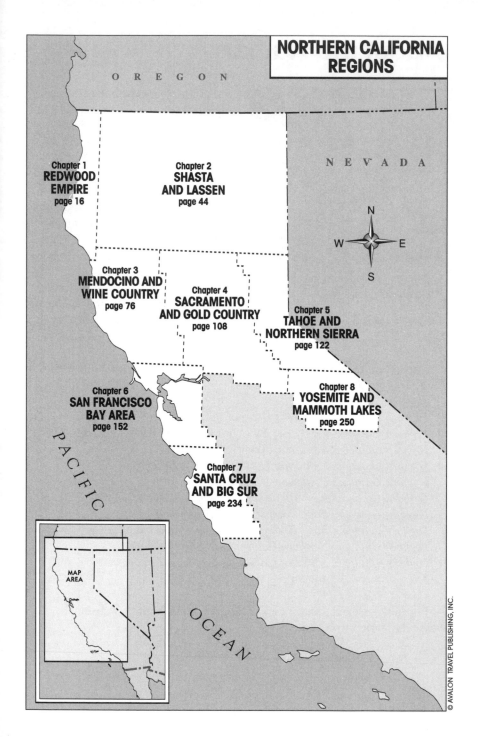

NORTHERN CALIFORNIA REGIONS

O R E G O N

N E V A D A

Chapter 1
REDWOOD EMPIRE
page 16

Chapter 2
SHASTA AND LASSEN
page 44

N
W—E
S

Chapter 3
MENDOCINO AND WINE COUNTRY
page 76

Chapter 4
SACRAMENTO AND GOLD COUNTRY
page 108

Chapter 5
TAHOE AND NORTHERN SIERRA
page 122

Chapter 6
SAN FRANCISCO BAY AREA
page 152

Chapter 8
YOSEMITE AND MAMMOTH LAKES
page 250

Chapter 7
SANTA CRUZ AND BIG SUR
page 234

P A C I F I C

O C E A N

MAP AREA

© AVALON TRAVEL PUBLISHING, INC.

Contents

How to Use This Book ix

About the Icons • About the Trail Descriptions • About the Maps

Introduction 2

Hiking Tips 3

What to Carry with You 3
About Hiking Boots 4
About Bears, Mountain Lions, and Snakes 5
About Ticks and Poison Oak 6
Getting Lost and Getting Found 7
Hiking with Kids 7
Protecting the Outdoors 8

Best Easy Hikes 9

5 Best Hikes with Toddlers .9
5 Best Waterfall Hikes 9
5 Best View Hikes 10
5 Best Hikes to See Wildlife 10
5 Best Coastal Hikes 10
5 Best Streamside Hikes 11
5 Best Lake Hikes 11
5 Best Hikes to Geologic Oddities 12

Chapter 1—Redwood Empire 13

Chapter 2—Shasta and Lassen 41
Chapter 3—Mendocino and Wine Country 73
Chapter 4—Sacramento and Gold Country 105
Chapter 5—Tahoe and Northern Sierra 119
Chapter 6—San Francisco Bay Area 149
Chapter 7—Santa Cruz and Big Sur 231
Chapter 8—Yosemite and Mammoth Lakes 247

Index 285

How to Use This Book

Foghorn Outdoors Easy Hiking in Northern California is divided into eight chapters that encompass the following geographical regions: Redwood Empire, Shasta and Lassen, Mendocino and Wine Country, Sacramento and Gold Country, Tahoe and Northern Sierra, San Francisco Bay Area, Santa Cruz and Big Sur, and Yosemite and Mammoth Lakes. Navigating this guide can be done easily in two ways:

1. If you know the general area you want to visit within one of the regions, turn to the map at the beginning of that chapter. This map shows by number all the hikes in that chapter. You can determine which hikes are in or near your destination by their corresponding numbers. Opposite the map is a table of contents listing each hike in the chapter by map number and page number. Turn to the corresponding page for the hike that interests you.

2. If you know the name of the specific trail you want to hike—or the name of the surrounding geographical area or nearby feature (town, national or state park or forest, lake, etc.)—look it up in the index and turn to the corresponding page.

About the Icons

Each trail has one or a series of icons provided at the top of the listing. These icons give you a snapshot of the trail's features, as follows:

 The trail visits a beach.

 The trail climbs to a high overlook with wide views.

 The trail passes through a special forest.

 The trail travels to a waterfall.

 The trail offers an opportunity for wildlife-watching.

 The trail features wildflower displays in spring.

The trail leads to a lake.

 The trail visits a historic site.

 Leashed dogs are permitted on the trail.

About the Trail Descriptions

At the top of each trail description, you find four pieces of key information:

Total distance—This is the total round-trip mileage for the hike.

Hiking time—This is the estimated time it will take to complete the hike. Remember that times may vary, and you may find that you require more or less time to complete each hike. Each of these trails was selected for its ease, but due to the variation in mileage, some hikes are easier and shorter than others.

Type of trail—This notes the kind of land you'll cover on the hike, such as mostly level terrain, rolling terrain, or some steep terrain.

Best season—This tells you the optimal time of year to hike each trail. In an area as diverse as Northern California, with its snow-covered mountain ranges, inland grasslands, and temperate coastline, it's smart to keep an eye on the calendar. That way, you'll have great hiking adventures year-round.

At the end of most trail descriptions, you'll find additional information under the heading Options. This section gives you some choices for other hikes in the same park or public land, or one nearby.

About the Maps

Each chapter in this book begins with a map of the region it covers. Every hike's starting point is noted by a number on the map. These points are placed as precisely as possible, but the scale of these maps often makes it difficult to pinpoint a hike's exact starting point. You may want to purchase a detailed map of the area, especially if it is new to you.

Our Commitment

We are committed to making *Foghorn Outdoors Easy Hiking in Northern California* the most accurate, thorough, and enjoyable hiking guide to the region. With this third edition you can rest assured that every hiking trail in this book has been carefully reviewed and accompanied by the most up-to-date information. Be aware that with the passing of time some of the fees listed herein may have changed, and trails may have closed unexpectedly. If you have a specific need or concern, it's best to call the location ahead of time.

If you would like to comment on the book, whether it's to suggest a trail we overlooked, or to let us know about any noteworthy experience—good or bad—that occurred while using *Foghorn Outdoors Easy Hiking in Northern California* as your guide, we would appreciate hearing from you. Please address correspondence to:

Foghorn Outdoors Easy Hiking in Northern California, third edition
Avalon Travel Publishing
1400 65th Street, Suite 250
Emeryville, CA 94608
email: atpfeedback@avalonpub.com
If you send us an email, please put "Easy Hiking in Northern California" in the subject line.

Introduction

© ANN MARIE BROWN

Introduction

I admit it; the idea for this book came from my own selfish perspective. Like so many of my friends and acquaintances, for years I had been working long hours in an office five or more days a week, putting in plenty of overtime and spending way too much time indoors. When I had time off, I tried to get out in the wilderness as much as possible, but with all of life's demands, I rarely had more than a free morning or afternoon to spend outside.

In response to the complexity and demands of my life, I decided to take up a weekly ritual: Every Sunday morning, no matter what else was happening, I would take a couple of hours to go for a walk in a beautiful outdoor place. I did this almost without fail for three years, only rarely missing a Sunday. It was during one of those walks that the idea for this book was born: a guide to great, easy hiking trails, for those of us who want to feel the peace of the wilderness but are short on time and also frequently short on energy.

What is great about the trails in this book is that they are suitable and fun for almost everybody. Bring along your children, your grandma, or your spouse who thinks the outdoors is all mosquitoes and poison oak. Every trail in this book was chosen because it offers a good payoff, a reason for going besides just for the exercise. These trails lead you away from the pavement, exhaust fumes, and crowds, to places where you'd rather be: sparkling waterfalls, scenic viewpoints, and peaceful forests. The best test for these trails is to try hiking one of them with someone who says they hate hiking, and just see if they don't have a good time.

To choose these hikes, I walked every trail in this book, some many times over. I also hiked plenty of other trails that didn't make the cut, often because they were too difficult or too dull to ensure that everybody would have fun. Sometimes I brought my less-than-enthusiastic-about-hiking friends with me. Sometimes I borrowed my friends' kids and took them along to see if they liked the hikes. Sometimes I met new friends on the trail—solitary female hikers, older hikers, hikers with babies in backpacks, hikers with dogs—and I asked them to suggest fun and easy trails.

What I found in researching this book is that there are plenty of Northern California trails designed for ordinary people, not just Mr. and Mrs. Hardcore Outdoors Enthusiast, and when people hike them, they feel good. It seems that fundamentally we aren't all that different from our canine companions, whom we call man's (and woman's) best friend. We seem to be happiest when we get to go for a good walk.

Hope to see you (and your children, grandmas, and spouses) out there.

Hiking Tips

What to Carry with You

1. Food and water

There's nothing like being hungry or thirsty to spoil a good time, or to make you anxious about getting back to the car. Even if you aren't the least bit hungry or thirsty when you park at the trailhead, you may feel completely different after 45 minutes or more of walking. A small daypack or fanny sack can keep you happily supplied with a quart or so of water and a few snacks. Always carry more than you think you'll need. If you don't bring your own water, make sure you carry a water filter or purifier so you can obtain water from a natural source, such as a stream or lake. Never, ever drink water from a natural source without first filtering, purifying, or boiling it. The risk to your health (from *Giardia lamblia* and other microorganisms) is too great.

2. Trail map

Get a current map of the park or public land you're visiting. Most of the trails featured in this book are thoroughly signed, but that isn't always enough to keep you on track. Signs get knocked down or disappear with alarming frequency, due to rain, wind, or park visitors looking for souvenirs. Also, signs will sometimes state the name of the trail you're walking on and sometimes state the name of a destination you're heading toward, but it isn't necessarily the information you need at that moment.

Maps are available from the managing agency of the place you're visiting. All their names and phone numbers are in this book. At state and national parks, you can usually pick up a map when you drive into the park entrance. If it costs a buck or so, pay it. At national parks, maps are included free with your entrance fee. For national forest lands, purchase maps at the ranger district offices noted for each trail, or order maps over the Internet at the Forest Service website: www.fs.fed.us/r5/maps/.

3. Extra clothing

On the trail, conditions can change at any time. Not only can the weather suddenly turn windy, foggy, or rainy, but your own body conditions also change: You'll perspire as you hike up a sunny hill, and then get chilled at the top of a windy ridge or when you head into shade. Always carry a lightweight jacket with you, preferably one that is waterproof and also wind resistant. Put it in your daypack or tie it around your waist. If your jacket isn't waterproof, pack along one of the $2, single-use rain ponchos that come in a package the size of a deck of cards (available at most drugstores and outdoor stores). If you can't part with two bucks, carry an extra-large garbage bag instead. If you need to, you can always poke a hole in the bottom of the bag, stick your head through, and stay dry.

If you are hiking in the mountains, carry gloves and a hat as well. You never know when you might need them.

4. Sunglasses and sunscreen
The dangers of the sun are well known. Wear both sunglasses and sunscreen, and/or a hat with a wide brim. Put on your sunscreen 30 minutes before you go outdoors so it has time to take effect, and don't forget about your lips. Coat them with lip balm with a high SPF to protect them.

5. Flashlight
Just in case your hike takes a little longer than you planned and darkness falls, bring at least one flashlight. Mini-flashlights are available everywhere, weigh almost nothing, and can save the day—or night. I especially like the tiny squeeze flashlights, about the shape and size of a quarter, which you can clip on to any key ring (the Photon Micro-Light is a popular brand). Since these flashlights are so small, carry two or three. That way you never have to worry about the batteries running out of juice.

6. First-aid kit and emergency supplies
Unless you're trained in first aid, nothing major is required here, but a few large and small adhesive bandages and moleskin for blisters, antibiotic ointment, ibuprofen, and an Ace bandage can be valuable tools. Also, if anyone in your party is allergic to bee stings or anything in the outdoors, carry their medication. If you are hiking where you might be bothered by mosquitoes, bring a small bottle of insect repellent.

For emergencies, always carry a Swiss Army-style pocket knife—one with several blades, a can opener, scissors, and tweezers on it. Matches in a waterproof container and a candle will ensure you can always build a fire if you need to. A whistle and small signal mirror can help you get found if you ever get lost. And if you know how to use a compass, carry one.

About Hiking Boots
Hiking boots are not always imperative for the trails in this book, but they can make your experience a lot more pleasant. Hiking boots offer more foot and ankle protection than running or athletic shoes (or most other types of footwear), and they provide better traction and grip on a rocky, wet, or muddy trail. These days, you'll find lots of lightweight hiking boots on the market. They feel as comfortable as your old tennis shoes, but offer much more protection for your feet and joints. Don't make the mistake of

purchasing heavy, expensive mountaineering or backpacking boots if you are simply going for day hikes. You can buy a decent pair of lightweight boots for $60–100 or so. If you plan to hike even once a month, they're worth it. They'll last a long time.

If you have hiking boots, don't forget to treat them with a waterproofing spray. You'll need to re-treat them every few months, especially if you've been out in the rain.

About Bears, Mountain Lions, and Snakes

All three of these creatures deserve your respect, and it's good to know a little bit about them. Chances are high you will never see a mountain lion, but you just might run into a bear or a snake somewhere.

You'll only find bears in bear country. For the trails covered in this book, that's all of the Sierra Nevada and parts of the Redwood Empire and the Shasta/Lassen region. The only bears found in California are black bears (even though they are usually brown in color). They almost never harm human beings, but with their impressive size and strength, they can make your hair stand on end.

There's only one important thing to remember about bears: They love snacks. Any time you see a bear, it's almost guaranteed that he's looking for food, preferably something sweet. When you are camping, keep your food—and anything scented, including toiletry items that a bear might mistake for food—packed away in bear-proof containers. Get an update from the rangers in the park you're visiting about suitable bear precautions. You're most likely to see a bear in or near a campground; it's less common to encounter one on a trail. When you're hiking, bears will usually hear you coming and avoid you.

Mountain lions are almost everywhere in California, but they are very shy and secretive animals and thus, rarely seen. When they do show themselves, they get a lot of media attention. If you're hiking in an area where mountain lions or their tracks have been spotted, remember to keep your children close to you on the trail and your dog leashed. If you see a mountain lion, it will most likely vanish into the landscape as soon as it notices you. If it doesn't, make yourself appear as large and aggressive as possible. Raise your arms, open your jacket, wave a big stick, and speak loudly and firmly or shout. If you have children with you, pick them up off the ground, but try to do so without crouching down or leaning over. (Crouching makes you appear smaller and more submissive, like prey.) Don't turn your back on the cat or run from it, but rather back away slowly and deliberately, always retaining your aggressive pose and continuing to speak loudly.

Rattlesnakes live where it's warm, and usually at elevations below 6,000 feet. If you see one, give it plenty of space to get away without feeling threatened. If you're hiking on a nice day, when rattlesnakes are often out sunning themselves, keep your eyes open for them so you don't step on one. Be especially on the lookout for rattlesnakes in the spring, when they leave their winter burrows and come out in the sun. They tend to prefer rocky, exposed areas. Although rattlesnake bites are painful, they are very rarely fatal. In the rare event that you should get bitten by a rattlesnake, your car key—and the nearest telephone—are your best first aid. Don't panic or run, which can speed the circulation of venom through your system. Call 911 as soon as you can, or drive to the nearest hospital.

Except for a handful of rattlesnake species, all other California snakes are not poisonous. Just give them room to slither by.

About Ticks and Poison Oak

Most hikers would say that these two are far worse than a whole convention of bears, mountain lions, and snakes. But you can avoid them with a little common sense. The easiest way to stay clear of ticks is to wear long pants and long sleeves when you hike. But if it's too hot to be covered up, don't worry. Just make sure you check yourself thoroughly when you leave the trail, and remove anything that's crawling on you. Check your clothes, and also your skin underneath. A good friend can be a useful assistant in this endeavor.

If you find a tick on your skin, remember that the larger brown ones are harmless. It's the tiny brown-black ones that are deer ticks and can possibly carry Lyme disease. Deer ticks about as small as the tip of a sharpened pencil. If you find a very small tick on you that's not crawling around, it's actually biting into your skin, do the following: Remove the tick very slowly and gently with tweezers or another tool, put it in a plastic bag, and take it to your doctor for examination to see if it is carrying Lyme disease.

Most tick bites cause a painful sting that will get your attention. But rarely, ticks will bite you without you noticing. If you've been in the outdoors, and then a few days or a week later you start to experience headaches, fever, nausea, or rashes, see a doctor immediately. Tell the doctor you are concerned about possible exposure to ticks and Lyme disease. Caught in its early stages, Lyme disease is easily treated with antibiotics.

If you stay on the trails when you hike, and if you perform tick checks faithfully after every trip outdoors, you should have few problems with ticks.

And as for poison oak, that old Boy Scout motto holds true: Leaves of three, let them be. If you can't readily identify poison oak, learn how. Poison oak disguises itself in different seasons. In spring and summer, when it's in full leaf, it looks somewhat like wild blackberry bushes. In late summer, its leaves turn bright red. But in winter, the plant loses all or most of its leaves and looks like clusters of bare sticks. Poison oak is poisonous year-round. To avoid it, stay on the trail and watch what you brush up against. If you're severely allergic to poison oak, wear long pants and long sleeves, and remove and wash your clothes immediately after hiking.

Getting Lost and Getting Found

If you're hiking with a family or group, make sure everybody knows to stay together. If anyone decides to split off from the group for any reason, make sure they have a trail map with them and know how to read it. Also, be sure that everyone in your group knows the key rules about what to do if they get lost:

- Whistle or shout loudly at regular intervals.
- "Hug" a tree, or a big rock or bush. Find a noticeable landmark, sit down next to it, and don't move. Continue to whistle or shout loudly. A lost person is easier to find if they stay in one place.

Hiking with Kids

Taking children along on a hiking trip can be immensely rewarding, for them and for you. That's the best scenario. In the worst scenario, hiking with kids can turn your day trip into a nightmare. Avoid the latter experience by following a few simple tips:

1. *Choose your trail wisely.* If you pick a trail that is too difficult for the age and ability level of your kids, no one will have fun. All of the trails in this book are rated "easy", but they aren't equally easy. If you have small children with you, a one- or two-mile hike will be challenging and time consuming enough (see Best Hikes for Toddlers suggestions on page 9). If your children are six years old or older, and eager to experience the outdoors, they can probably hike five or six miles round-trip quite comfortably. When in doubt, choose a shorter trail. If the kids are disappointed when the hike is over so quickly, choose a longer trail next time.

2. *Bring more snacks than you think you will need.* Adults burn a lot of calories while exercising, but kids burn even more. Offer them a variety of snacks—both salty and sweet—and don't forget to have them drink plenty of water. You'll have to carry most of the foodstuffs in your own pack, but also let your kids carry their own small day packs filled with snacks and a small bottle of water. Just make sure their packs are not too heavy.

3. *Let your child take the lead.* Kids love to be out in front on the trail. If you have more than one child with you, rotate leaders from time to time. Don't let anyone get too far out in front—or too far behind, either. For safety's sake, the entire group should always stay close together.

4. *Distract when necessary.* Remember that kids' attention spans are shorter than yours, and children are not always enthralled by the scenery and fresh air the way adults are. To keep your child interested and motivated on the trail, distract him or her by singing songs, making up games, or telling stories. If necessary, use the promise of snacks or rest stops as an impetus

for continuing up the trail (but make sure you deliver on the promise). Education also makes an excellent distraction, if it is accomplished in a fun, non-lecturing manner. Teach children about what they are seeing along the trail. Show them the difference between various types of conifer cones. Let them smell the scent of the Jeffrey pine's bark. Have them look for fish in streams or lakes, and birds in the high branches of trees.

5. *Have children keep a scrapbook of their outdoor experiences.* This could include feathers or leaves found along the trail, photographs taken on hiking trips, or a list of the birds or animals they have seen. At the same time, teach children that some things, like wildflowers and pine cones, should always be left where they are, and not taken home as souvenirs.

6. *Slow down.* Let your children determine the hiking pace, which may be a lot slower than you would like. Take plenty of stops for rests and snacks. If you don't make it to your chosen destination, who cares? With children, the joy is in the going, not in getting there.

7. *Set ground rules.* Teach children that hiking is fun, but that nature is no place for yelling loudly, running ahead of the group, or destroying plants or wildlife. Make these rules clear before you set out on the trail, so everyone understands what is acceptable. Children can easily learn respect for nature at an early age, but they must be taught.

8. *Offer praise, not nagging.* Give plenty of positive reinforcement when a child makes it up a hill or reaches a destination. The words, "Wow, you're a great hiker" go a long way with children. If your kids don't perform as well as you would like them to, keep it to yourself. The goal is to keep their feelings about outdoor adventures positive, so they will be willing to try again on the next trail.

Protecting the Outdoors

Take good care of this beautiful land you're hiking on. The basics are simple: Leave no trace of your visit. Pack out all your trash. Do your best not to disturb animal or plant life. Don't collect specimens of plants, wildlife, or even pine cones. Never, ever carve anything into the trunks of trees. If you're following a trail, don't cut the switchbacks. Leave everything in nature exactly as you found it, because each tiny piece has its place in the great scheme of things.

You can go the extra mile, too. Pick up any litter that you see on the trail. Teach your children to do this as well. Carry an extra bag to hold picked-up litter until you get to a trash receptacle, or just keep an empty pocket for that purpose in your day pack or fanny sack.

If you have the extra time or energy, join a trail organization in your area or spend some time volunteering in your local park. Anything you do to help this beautiful planet will be repaid to you, many times over.

Best Easy Hikes

Can't decide where to hike this weekend? Here are my picks for the best easy hikes in Northern California in the following categories:

5 Best Hikes with Toddlers

La Laguna Trail, Mendocino and Wine Country, p. 78. Kids will easily spot birds and wildlife as they stroll this level path around the edge of a freshwater lake.

Lily Lake & Fern Falls Trails, Tahoe and Northern Sierra, p. 131. Two short walks in Plumas National Forest let small children travel at their own speed and explore the woodland surroundings.

Sand Pond Interpretive Trail, Tahoe and Northern Sierra, p. 134. Kids are fascinated by cute, furry mammals, and they'll have fun searching for beavers and finding beaver evidence on this short interpretive trail.

Lagoon Trail, San Francisco Bay Area, p. 191. This easy walk alongside a bird-filled lagoon ends at the sandy shores of Rodeo Beach, a great place to look for semiprecious stones.

Davenport Beach Walk, Santa Cruz and Big Sur, p. 236. Follow a natural sandstone staircase to a windswept cove and let the toddlers play in the sand at Davenport Beach.

5 Best Waterfall Hikes

McCloud Falls Trail, Shasta and Lassen, p. 50. Three waterfalls on the McCloud River, plus an extraordinary view of Mount Shasta, can be seen on this easy, 3.5-mile hike.

Headwaters & Pacific Crest Trails, Shasta and Lassen, p. 56. Watch as 100 million gallons of water pour over a cliff on this loop hike to spectacular Burney Falls.

Fern Canyon & Falls Loop Trails, Mendocino and Wine Country, p. 88. The reward for this easy streamside walk near Mendocino is a close-up view of 36-foot Russian Gulch Falls as it plunges into a fern-filled, redwood-lined grotto.

Frazier Falls Trail, Tahoe and Northern Sierra, p. 132. This 178-foot-tall free fall is a showstopper in the early months of summer, and can be visited via a wheelchair-accessible trail.

Devils Postpile & Rainbow Falls, Yosemite and Mammoth Lakes, p. 277. Rainbow Falls, a voluminous 101-foot cataract on the San Joaquin River, is best seen in late morning or midday, when its namesake rainbow appears.

5 Best View Hikes

Rubicon Trail, Tahoe and Northern Sierra, p. 141. Stare down into the
crystal clear waters of Lake Tahoe from your high perch on the lakeside
Rubicon Trail.

Coastal & Matt Davis Trails, San Francisco Bay Area, p. 186. Wide coastal
views are yours for the taking from these trails on the upper slopes of
Mount Tamalpais.

Skyline Trail to Summit Rock, San Francisco Bay Area, p. 218. The whole
of the South Bay lies at your feet from the base of Summit Rock, one of
the most popular rock climbing sites in the Bay Area.

Sentinel Dome Trail, Yosemite and Mammoth Lakes, p. 264. Many consider
the view from 8,122-foot Sentinel Dome, which takes in five waterfalls plus
Half Dome and all its granite neighbors, to be the best in all of Yosemite.

Panorama Trail, Yosemite and Mammoth Lakes, p. 268. Walk right into a
picture-postcard view of Yosemite Valley and Tenaya Canyon on this trail
that starts at Yosemite's Glacier Point.

5 Best Hikes to See Wildlife

Fern Canyon Trail, Redwood Empire, p. 24. Sighting a herd of 1,000-
pound Roosevelt elk is a thrilling wildlife experience at Prairie Creek
Redwoods State Park.

Hookton Slough Trail, Redwood Empire, p. 36. September through March
is the best birding season at Hookton Slough on Humboldt Bay, when
more than 200 species of birds make a rest stop at this marsh.

Headlands Trail, Mendocino and Wine Country, p. 80. A 200-plus resident
population of harbor seals can be seen on this short walk at MacKerricher State Park.

Tomales Point Trail, San Francisco Bay Area, p. 154. You have a near
guarantee of seeing large herds of tule elk on this trail in northern Point
Reyes National Seashore.

Mark Twain Scenic Tufa Trail, Yosemite and Mammoth Lakes, p. 272.
Mono Lake is the birthplace of 85 percent of the gulls that live on the California coast, and also a popular spot for hundreds of migratory species.

5 Best Coastal Hikes

Yurok Loop & Coastal Trail, Redwood Empire, p. 22. This easy trail accesses
Hidden Beach, a classic Northern California stretch of sand complete with
jagged rocks, mighty waves, and driftwood of all shapes and sizes.

Rim Trail: Wedding Rock to Rocky Point, Redwood Empire, p. 34. This
trail at Patrick's Point State Park offers many opportunities to gaze at
the dramatic Trinidad coast and its 100-foot-high, cliff-like sea stacks
poking out of the swirling sea.

Headlands & Devil's Punchbowl Trails, Mendocino and Wine Country, p. 86. See blowholes and sea caves up close on this blufftop walk in Russian Gulch State Park.

Bluff Trail, Mendocino and Wine Country, p. 93. Time your trip for the spring wildflower bloom and pack a picnic lunch for this pleasant meander along the blufftops at Salt Point State Park.

Old Landing Cove Trail, Santa Cruz and Big Sur, p. 238. Hike along the tops of sandstone bluffs to a secret fern grotto hidden in the back of a sandy cove.

5 Best Streamside Hikes

Fern Canyon Trail, Redwood Empire, p. 24. You'll cross multiple bridges over Home Creek as you make your way between the fern-covered, tunnel-like walls of Fern Canyon.

Hat Creek Trail, Shasta and Lassen, p. 58. This hike travels smack in between two waterways—Hat Creek and the Pit River—and borders a big meadow filled with wildflowers and leafy oaks.

Kings Creek Falls, Shasta and Lassen, p. 65. This trail's destination waterfall is memorable, but even better is the walk to reach it alongside the rushing white water of Kings Creek.

Horsetail Falls Trail, Tahoe and Northern Sierra, p. 147. You won't actually reach the base of Horsetail Falls on this trail, but you will find many spots to linger alongside the rushing cascades of Pyramid Creek.

Devils Postpile & Rainbow Falls, Yosemite and Mammoth Lakes, p. 277. Stroll near the edge of the San Joaquin River and pass a geological phenomenon on the way to the river's 101-foot drop at Rainbow Falls.

5 Best Lake Hikes

Castle Lake Trail, Shasta and Lassen, p. 48. This hiking trail in Shasta-Trinity National Forest offers an easy walk to a spectacular lookout high above a granite-lined lake.

Terrace, Shadow, & Cliff Lakes, Shasta and Lassen, p. 67. Visit three picturesque lakes in one short walk in Lassen Volcanic National Park.

Smith Lake Trail, Tahoe and Northern Sierra, p. 129. A heart-pumping climb up and over a ridge brings you to this classically beautiful glacial lake in Plumas National Forest.

Lukens Lake Trail, Yosemite and Mammoth Lakes, p. 254. In early summer, the wildflowers at Lukens Lake will wow you, and in the later months, its warm waters are ideal for a swim.

Parker Lake Trail, Yosemite and Mammoth Lakes, p. 275. A streamside walk alongside fish-filled Parker Creek leads to postcard-perfect Parker Lake, set at the base of 12,861-foot Parker Peak.

5 Best Hikes to Geologic Oddities

Bumpass Hell Trail, Shasta and Lassen, p. 69. Bumpass Hell is geology in action—16 acres of boiling springs, hissing steam vents, noisy fumaroles, and bubbling mud pots.

Taft Point Trail, Yosemite and Mammoth Lakes, p. 266. It's a dizzying experience to stand 3,500 feet above Yosemite Valley at Taft Point and look straight down to the Valley floor.

Mark Twain Scenic Tufa Trail, Yosemite and Mammoth Lakes, p. 272. Mono Lake is one of the oldest lakes in North America at an estimated 700,000 years, and it's three times as salty as the ocean.

Devils Postpile & Rainbow Falls, Yosemite and Mammoth Lakes, p. 277. Visit a remarkable assemblage of volcanic rock columns made from lava that was forced up from the earth's core less than 100,000 years ago.

Hot Creek Geothermal Area Trail, Yosemite and Mammoth Lakes, p. 281. Hike to Hot Creek and you can admire azure, boiling-hot pools and soak in a more temperate natural hot spring while cold, river water flows past you.

Chapter 1

© ANN MARIE BROWN

Redwood Empire

Redwood Empire

Land of the tallest trees, dwelling place of the giants . . . the Redwood Empire is home to some of the largest remaining stands of old-growth *sequoia sempervirens,* or coast redwoods—magnificent trees that grow to more than 350 feet tall and live as long as 2,000 years. This is one of the most unique habitat areas in California, and in fact, the world.

It's these behemoth trees that attract visitors from around the globe to the Redwood Empire. Although the area boasts a rugged and beautiful coastline, quaint towns like Arcata and Trinidad, and wide, free-flowing rivers, the redwoods draw the visitors. Nowhere else in California can you gaze up at such an abundance of the world's tallest living things.

Although a redwood forest is considered to be a monosystem (an ecological system in which only one tree or plant species predominates), many other plants live alongside the big trees, including ferns of all kinds, vine maples, huckleberry, salmonberry, and redwood sorrel. Visitors frequently say they get the feeling these woods are "alive," and in fact, they are more alive than almost any other place on earth.

Per square inch of land surface, redwood forests have the greatest volume of living matter of any ecosystem in the world.

The Redwood Empire also features a wealth of wildlife, most notably its herds of giant Roosevelt elk. An adult male elk can weigh more than 1,000 pounds; its larger-than-life stature and huge antlers seem strangely appropriate among the giant redwoods. Black bears roam the redwood forests, searching for acorns and berries. Mountain lions and bobcats prefer the high grassland prairies, which are also good birding spots. The rivers and streams of the Redwood Empire, particularly the Smith and Klamath Rivers, are renowned for steelhead and salmon fishing.

No wonder these precious resources are preserved under the umbrella of Redwood National and State Parks, a co-managed park system that extends for 50 miles up the California coast and includes Redwood National Park, Jedediah Smith Redwoods State Park, Prairie Creek Redwoods State Park, and Del Norte Coast Redwoods State Park. Clearly this is land worth protecting. It's also land worth seeing for yourself. Don't forget your hiking boots, and also an impermeable layer for those infamous rainy and foggy days among the big trees.

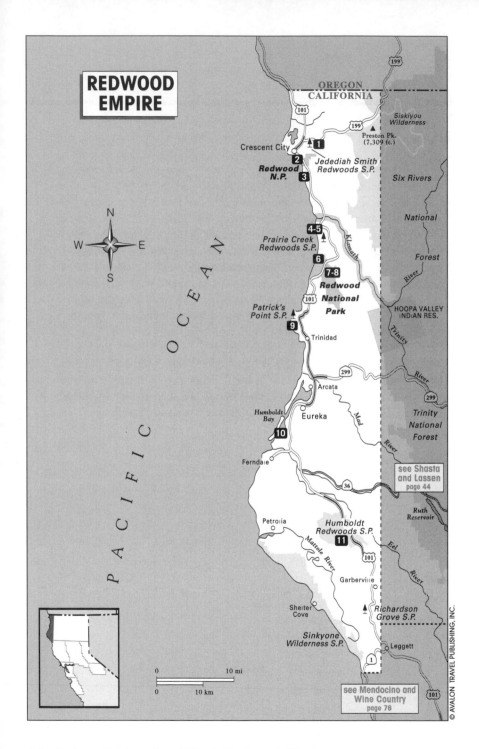

Contents

1. Simpson-Reed & Peterson Trails 18
2. Enderts Beach Trail 20
3. Yurok Loop & Coastal Trail. 22
4. Fern Canyon Trail 24
5. Brown Creek, Rhododendron, & South Fork Loop 26
6. Skunk Cabbage & Coastal Trail 28
7. Lady Bird Johnson Grove 30
8. Tall Trees Grove 31
9. Rim Trail: Wedding Rock to Rocky Point 34
10. Hookton Slough Trail 36
11. Big Tree Area: Bull Creek Flats Trail 38

1 SIMPSON-REED & PETERSON TRAILS
Jedediah Smith Redwoods State Park,
off U.S. 101 near Crescent City

Total distance: 0.75 mile round-trip

Type of trail: mostly level terrain

Hiking time: 30 minutes

Best season: year-round

If you haven't had much exposure to coast redwoods and their ecosystem, hiking in the forests of northwestern California can raise a lot of questions. This loop trail answers them, and provides a half hour of pleasant walking in the process. The Simpson-Reed Trail serves as an excellent introduction to the redwoods; the connecting Peterson Trail extends the trip by making a figure-eight loop.

Get out your notebooks and number two pencils. Here's the kind of information you'll gather on the Simpson-Reed Trail: California has two species of native redwoods, the coast redwood and Sierra redwood, or Sequoia. Sequoias grow wider and bulkier, but coast redwoods grow taller—as tall as 360 feet. They are the tallest living things on earth. Coast redwoods like fog and rain, and grow best at less than 2,000 feet in elevation. These giants can live for more than 2,000 years.

You'll also notice the many neighbors of the redwoods— including ferns of all kinds, vine maples, huckleberries, salmonberries, and redwood sorrel—as you walk the Simpson-Reed Trail, and learn how to identify them. Sorrel, for instance, has distinctive, clover-like leaves with purple undersides and pink flowers.

Other trees may grow in a redwood grove, including

Hikers lunch at the base of a giant redwood on the Simpson-Reed trail.

Douglas firs and maples. One of the redwood's most interesting cohabitants can be seen on this walk; it's a special type of tree nicknamed the "octopus tree." These are western hemlocks that have sprouted on the tops of redwood stumps, then grown over and around them, clutching the stumps in their roots or "legs." When the fallen redwood has finally rotted away, the hemlock remains standing on its long, thick roots.

An old-growth forest doesn't support an abundance of wildlife, but you may hear the sounds of busy woodpeckers drilling holes in trees with the precision of miniature jackhammers. The huge redwood stumps also make perfect nesting grounds for the spotted owl.

As you walk this redwood needle–lined path, you'll see firsthand how redwood trees reproduce and grow. Unlike other conifers, redwoods can sprout additional trunks as well as reproduce by seed. Often you'll see a circle of baby redwoods, called cathedral trees or fairy rings, surrounding an old redwood that has been fire-scarred or felled. The sprouts begin as dormant buds that are stored in burls, the large bumpy growths found near the base of the redwood. The dormant buds, or sprout seeds, are released during forest fires or as the tree gradually decays.

As you loop around to the east side of the Simpson-Reed Trail, be sure to take the connecting loop to the Peterson Trail. This .25-mile path shows off a riparian area with impressive big-leaf maples, skunk cabbage, and many charming footbridges over cascading streams.

Options

If you're seeking more big trees and a longer walk, head across the road to the trailhead for the Hatton Trail. Walk out-and-back on the 1.2-mile Hatton-Hiouchi Trail, which parallels the road, or just follow the .3-mile Hatton Loop Trail.

Information and Contact

A $6 day-use fee is charged per vehicle. An interpretive brochure is available at the trailhead. For more information, contact Jedediah Smith Redwoods State Park, 1375 Elk Valley Road, Crescent City, CA 95531, 707/464-6101 or 707/445-6547, website: www.parks.ca.gov.

Directions

From Crescent City, drive five miles north on U.S. 101, then turn east on U.S. 199. Drive just under three miles to mile marker 2.84. The Simpson-Reed Trailhead is on your left. Park in the gravel pullout alongside the road.

2 ENDERTS BEACH TRAIL

Redwood National Park, off U.S. 101 near Crescent City

Total distance: 1.8 miles round-trip

Hiking time: 1 hour

Type of trail: rolling terrain

Best season: year-round

The Enderts Beach Trail leads to a terrific stretch of beach with pristine sand and good tidepooling opportunities. The trail goes right past Nickel Creek Campground, an easy-to-reach backpacking camp that makes a great first-time overnight trip for families or couples.

The trip begins where Enderts Road ends near Crescent Beach Overlook, just a few miles south of Crescent City. The trail consists of an old abandoned road that has partially collapsed into the sea. Clearly Mother Nature isn't finished yet: you'll pass by an impressive landslide just a few yards from the parking area.

Most of the route is wide enough for hand-holding, and it's just a sim-

walking through trees covered with licorice ferns en route to Enderts Beach

ple downhill walk of .6 mile to a three-way trail junction. A short nature trail alongside Nickel Creek leads left, straight ahead is the Coastal Trail heading south, and to the right is the path to Nickel Creek Campground and Enderts Beach. Before you make a beeline for the beach, take a side trip on the .25-mile Nickel Creek Nature Trail, which passes by a grove of remarkable fern-covered trees. The ferns are licorice ferns, which grow high off the ground on tree branches and trunks. Alongside Nickel Creek they hang off tree limbs from every possible angle, looking like massive, leafy beehives on the trees. The trail ends abruptly at a viewing bench by the creek. Have a seat and remind yourself that you're in the northwest corner of California—this short stretch of trail is like a walk in the Florida Everglades.

From Nickel Creek, return to the junction and follow the opposite trail into Nickel Creek Campground. Check out its five campsites and make a plan for a future overnight trip, then take the right fork that leads uphill above the restroom. In a matter of minutes you reach a grassy bluff above a long, crescent-shaped beach. You can easily descend to the beach, or pick a high perch on the bluffs to survey the scene. Enderts Beach is rocky and driftwood-strewn, but it also has large sandy stretches where you can lay out your towel.

If you like exploring tidepools, consult your tide chart before you visit. During low tides, Enderts Beach has some excellent pools at its southern end. At certain times of the year, park rangers lead visitors on guided tidepool walks. Check with the ranger station in Crescent City for information on current dates and times.

Options
After visiting Enderts Beach, return to the junction before Nickel Creek Campground where the Coastal Trail heads south. Hike south on the Coastal Trail for as far as you like, passing through redwood, spruce, and red alder forests interspersed with open coastal bluffs. You'll have plenty of opportunities for bird-watching and photographing the coast.

Information and Contact
There is no fee. A free map is available from park headquarters or the Thomas H. Kuchel Visitor Center near Orick. For more information, contact Redwood National Park Headquarters, 1111 Second Street, Crescent City, CA 95531, 707/464-6101, website: www.nps.gov/redw.

Directions
From Crescent City, drive three miles south on U.S. 101 and turn right (south) on Enderts Beach Road. Drive 2.2 miles to the end of road. The trailhead parking lot is just beyond Crescent Beach Overlook.

🖪 YUROK LOOP & COASTAL TRAIL

Redwood National Park, off U.S. 101 near Crescent City

Total distance: 2.25 miles round-trip

Type of trail: rolling terrain

Hiking time: 1 hour

Best season: year-round

Everybody likes walking along a beach at the end of a day, watching the waves come in and the sun dip into the water. But few enjoy facing the gale-force winds that attack the coast on so many days in Northern California. That's what makes the semi-protected Yurok Loop a great little trail, especially when combined with a short section of the Coastal Trail that leads to spectacular Hidden Beach.

Begin hiking at the northwest end of the Lagoon Creek parking lot. You'll cross a bridge and then head north toward the ocean. The Yurok Loop is an interpretive trail with numbered posts keyed to its brochure, which is usually available from a box at the bridge. If you pick up a brochure, you'll learn about Yurok American Indian culture and their many uses of the land in this area. The trail itself is an ancient Yurok pathway leading south along the sea bluffs. It alternates through an oak and alder forest and open, grassy areas. What captures your attention are the views of driftwood-laden False Klamath Cove to the north and massive

Hidden Beach

False Klamath Rock to the west. At 209 feet tall, this huge rocky outcrop dwarfs all the other sea stacks in the area. The Yurok used to dig for the bulbs of *brodiaea* plants (called "Indian potatoes") by this rock.

Stay to the right when the trail forks at the sign for the Coastal Trail, saving the second part of the Yurok Loop for your return. Ramble along the Coastal Trail, a forested, fern-lined route. In .5 mile of mostly level walking, you'll meet up with the spur trail to Hidden Beach. Follow it to the right for 100 yards to reach a classic Northern California stretch of sand, complete with jagged rocks, mighty waves, and driftwood of all shapes and sizes. The beach is prime for watching the sunset. Bring a flashlight in case it gets dark sooner than you expect.

After visiting Hidden Beach, head back the way you came on the Coastal Trail. This time turn right and walk the other side of the Yurok Loop, descending through a tunnel-like canopy of alders.

When you return to the parking lot, be sure to explore around the freshwater pond on Lagoon Creek. It's covered with big yellow pond lilies and happy water birds, including ducks, egrets, and herons. The pond is also popular with trout fishermen.

Options

From Hidden Beach, you can continue south on the Coastal Trail. The path leads another three miles to Klamath Overlook.

Information and Contact

There is no fee. A free map is available from park headquarters or the Thomas H. Kuchel Visitor Center near Orick. For more information, contact Redwood National Park Headquarters, 1111 Second Street, Crescent City, CA 95531, 707/464-6101, website: www.nps.gov/redw.

Directions

From Crescent City, drive south on U.S. 101 for approximately 14 miles. Turn right at the sign for Lagoon Creek Fishing Access. The trail begins on the west (ocean) side of the parking lot. (Coming from the south, the trailhead is located six miles north of Klamath.)

4 FERN CANYON TRAIL
Prairie Creek Redwoods State Park, off U.S. 101 near Orick

Total distance: 0.75 mile round-trip

Type of trail: mostly level terrain

Hiking time: 30 minutes

Best season: year-round

When you hike the Fern Canyon Trail, the drive to the trailhead is part of the day's adventure. Unpaved Davison Road runs through the middle of the Elk Prairie section of Prairie Creek Redwoods State Park, home to a large herd of Roosevelt elk. You'll have several chances to see these enormous creatures, which have the distinction of being California's largest land animals. Some weigh nearly 1,000 pounds. Large groups of elk will frequently stand just a few feet from Davison Road, grazing on the roadside grasses. For the most part, they ignore park visitors. The elk are extremely docile, although you shouldn't mess with the bulls, especially during mating season.

But the wildlife is not the only excitement on a trip to Fern Canyon. Your destination is a secluded fern grotto—a hidden paradise of giant ferns growing on 50-foot-high rock walls on both sides of a forest

Roosevelt elk near the Fern Canyon Trail

stream. After driving the length of Davison Road, park at the Fern Canyon Trailhead, just steps away from beautiful Gold Bluffs Beach. Put on your waterproof hiking boots and start walking to your right, heading up the gravel streambed of Home Creek. You may or may not have to do some rock-hopping to get across the stream. From late spring through fall, park rangers make the hiking easy by installing small footbridges. In the rainy season, the creek runs with a fury, so the bridges are removed.

Make your way up the streambed, observing as the canyon walls grow taller and squeeze tighter. The going may be slow, but you won't mind in the slightest. Dense ferns line the canyon walls like wallpaper. Home Creek gushes near your feet. Miniature waterfalls pour down the rock walls. Moss grows everywhere, and combined with the multitude of ferns, the canyon feels like a rainforest. Green is the color of the day.

Look for the many frogs, salamanders, and newts that make their home in the canyon, including the rare Pacific giant salamander. If you're very lucky, you might spot the coastal cutthroat trout, which travels from the ocean in spring to lay its eggs in the gravel streambed. Practice your fern identification as you walk. An interpretive sign at the trailhead explains the identifying characteristics of various fern varieties, including sword, lady, five-finger, chain, and bracken ferns—up to eight different species, each waving delicately in the breeze.

Continue up the canyon for .5 mile until you reach a signed trail on the left that climbs out of the canyon on wooden stairsteps, then returns through the forest to the parking lot. This is a short section of the James Irvine Trail and the return leg of your loop. Follow it, or do what so many Fern Canyon visitors do: Just turn around and meander back out through the canyon. It's hard to resist seeing this place all over again.

Options
To extend the trip, turn right on the James Irvine Trail after you climb out of Fern Canyon. A mile or two out-and-back on this densely forested trail would be a fine addition to your day. Or, from the trailhead parking area, cross the access road and walk down to pristine, windswept Gold Bluffs Beach. Wander on the beach as far as you please.

Information and Contact
A $6 day-use fee is charged per vehicle. A trail map is available at the entrance kiosk. For more information, contact Prairie Creek Redwoods State Park, Orick, CA 95555, 707/464-6101 or 707/445-6547, website: www.parks.ca.gov.

Directions

From Eureka, drive north on U.S. 101 for 41 miles to Orick. Continue
north for 2.5 more miles to Davison Road, then turn left (west), and drive
seven miles to the Fern Canyon Trailhead. The access road is gravel and
may be rough; no trailers or motor homes are permitted.

5 BROWN CREEK, RHODODENDRON, & SOUTH FORK LOOP

Prairie Creek Redwoods State Park, off U.S. 101 near Orick

Total distance: 3.6 miles round-trip

Type of trail: rolling terrain

Hiking time: 2 hours

Best season: year-round

This loop trail through the redwoods may give you a neck ache. It leads
through a colossal old-growth forest in which you will walk with your head
raised, neck craned, and eyes gazing toward the sky. You won't be check-
ing for rain or gawking at skyscrapers—just gaping at big trees.

The loop is a combination of three trails: Brown Creek, Rhododendron,
and South Fork. Start walking from the South Fork trail sign, following
the South Fork Trail for .2 mile. Turn left on the Brown Creek Trail and
prepare your neck for a workout. The path leads through prime redwood
forest, complete with virgin groves and lots of old growth. It meanders
along a perfectly charming stream, which serves as the lifeblood for the
towering trees. You simply follow the creek, crossing it on a footbridge at
a half-mile out. Be sure to take one or more of the short spur trails that
lead to memorial groves and trees.

The size of the redwoods is truly inspiring. Try as you may, it's impossible to see their tops, which are as much as 300 feet off the ground. Often
the trees that make the greatest impression are the fallen giants lying on
the ground, toppled by centuries of weather. Their huge root balls look
like intricate sculpted knots, and their horizontal trunks serve as natural
planters for entire microcosms of ferns, moss, mushrooms, and sorrel.
Some of these tree trunks make such perfect garden boxes that you'll
wonder if Mother Nature hasn't hired elfin landscape architects to help
her do her work.

The Brown Creek Trail junctions with the Rhododendron Trail at 1.3 miles
from the start. Turn right to continue the loop. The path climbs a bit steeply,
then curves across the hillside, with views back down into the canyon. True

to the trail's name, bright pink rhododendrons are plentiful, adding splashes of vibrant color to the forest's myriad shades of green. The giant redwoods continue, although the forest gets drier and less dense as you climb.

At 2.5 miles, you'll meet up with the South Fork Trail. Turn right and finish out the loop with a switchback descent. Look for orange leopard lilies in the spring, growing as tall as five feet. They are mixed in with redwoods, huckleberries, and rhododendrons. As you lose elevation, you'll get a wider perspective on the big trees with views across the wooded slopes. When you reach the Brown Creek Trail again, turn left and follow the South Fork Trail for .2 mile back to your car. Now, how does your neck feel?

a redwood bridge in the redwood forest, Prairie Creek Redwoods State Park

Options

At the 2.5-mile mark, where Rhododendron Trail meets up with South Fork Trail, you can remain on Rhododendron Trail heading south for up to 2.5 miles more. Hike out and back, or extend your trip into a much longer loop by following Rhododendron Trail to Cathedral Trees Trail, turning right, and then following Cathedral Trees Trail and Foothill Trail back to the Brown Creek Trail/South Fork Trail junction. Make sure you bring along a map.

Information and Contact

A $6 day-use fee is charged per vehicle. A trail map is available at the entrance kiosk. For more information, contact Prairie Creek Redwoods State Park, Orick, CA 95555, 707/464-6101 or 707/445-6547, website: www.parks.ca.gov.

Directions

From Eureka, drive north on U.S. 101 for 41 miles to Orick. Continue
north for approximately five more miles, then take the Newton B. Drury
Scenic Parkway exit and turn left. Drive 2.6 miles to the parking pullout
near mileage marker 129. The trail is signed "South Fork Trail."

6 SKUNK CABBAGE & COASTAL TRAIL

Redwood National Park, off U.S. 101 near Orick

Total distance: 6.0 miles round-trip

Type of trail: rolling terrain

Hiking time: 2.5 hours

Best season: March–June

Sometimes it takes a while for the obvious to become apparent. My hiking
partner and I were walking on the Skunk Cabbage Trail, marveling at the
dense forest and especially the huge, leafy plants that grew on the ground
near every stream or spring. But we kept shaking our heads, puzzled by
the plants' identification. Neither one of us had a clue about what the
large-leafed foliage could be. It took almost three miles of hiking before
the light bulb in my brain turned on. "Hey! I bet these big leafy plants are
the trail's namesake—skunk cabbages!"

Indeed they were. The Skunk Cabbage Trail is a section of the Coastal
Trail in Redwood National Park. It leads deep into a lush, jungle-like alder
and spruce forest—so dense with foliage that you may think you've walked
onto the set of *Jurassic Park*. Then, without any advance notice, the trail
suddenly opens out to a wide stretch of coast at Gold Bluffs Beach.

The out-and-back trail is three miles each way, but with very little elevation change. The scenery will capture your imagination, particularly from
about a half mile in where the trail begins to follow Skunk Cabbage Creek.
Here you'll find the largest numbers of skunk cabbages growing near the
stream. They are vibrant green and as large as five feet across, with individual leaves growing a foot wide. The plants look something like cabbage
heads on steroids, but they are actually a relative of the corn lily. Spring is
the time to see them.

The skunk cabbages grow in dense clusters under a canopy of alders,
Sitka spruce, and occasional big redwoods. The white bark of the alders
shines bright white in the dimly lit forest. Where you don't see skunk cabbages, you'll see massive clumps of sword ferns and redwood sorrel. Your
trail weaves among all this foliage, crossing and re-crossing Skunk Cabbage Creek on wooden footbridges.

A hiker stands among the giant skunk cabbage.

After two delightful miles, the trail ceases its mostly level meandering and suddenly starts to climb. Leaving the creek behind, you continue up a ridge through a dense alder forest. (We saw probable bear evidence here in one stand of trees, where the bark on several alders had been torn to shreds as high as eight feet off the ground.) At 2.7 miles out, you round a curve in the trail, and—surprise—you're high on a bluff overlooking the ocean. It's quite startling to see the dense, terrarium-like forest end so abruptly at a broad expanse of open coastline.

Here, at a trail junction, you must make a choice: right is the continuation of the Coastal Trail that eventually leads to Gold Bluffs Beach, and left is a spur trail that beckons you to the beach directly below. Just a few yards west of this junction there is a fine view of the coast, and perhaps a spot to sit and have lunch. A descent of about 300 feet over .25 mile of moderate switchbacks will take you to the dune-like stretch of sand below. Once there, what will you find? Mussel Point, a rocky outcrop, lies about three-quarters of a mile to the south. Other than that, there's plenty of driftwood, sand verbena, and precious solitude.

Options

If you turn right at the junction at 2.7 miles, you can continue on the Coastal Trail all the way to Gold Bluffs Beach, 2.5 miles away.

Information and Contact

There is no fee. A free map is available from park headquarters or the Thomas H. Kuchel Visitor Center near Orick. For more information, contact Redwood National Park Headquarters, 1111 Second Street, Crescent City, CA 95531, 707/464-6101, website: www.nps.gov/redw.

Directions

From Eureka, drive north on U.S. 101 for 41 miles to Orick, then continue north for 1.1 mile. Just past the right turnoff for Bald Hills Road, take the left turnoff that is signed for the Skunk Cabbage Section of the Coastal Trail. Drive .5 mile down the road to the parking area and trailhead.

7 LADY BIRD JOHNSON GROVE
Redwood National Park, off U.S. 101 near Orick

Total distance: 1.0 mile round-trip

Type of trail: mostly level terrain

Hiking time: 30 minutes

Best season: year-round

It was on the Lady Bird Johnson Grove that I first had "The Redwood Experience." In case you've never felt it, it happens something like this: You are wandering among ancient redwood trees that are hundreds of feet tall. Perhaps the fog has moved in, casting eerie filtered shadows in the forest. Your footsteps begin to slow. You find yourself noticing the most minute details, like the dewdrops on the pink petals of a rhododendron, or the bark pattern on one square inch of a 300-foot-tall redwood tree. Your voice drops to a whisper; you walk very softly, almost on tiptoe. The redwood forest has wrapped you in its embrace, and you may never want to leave.

That's "The Redwood Experience." It has happened to many hikers on many trails in Redwood National Park. It's this kind of feeling that makes visitors return to the redwoods, year after year. The Lady Bird Johnson Grove is one of the easiest places to get a taste of it.

From the trailhead parking area, cross the sturdy bridge over Bald Hills Road to access the trail. The 300-acre Lady Bird Johnson Grove was named for President Lyndon Johnson's wife, who dedicated the park in 1969. President Johnson signed the bill that created Redwood National Park in 1968, protecting these trees for generations to come.

The trail through the redwoods is only one mile round-trip, but you may find it takes you a while to hike it. You'll want to stop to read the interpretive signs, which explain about the history of white men in the redwood region. Jedediah Smith first explored this area in 1828, and Josiah Greg took the first recorded measurements of the redwood trees in 1849. Not surprisingly, the logging industry moved in next, although the loggers did not touch this particular grove.

In the understory of the redwoods, you'll see salmonberry, huckleberry, salal, and rhododendron. Sword ferns and sorrel grace the forest floor. If you picked up an interpretive brochure at the trailhead, you'll learn to identify "goose pens" (hollowed out redwood trunks that early settlers used for keeping poultry) and "sprout trees" or "cathedral trees" (redwoods that have sprouted additional trunks instead of reproducing by seed).

On the return half of the loop, you'll notice more Douglas fir and western hemlock trees in addition to the coast redwoods. The trail is short and simple, but it's likely to leave you feeling different from when you started. In the words of Lady Bird Johnson: "One of my most unforgettable memories of the past years is walking through the redwoods last November, seeing the lovely shafts of light filtering through the trees so far above, feeling the majesty and silence of that forest, and watching a salmon rise in one of those swift streams. All our problems seemed to fall into perspective and I think every one of us walked out more serene and happier."

Options

Combine this walk with a hike on the Skunk Cabbage section of the Coastal Trail, described in the previous trail description. The trailheads are only three miles apart.

Information and Contact

There is no fee. A free map is available from park headquarters or the Thomas H. Kuchel Visitor Center near Orick. For more information, contact Redwood National Park Headquarters, 1111 Second Street, Crescent City, CA 95531, 707/464-6101, website: www.nps.gov/redw.

Directions

From Eureka, drive north on U.S. 101 for 41 miles to Orick, then continue north for one mile. Turn right on Bald Hills Road and drive 2.7 miles to the trailhead parking area on the right.

8 TALL TREES GROVE
Redwood National Park, off U.S. 101 near Orick

Total distance: 3.0 miles round-trip   **Hiking time:** 1.5 hours

Type of trail: some steep terrain   **Best season:** year-round

It might sound like too much trouble to go to the visitors center, pick up a permit and a gate combination for the Tall Trees Access Road, then drive 16 miles to the trailhead—just to hike a trail that features big redwoods.

After all, there are plenty of other redwood trails in the area that don't require a permit. But these aren't your average big redwoods; the Tall Trees Grove includes what was once considered the world's tallest tree at 367 feet high, but in 1999 was downgraded in status after losing about 10 feet of height in a storm. (The honor of being the world's tallest now goes to the Mendocino Tree in Montgomery Woods State Reserve near Mendocino.) Still, a few trees in the top 10 list are found in the Tall Trees Grove. The fact is, every redwood in this grove is immense. It's impossible to see all the way to their skyscraping summits.

massive trees and ferns at the Tall Trees Grove

The permit system is necessary because the Tall Trees Access Road (also called C-Line Road) is narrow and winding; too many cars at once would surely result in accidents. But the side benefit of the permit system is that it limits the number of hikers in the grove and adds to the serenity of the experience. (Only 50 cars are given a permit each day, but that limit is rarely reached except on peak summer weekends. If you are concerned about getting a permit on a particular day, just show up at the visitors center first thing in the morning.)

At the Tall Trees Trailhead, pick up an interpretive brochure at the kiosk and head downhill. You'll pass a junction with the Emerald Ridge Trail in the first 100 yards; stay right. The first stretch of trail leads gently downhill through a mixed forest with myriad rhododendrons—no big redwoods yet. At 1.2 miles, you pass a restroom, which seems oddly out of place with the natural beauty of the forest. Just beyond it, the trail bottoms out and you reach the start of the loop trail through the grove. Follow the trail clockwise (to the left). Take the left spur trail to see Redwood Creek; in summer a bridge spans the creek to connect hikers to the Redwood Creek Trail. In winter and spring the creek is wide and powerful—more on the order of a river. The rich soils from its streambed, combined with the coastal climate, cause the redwoods here to grow to their enormous size.

Back on the main trail, you reach the base of what was once the world's tallest tree in short order. But don't turn around there, because this trail isn't about numbers, or about any one specific tree. The entire grove is remarkable. There are so many mammoth-sized trees in such close proximity that humans feel ant-sized in comparison. Even the rhododendrons grow extra large—as tall as 15 feet. They display flashy pink blooms among the dark shadows of the redwoods.

The trail continues past more huge redwoods to the north end of the loop, where you walk through a quarter-mile stretch of big leaf maples and California bays—a distinct contrast to the giant redwoods. This no-redwood area is beautiful in its own way, especially in autumn when the maples turn colors. The loop eventually heads back into the big trees and finally rejoins the main trail to head back uphill. Linger a while among the giants before you go.

Options

If the summer bridge is in place across Redwood Creek, cross it and hike for as far as you like on the opposite side of the stream. You'll pass a small backpacker's camp, which makes a good picnic spot.

Information and Contact

There is no fee. A free map is available from park headquarters or the Thomas H. Kuchel Visitor Center near Orick. For more information, contact Redwood National Park Headquarters, 1111 Second Street, Crescent City, CA 95531, 707/464-6101, website: www.nps.gov/redw.

Directions

From Eureka, drive north on U.S. 101 for 40 miles to the Thomas H. Kuchel Visitor Center on the west side of the highway. (It's two miles south of the town of Orick.) At the visitors center, pick up a Tall Trees Grove permit and the gate combination for the access road. Then drive north on U.S. 101 for three miles and turn right on Bald Hills Road. Drive seven miles to the Tall Trees Access Road on the right (just past Redwood Creek Overlook). Turn right, stop at the gate, use your combination to open it, then drive through. Close and lock the gate behind you. Drive six miles on the Tall Trees Access Road (also called C-Line Road) to the trailhead parking lot.

⑨ RIM TRAIL: WEDDING ROCK TO ROCKY POINT

Patrick's Point State Park, off U.S. 101 near Trinidad

Total distance: 1.0–4.0 miles round-trip

Hiking time: 30 minutes–2 hours

Type of trail: mostly level terrain   **Best season:** year-round

---

Although I had heard the phrase "sea stack" before, I never knew exactly what it meant until I came to Patrick's Point State Park. Thousands of years ago, the main part of this seaside park was once entirely submerged in the ocean. When the water receded, dozens of 100-foot-high, precipitously balanced, cliff-like outcrops were left standing high and dry. The park today shows off numerous examples of sea-stack geology.

Two of these sea stacks, dubbed Ceremonial Rock and Lookout Rock, are a part of the main land mass of Patrick's Point State Park. They have many isolated rocky cousins located just off the coast. On land and in water, the sea stacks provide plentiful coastal drama for hikers. The best way to see them is with a short trek on the park's Rim Trail.

Wedding Rock at Patrick's Point State Park

The entire trail is two miles in length, or four miles round-trip, which is just fine if you feel ambitious. If you don't, you can sample the park's highlights by hiking only a section of the Rim Trail and then adding on the short spur trails that connect to three ocean overlooks— Wedding Rock, Patrick's Point, and Rocky Point.

If you start at the parking lot near Wedding Rock, you can take the connector trail from the Rim Trail to Wedding Rock, a majestic, castle-like rock terrace. From there, you can head left (southwest)

on the Rim Trail and follow a wheelchair-accessible cutoff to Patrick's Point, and then head farther southwest on the Rim Trail to your final destination, the cutoff to Rocky Point.

In between the three overlook points, you'll walk through a mixed forest of Sitka spruce, Douglas fir, red alder, and pine. Wildflowers are abundant in spring, including Douglas iris, trillium, rhododendron, and salal. In spring and fall, be sure to scan the ocean horizon for migrating California gray whales.

While the Rim Trail itself is fairly level, the cutoff trails to the three overlooks have some ups and downs, especially the spur trail to Rocky Point. Even though you won't walk many miles on this route, you'll feel like you are getting a bit of a workout, especially if the wind is howling, which is a common occurrence. Coastal fog can also be problematic—especially if you came for the views. But never mind. Patrick's Point State Park is one of the crown jewels of the state park system, with dramatic coastal scenery and geology that will knock your socks off, even on the worst weather days.

Options

Drive your car .5 mile east to the Agate Campground parking area, then take a walk on the Agate Beach Trail to Agate Beach. This is the only large sand beach in the park. Rock collectors flock to Agate Beach for its semiprecious agates, which are found right at the surf line. This will add 1.2 miles to your day.

Information and Contact

A $6 day-use fee is charged per vehicle. A trail map/brochure is available at the entrance station. For more information, contact Patrick's Point State Park, 4150 Patrick's Point Drive, Trinidad, CA 95570, 707/677-3570 or 707/445-6547, website: www.parks.ca.gov.

Directions

From Eureka, drive north on U.S. 101 for 25 miles, past the town of Trinidad, and take the Patrick's Point Drive exit. Follow the signs to the entrance station for Patrick's Point State Park, then continue past the Bishop Pine Group Picnic Area. Turn left and park at the paved parking lot near Wedding Rock and Patrick's Point.

10 HOOKTON SLOUGH TRAIL
Humboldt Bay National Wildlife Refuge,
off U.S. 101 near Eureka

Total distance: 3.0 miles round-trip   **Hiking time:** 1 hour

Type of trail: mostly level terrain   **Best season:** September–April

---

The Hookton Slough Trail is a level, wide, and easy trail that practically gives you a guarantee of seeing wildlife as you walk. You want to see birds? No problem. Waterfowl, raptors, shorebirds—the Hookton Slough Trail has 'em all. You want a chance to see harbor seals basking in the mud? Your chances are good if the tide is high; that's when the seals swim up the slough from Humboldt Bay in search of a meal. Sand dabs, leopard sharks, and salmon also migrate through this estuary.

The key to all this wildlife diversity is the eelgrass, mudflats, and wetlands that provide habitat for thousands of living creatures—from tiny invertebrates to crabs and clams, from more than 200 species of birds to migratory fish and mammals like the harbor seals.

In one trip here, I saw dozens of white egrets, plus several species of ducks and gulls. Huge flocks of western sandpipers clustered by the edge

© ANN MARIE BROWN

A level trail runs alongside Hookton Slough.

of the bay, racing back and forth within inches of the water but never getting wet. Every 100 feet or so on the trail, I encountered giant goose eggs that had been cracked open, their contents either given over to predators or hatched to life.

September through March is the main bird viewing season, but the most interesting show comes from mid-March–late April, when black brants (also called sea geese) pass through town on their way from Alaska to Baja. Humboldt Bay is an important resting stop for these weary and hungry birds, because it provides the largest beds of eelgrass south of Washington.

The hike is simple: Begin at the parking lot, walk 1.5 miles out to the end of the trail (clearly marked at a boundary), and then walk back. On the return trip, when I took my eyes off the mudflats and looked ahead to the farms and hillsides in the west, I noticed large white spots in the tops of the trees. The "spots" were actually a few dozen white egrets, nesting in the tallest treetops.

Options
Add on a hike on the 1.75-mile Shorebird Loop Trail, which passes near some of the refuge's best shorebird viewing areas. This trail is located off Ranch Road near the refuge office.

Information and Contact
There is no fee. Free trail maps/brochures are available at the trailhead. The Hookton Slough Trail is open every day sunrise–sunset. The refuge office is open on weekdays 7 A.M.–4 P.M. For more information, contact Humboldt Bay National Wildlife Refuge, 1020 Ranch Road, Loleta, CA 95551, 707/733-5406, website: http://pacific.fws.gov/humboldtbay/.

Directions
From Eureka, travel 10 miles south on U.S. 101. Take the Hookton Road exit and drive 1.2 miles west on Hookton Road to the Hookton Slough parking area. (The refuge office is located off the same exit but on Ranch Road. It's not necessary to go to the refuge office; you can drive directly to Hookton Slough.)

11 BIG TREE AREA: BULL CREEK FLATS TRAIL

Humboldt Redwoods State Park,
off U.S. 101 near Garberville

Total distance: 2.5 miles round-trip

Type of trail: mostly level terrain

Hiking time: 1.5 hours

Best season: year-round

Humboldt Redwoods State Park encompasses more than 51,000 acres, making it one of the largest state parks in California. This results in it having seven separate exits off the freeway and an overflowing abundance of trails to choose from. A first-time visit here can seem daunting. The trick, of course, is to know where to go.

If you're an avid fan of gargantuan *sequoia sempervirens* and lovely streamside walks, the park's Big Tree Area is your ticket. Just driving to the trailhead on Bull Creek Flats/Mattole Road is a thrill. The road is winding, shaded, and narrow, with big trees so close that you can touch them by leaning out your car window.

From the parking area, walk straight ahead across a long, narrow footbridge, which rises 20 feet above Bull Creek. Turn left on the trail to see the Giant Tree, which is recognized by the American Forestry Association as the National Champion Coast Redwood. It's a colossal 363 feet tall and 53.2 feet in circumference. Next, follow the trail signs back to the Flatiron Tree, a huge fallen tree that is flat on one side, looking nearly triangular in shape instead of round.

To find more big trees, retrace your steps across the bridge to the parking area, walk across the lot, and locate the trail to the Tall Tree. How tall, you ask? It's a whopping 359.3 feet, and a pleasant little loop trail travels around it.

If you've had your fill of trees named every possible synonym for "big," continue from the Tall Tree, heading west on the Bull Creek Flats Trail and paralleling Bull Creek. You can take the trail from the Tall Tree all the way to Albee Creek Campground, a distance of just under one mile. The trail travels along the creek, where you'll find plenty of horsetails and Douglas irises in the spring. When you come to Bull Creek Flats/Mattole Road and the access road for the camp, turn around and head back to your car.

Options

You can also hike the Bull Creek Flats Trail in the opposite direction, heading east along Bull Creek. From the Big Tree Area it is about three miles to the Rockefeller Loop Trail at the Bull Creek Flats Area.

Information and Contact

There is no fee. For more information and a park map, contact Humboldt Redwoods State Park, P.O. Box 100, Weott, CA 95571, 707/946-2409 or 707/445-6547, website: www.parks.ca.gov.

Directions

From Garberville, travel north on U.S. 101 for about 20 miles, heading into Humboldt Redwoods State Park. Take the Founder's Grove/Rockefeller Forest exit and drive approximately four miles on Bull Creek Flats Road/Mattole Road to the Big Tree Area of Rockefeller Forest. Turn left at the Big Tree Area and park in the lot. The trail begins from the south side of the lot, at the bridge over Bull Creek.

Chapter 2

© ANN MARIE BROWN

Shasta and Lassen

Shasta and Lassen

In the northeastern corner of California lies a part of the state where most people have never set foot. Ranging from the Oregon border south to Redding and from the Nevada border west through the Klamath Mountains, this northern interior is both the least populated and least visited region of the Golden State. Yet it is bestowed with some of California's most spectacular scenery: a landscape of rugged mountains, raging rivers in steep canyons, and vast expanses of sagebrush flats and pine- and fir-covered ridges. This is the land where oprey and eagles soar, and remnants of volcanoes sputter and fume.

Two national parks are found here, both celebrating the region's volcanic past: Lava Beds National Monument, with its 300 lava tube caves, vast volcanic cinder landscape, and western juniper forests; and Lassen Volcanic National Park, California's best example of recent geothermal activity. How recent? In May 1914, Lassen Peak began a seven-year stint of volcanic outbursts. Even today, visitors can witness volcanic action including seething hot springs, steaming volcanic vents, and boiling mud pots (springs filled with hot mud).

Then there is the 2.1 million acres of Shasta-Trinity National Forest, dominated by mighty Mount Shasta, a dormant volcano whose summit attains the lofty height of 14,162 feet. At its base lies Shasta Lake, the largest reservoir in California, which is part of another federally managed parkland: Whiskeytown-Shasta-Trinity National Recreation Area. Both Shasta and Whiskeytown Lakes provide an uncrowded playground for hikers and bikers, with miles of winding trails to explore around the lakes' shores.

Not surprisingly, since water is so abundant in the Shasta and Lassen region, so are waterfalls. East of Mount Shasta is McArthur Burney Falls State Park and its showpiece Burney Falls, which President Theodore Roosevelt called "the eighth wonder of the world." Several other impressive cataracts are found near Mount Shasta, including Hedge Creek Falls and McCloud Falls, both accessible by short, easy hikes.

It probably isn't an overstatement to say that the Shasta and Lassen region has it all. The fact is, the only thing you won't find in this part of California is a crowd. Perhaps that is the best reason of all to come here and take a hike.

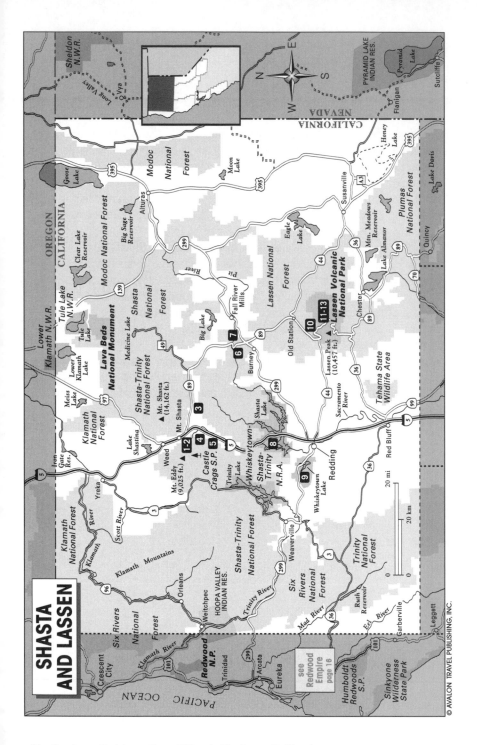

Contents

1. Sacramento River & Cantara Loop Trail 46
2. Castle Lake Trail 48
3. McCloud Falls Trail 50
4. Hedge Creek Falls Trail 52
5. Root Creek Trail 54
6. Headwaters & Pacific Crest Trails 56
7. Hat Creek Trail 58
8. Lake Shasta Overlook Trail 60
9. Mill Creek Trail 61
10. Chaos Crags & Crags Lake 63
11. Kings Creek Falls 65
12. Terrace, Shadow, & Cliff Lakes 67
13. Bumpass Hell Trail 69

1 SACRAMENTO RIVER & CANTARA LOOP TRAIL

Shasta-Trinity National Forest, off I-5 near Dunsmuir

Total distance: 1.5 miles round-trip

Type of trail: mostly level terrain

Hiking time: 45 minutes

Best season: April–October

John Muir once said that "Nature is always lovely, invincible, glad, whatever is done and suffered by her creatures. All scars she heals, whether in rocks or water or sky or hearts." In few places is Nature's healing more evident than on the Cantara Loop Trail along the Sacramento River.

The Cantara Loop is a stretch of horseshoe-shaped railroad track that bridges the Sacramento River upstream of the town of Dunsmuir. In July of 1991, California's worst inland toxic spill occurred on this stretch of track when an improperly loaded Southern Pacific freight train derailed. It dumped 19,000 gallons of metam sodium, an inert plant and insect killer, into the river. The poison, when mixed with water, did exactly what it was manufactured to do: It killed every living organism within its reach, and also sickened people and animals in nearby Dunsmuir.

That terrible event happened not very long ago, and yet when you hike the Cantara Loop today, it seems as if you're in one of the most pristine places on earth. The river runs strong and clear, the streambeds and shorelines are teeming with plants and birds, and even the fishing has returned to its pre-disaster status. If you didn't know about the toxic spill, you would never guess it had occurred.

Begin your hike by following the trail that parallels the river, heading downstream. Just after crossing the train tracks, you'll gain a good view of the Cantara Bridge. You can see how the train route curves through the valley, making a perfect "U" at the bridge. This tight turn is where the train derailed.

Where the trail splits, head away from the water and through lovely meadows filled with daisies and Canada thistle. Then follow the trail back down toward the river again. The path eventually disappears in thick brush, forcing you to turn around and retrace your steps.

While hiking, your peaceful meandering may be interrupted by the sound of an oncoming train. It happened to me on my trip: A long, 100-plus-car freight train rolled through the loop, its cars following in an seemingly endless chain after the engine had passed, screeching through the tight curve around the bridge. The conductor of this freighter, who was

fields of wildflowers along the Cantara Loop Trail

surely accustomed to this routine, leaned out the engine window and kept his eye on the bridge tracks. I wondered if he was crossing his fingers.

Options
If you want to extend your walk, you can also take this trail in the other direction from the parking area, heading upstream along the river.

Information and Contact
There is no fee. For more information, contact Shasta-Trinity National Forest, Mt. Shasta Ranger District, 204 West Alma Street, Mt. Shasta, CA 96067, 530/926-4511, website: www.fs.fed.us/r5/shastatrinity.

Directions
From Redding, drive north on I-5 for 65 miles to the town of Mt. Shasta, then take the Central Mt. Shasta exit. At the stop sign, turn left, cross the overpass, and continue for .5 mile to South Old Stage Road. Turn left on South Old Stage Road and drive .2 mile to a Y in the road, where you bear left and continue on South Old Stage Road for 2.1 miles to Azalea Road. Turn right at Azalea, drive over the train tracks, and continue for .5 mile to Cantara Road. Turn right on Cantara Road and drive .8 mile to the parking area along the Sacramento River. The trailhead is on the left; head downstream.

2 CASTLE LAKE TRAIL

Shasta-Trinity National Forest, off I-5 near Dunsmuir

Total distance: 1.6 miles round-trip

Type of trail: rolling terrain

Hiking time: 1 hour

Best season: May–October

While national and state parks always seem to be bustling with visitors, fewer travelers plan their vacations around visiting the national forests, a 20-million-acre wonderland in California. Maybe that's because the Forest Service people don't exactly string up neon lights and shout from a megaphone, alerting everyone to the presence of their lands. So if you are seeking an escape from the crowds, you have a chance at finding it in Shasta-Trinity National Forest. A hiking trip at Castle Lake is a perfect start; it offers an easy trail to a spectacular lookout high above a granite-lined lake.

When you pull into the parking area at Castle Lake's edge, you may gasp in surprise—this lake is a stunner. Set in a glacial bowl at 5,450 feet in elevation, its waters are backed by a high rock cliff and views of Mount Shasta on clear days.

The trail starts at the parking lot, where a small but popular campground is located. The first 200 feet of trail are the trickiest: You have to boulder-hop across a stream, which ranges from two feet wide in summer to 25 feet wide after winter snow and rain. The path laterals around the lake, ascending gradually through a sparse forest of red and white firs. Your views keep getting wider as you climb. When you reach a saddle on the ridge above the lake, after hiking about three-quarters of a mile, you're at 5,900 feet in elevation. Have a seat on a rock, pull out your picnic, and stay a while.

The Shasta and Wintu American Indians called Castle Lake

Castle Lake

"Castle of the Devil." They believed an evil spirit lived in the lake and made the eerie echoing noises frequently heard in winter. The sound is actually just the movement of ice—and maybe the grumbles and moans of people who come here to ice fish. They don't catch much. Ice-skating is also popular in winter. The crystal clear lake has 47 surface acres of water and a depth of 120 feet against its back granite wall.

Some people claim that Castle Lake has rejuvenating powers; they swear that swimming in Castle Lake is like being dipped in magic water. I would venture that it is more like being dipped in ice cubes—the lake's water is mostly snowmelt from Mount Shasta.

Options
You can add on a hike from the ridge above Castle Lake to Little Castle Lake and/or Heart Lake. Just beyond the saddle and lake overlook, turn right on an unmarked trail to reach Heart Lake, .5 mile away. The little lake is clearly heart-shaped. Or, stay straight on the main trail to head for Little Castle Lake. This requires a 300-foot elevation drop over .5 mile, which you will have to gain back on your return. When you reach a small meadow, leave the main trail and turn right on an unmarked side trail to Little Castle Lake. This lake is really more of a shallow pond, but it features a great mirror-image reflection of Mount Shasta on its surface.

Information and Contact
There is no fee. For more information, contact Shasta-Trinity National Forest, Mt. Shasta Ranger District, 204 West Alma Street, Mt. Shasta, CA 96067, 530/926-4511, website: www.fs.fed.us/r5/shastatrinity.

Directions
From Redding, drive north on I-5 for 65 miles to the town of Mt. Shasta, then take the Central Mt. Shasta exit. At the stop sign, turn left, cross the overpass, and continue for .5 mile to South Old Stage Road. Turn left on South Old Stage Road and drive .2 mile to a Y in the road, where you bear right and continue on W. A. Barr Road. Drive 2.1 miles on W. A. Barr Road, crossing over the dam at Lake Siskiyou; then turn left on Castle Lake Road and drive 7.1 miles to the parking area for Castle Lake. The trailhead is at the edge of the parking lot to the left of the lake.

3 McCLOUD FALLS TRAIL

Shasta-Trinity National Forest, off Highway 89 near McCloud

Total distance: 3.5 miles round-trip

Type of trail: rolling terrain

Hiking time: 30 minutes

Best season: year-round

The small, easy-to-miss Forest Service sign on Highway 89 says simply "River Access," giving no indication of the impressive waterfalls nearby. This is clearly a case of understatement. Showstopping Middle McCloud Falls and its siblings Lower and Upper Falls are located by Fowlers Camp near the town of McCloud, and are easily visited by a 3.5-mile round-trip trail. You get a lot more than "river access" if you make the turn into Fowlers Camp.

Lower McCloud Falls is the easiest to access; you drive right up to it. The 12-foot-high plunge is a popular put-in spot for kayakers heading down the McCloud River, and for swimmers who want to jump in and cool off in summer. Start your trip at Lower Falls; this will get you in the

Middle McCloud Falls

waterfall mood. Then follow the paved trail along the river into the campground, where the McCloud Falls Trail begins.

For the next .5 mile, you'll walk on a level, fir-needle-strewn route along the Mc-Cloud River, with water views the whole way. Soon you'll hear a furious rush of water, and then suddenly Middle McCloud Falls appears—tall, wide, and majestic. The gushing water drops about 50 feet over a cliff, forms a deep pool at its base, then continues its way downstream. After heavy winter rains, the usually serene and pretty waterfall can look downright dangerous. Catch a sight of these falls after a winter storm and you'll see water not falling but rocketing over the cliff, hitting its pool with such force and fury that it creates a tremendous upsurge. It's difficult to imagine that in the summertime, bold teenagers sometimes jump off the basalt cliffs on the fall's left side, diving into the chilly waters. Plenty of boulders downstream make good perches for watching the scene. Elephant ears grow in and around the falls, and water ouzels somehow manage to build their homes behind the fall's tremendous flow of water.

From Middle McCloud Falls, follow the trail uphill and through a few switchbacks to an overlook of Upper McCloud Falls. The upper fall is the hardest of the three waterfalls to get a good look at, but from several points on the trail you can catch sight of its narrow funnel of water plunging into a rocky bowl.

You'd think three waterfalls would be about all the excitement you could take on one trail, but another surprise awaits on your return trip, as you retrace your steps: an extraordinary view of Mount Shasta, which was hiding behind your back on the way in. It appears to be so close that you could reach out and touch it.

Here's a tip for your visit: Locals and campers who know about Middle McCloud Falls are most likely to be here in summer, when the air and water temperatures heat up. But the best time to see the falls is in late winter and spring, when the water is running hard and fewer people are around. Plan your trip for April or early May and you'll have a good chance of having the waterfalls all to yourself.

Options
If you'd like to see more of the beautiful McCloud River, pay a visit to the Nature Conservancy's McCloud River Preserve, off Squaw Creek Road near the town of McCloud. Take Squaw Creek Road south from Highway 89, and 2.5 miles after passing the McCloud Reservoir, turn right on Road 38N53, a dirt road. Follow the signs to Ah-Di-Na Campground and you'll reach the Preserve parking lot at 18.5 miles from the highway (one mile beyond the campground). An easy trail leads alongside the river.

Information and Contact
There is no fee. For more information, contact Shasta-Trinity National Forest, McCloud Ranger District, P.O. Box 1620, 2109 Forest Road, McCloud, CA 96057, 530/964-2184, website: www.fs.fed.us/r5/shastatrinity.

Directions
From Redding, drive 65 miles north on I-5. Take the Highway 89/McCloud/Reno exit and drive east on Highway 89. Pass the town of McCloud

in nine miles, then continue five miles farther east to a small Forest Service sign on the right for "River Access." Turn right and follow the signs to the McCloud River Picnic Area and Lower McCloud Falls. (Bear right at the road forks, driving past Fowlers Camp.) Park in the day-use area.

4 HEDGE CREEK FALLS TRAIL

City of Dunsmuir, off I-5 in Dunsmuir

Total distance: 0.4 mile round-trip   **Hiking time:** 20 minutes

Type of trail: rolling terrain   **Best season:** year-round

Imagine you're hightailing it up I-5 with the kids, on your way to visit grandma in Portland. They are going berserk from being locked in the car for hours, and you're about to lose it if you see any more concrete, guardrails, or fast-food restaurants. But then you reach the town of Dun-smuir, 57 miles north of Redding, and you remember a freeway antidote: Hedge Creek Falls.

Get off the highway and head to Dunsmuir Avenue. Park in the small picnic area's parking lot, do a few warm-up stretches, and then hike down the path. Blink and you'll miss it—not the waterfall but the walk to it. You'll reach the falls in about five minutes of downhill cruising.

Hedge Creek Falls drops 30 feet over a sheer granite slab into a shallow pool and a babbling stream. The cliff that creates the fall is so sheer that it makes the water chute appear much grander than it really is. A large indentation in the bottom of the cliff, near where the fall hits the

Hedge Creek Falls

pool, creates a small cave. When the water flow is somewhat diminished in summer, you can sneak behind the falls and pretend you are a water ouzel, that funny bird that makes its home behind waterfalls.

Prolong your visit to this paradise just off the freeway by settling in on the bench by the falls. Consider the history of this pastoral spot: It is said to have been a secret hideout of the notorious 1850s stagecoach robber, Black Bart. In the 20th century, it was saved from the bulldozers when I-5 was built through Dunsmuir. Local citizens rallied to move the freeway a few yards to the east, just far enough to preserve Hedge Creek Falls.

More benches are positioned up and down the trail, which may come in handy on the return climb. When you hike back uphill, be sure to turn around a few times for parting glances at the falling water. At a few spots, about 20–30 feet from the waterfall, you can peer through the lush canopy of leaves and see another cataract directly above this one, set back in the canyon about 50 feet.

When you return to the trailhead, make sure you take a long drink out of the water fountain at the picnic area. This is Dunsmuir's pride and joy, what they call "The Best Water on Earth."

Options

To see another easily visited waterfall near the town of Dunsmuir, take the Sweetbriar exit off I-5 (two miles south of Castle Crags State Park). Drive east for .5 mile and park alongside the train tracks (just before crossing them, on their west side). Cross the tracks and walk up Sweetbriar Road toward the Sacramento River, passing several cabins. Cross the river bridge and walk 50 feet to your right, downstream on the river trail. This puts you smack in front of small Sweetbriar Falls. A wooden footbridge crosses the creek near the fall's base, giving you the option to continue hiking along the river.

Information and Contact

There is no fee. For more information, contact the Dunsmuir Chamber of Commerce, 4118 Pine Street, Dunsmuir, CA 96025, 530/235-2177 or 800/386-7684, website: www.dunsmuir.com.

Directions

From Redding, drive 57 miles north on I-5 to Dunsmuir and take the Dunsmuir Avenue/Siskiyou Avenue exit. Turn left at the stop sign and cross under the freeway, then turn right (north) on Dunsmuir Avenue, travel about 20 yards, and turn left into the small parking area.

5 ROOT CREEK TRAIL
Castle Crags State Park, off I-5 north of Lake Shasta

Total distance: 2.0 miles round-trip

Type of trail: mostly level terrain

Hiking time: 1 hour

Best season: April–October

Have you ever driven north on I-5, gaping at looming Mount Shasta ahead, and then suddenly looked over your left shoulder and seen those big, gray, craggy rocks looming over you—the unmistakable jagged outline of Castle Crags's ancient granite spires?

Admiring the crags from afar is good, but getting close to them is even better. The problem is that the spires of Castle Crags go straight up, jutting abruptly into the stratosphere at 6,500 feet in elevation. The trails to reach them are remarkably steep. Although you can ascend the Crags Trail all the way to Castle Dome's base—gaining 2,300 feet in nearly three miles, a prodigious climb—let's dispense with our summit illusions and go for something more manageable.

Starting from the vista point parking lot, the first trip you should take is the short walk to the vista point. You'll get an eyeful of Castle Crags and, on a clear day, Mount Shasta to your right and Grey Rocks to your left. Conical Mount Shasta at 14,162 feet is obviously a volcano, albeit one that's not currently in service. But Castle Crags is a completely different type of geological formation, made of a granite material (granodiorite) that was formed below the earth's surface millions of years ago and then slowly forced upward. The formation called Grey Rocks looks vastly different from either Mount Shasta or Castle Crags; it is of yet another geologic type, composed of greenstone and slate metamorphic rock that has been thrust upward and sideways from the earth and weathered by the centuries.

Retrace your steps from the vista point, cross the parking lot, and head down the access road for about 40 yards to the trailhead for the Root Creek Trail. This pleasant trail is mostly level and travels through a conifer and hardwood forest to its destination, Root Creek. At trail's end you get a surprising look straight up at Castle Dome-the big, smooth, rounded rock formation that leads the parade of crags.

At different times of the year you may spot the crags from other points along the trail, not just at the end, depending on the thickness of the forest canopy. But views or no views, the walk is terrific, with conifer needles at your feet and five-finger and deer ferns pointing the way. Root Creek bubbles over rounded rocks and is framed by plentiful elephant ears growing along its banks. Also known as Indian rhubarb, elephant ears are foot-

Root Creek is lined with boulders and Indian rhubarb.

high, giant-leafed green plants that grow along many streams in Northern California. It's easy to understand how they got their moniker.

When you reach the trail's end at Root Creek, you can hang out for as long as you like (there's a wooden bench for that purpose) and then backtrack to the parking area.

Options

The Root Creek Trail connects with both the Crags Trail and the Pacific Crest Trail. You can add on an out-and-back hike on either of these trails. The Pacific Crest Trail has an easier grade. Or, try out a few of the park's other easy-hiking trails: Indian Creek Trail is an interpretive trail that identifies 21 different plants and trees; and the Flume Trail visits an old wooden flume that once brought water to the town of Castella.

Information and Contact

A $5 day-use fee is charged per vehicle. A trail map is available from the ranger kiosk. For more information, contact Castle Crags State Park, P.O. Box 80, Castella, CA 96017-0080, 530/235-2684, website: www.parks.ca.gov.

Directions

From Redding, drive 50 miles north on I-5 and take the Castle Crags State Park exit, four miles south of the town of Dunsmuir. Turn west and follow the signs to the park entrance. After paying at the kiosk, turn right and follow the road to its end at the Vista Point parking area. The trail for the vista point is at the parking lot; the Root Creek Trail begins about 40 yards downhill from the parking lot.

6 HEADWATERS & PACIFIC CREST TRAILS
McArthur-Burney Falls Memorial State Park,
off Highway 89 near Burney

Total distance: 1.0 mile round-trip

Hiking time: 30 minutes

Type of trail: rolling terrain

Best season: year-round

Plenty of people drive to McArthur-Burney Falls Memorial State Park each spring and summer, park in the main lot, get out of their cars, and look over the railing at the falls. Maybe they even walk 50 yards or so to get a little closer to the huge surge of plunging water and mist. Then they take a few pictures, jump back in their cars, drive home, and brag to all their friends about how they ventured into the wilderness.

Sure, Burney Falls is worth the trip—even if all you do is sightsee. Watching 100 million gallons of water pour over a cliff is a breathtaking experience. President Theodore Roosevelt, a devout nature-lover, went so far as to call Burney Falls the eighth wonder of the world. But if you want to spend a little more time in this beautiful state park, you can leave the crowds behind and take a lovely loop hike to reach the waterfall.

Park your car in the small lot to the left of the entrance kiosk (not the main lot to the right), then begin walking on the Headwaters Trail, heading upstream and away from the falls. The woods are filled with conifers, including ponderosa pines (easily identified by their clearly delineated, jigsaw-puzzle bark) and huge Douglas firs, plus hardwoods such as white oaks and black oaks. If you visit in spring or early summer, you may notice the lovely sweet scent of mountain misery, a small shrub with tiny, light-blue or white flowers.

In .5 mile, you'll reach a long footbridge over Burney Creek and an intersection with the Pacific Crest Trail. Cross the bridge and follow this short section of the Pacific Crest Trail, heading downstream toward the falls. In another .5 mile, turn right on the Falls Trail. As you hike, keep your eyes open for two unusual bird species who frequent this park: Migratory black swifts, who build their nests on the sheer cliffs of the waterfall in early summer; and bald eagles, who nest at nearby Lake Britton.

© ANN MARIE BROWN

Burney Falls

After a couple minutes of walking on gentle downhill switchbacks, you'll come to a placard for the Burney Falls lookout and a small clearing through the woods, where the rushing cataract is framed by trees. It could be argued that the waterfall view from this angle is more dramatic than from the other, more photographed side of the creek.

At 129 feet, Burney Falls is not the highest waterfall in California, but what makes it unusual is that it flows at basically the same rate all year long, with no change in the dry season. This is because the water for Burney Creek comes from underground springs and stored snowmelt in the basalt rock layers that make up the falls. If you look closely, you can see that much of the water actually pours out of the face of the cliff, rather than running over the top of the cliff. Due to its underground water source, the water temperature below the falls, even on warm summer days, is a chilly 42°F. Swimming here would be a really bad idea.

To return to the parking area, backtrack up the paved Falls Trail for a few hundred yards and then turn left onto another footbridge.

Options

From the main waterfall overlook, hike in the opposite direction of the loop described above, following Burney Creek Trail to the edge of Lake Britton. Loop back on Rim Trail for a four-mile round-trip. Pick up a map at the ranger kiosk before you go.

Information and Contact

A $6 day-use fee is charged per vehicle. A trail map is available from the ranger kiosk. For more information, contact McArthur-Burney Falls Memorial State Park, 24898 Hwy. 89, Burney, CA 96013, 530/335-2777, website: www.parks.ca.gov.

Directions

From Burney, drive approximately four miles east on Highway 299 to the intersection of Highways 89 and 299. Turn left and drive north on Highway 89 for approximately six miles to the main entrance to the park. Pay at the kiosk, then drive past it and to the left. (The visitors center and main parking area is to the right.) Park in the small parking area a few hundred yards to the left of the kiosk. The trailhead for the Headwaters Trail is on the left side of the parking lot.

7 HAT CREEK TRAIL

Shasta-Hat Creek County Park,
off Highway 299 between Burney and Fall River Mills

Total distance: 4.0 miles round-trip

Type of trail: mostly level terrain

Hiking time: 2 hours

Best season: April–October

There's nothing quite as nice as watching a big stream roll by, unless of course you're watching two big streams roll by. That's what you get on this hike along Hat Creek and the Pit River. It's a perfect walk to do with a loved one or ones, because the trail is level, easy, and wide enough so that you can walk side by side.

Your hike is an easy stroll down an old dirt road that soon diminishes to a trail. The Pit River flows by on your right and Hat Creek on your left. You walk smack in between the two waterways for most of the trip, in a big meadow filled with wildflowers and bordered by black oaks and white oaks. After a mile or so, the trail brings you closer to the Pit River side, and then curves around to your left to the confluence of the Pit River and Hat Creek. On your return, you stay closer to the Hat Creek side for a few hundred yards until you are led back to the main trail.

The faint spur trails you'll see along the way are mostly used by fishing enthusiasts. You can take any or all of them without fear of getting lost, because the two waterways always keep you on track. As you wander, watch for birds. This type of meadow and woodland environment attracts numerous songbirds and birds of prey. Look for stellar's jays, robins, meadowlarks, blackbirds, red-tailed hawks, and Cooper's hawks. A local birding group has put up nesting boxes along the river in the hope of attracting more songbirds.

The broad open fields and oak woodlands that divide the Pit River and Hat Creek seem to naturally encourage good conversation, and the inter-

hikers alongside Hat Creek

section where the two waters meet is the perfect place to lay out a blanket and have a picnic. Linger in this special place as long as you can.

On your return hike along Hat Creek, you'll notice a small dam and a five-foot waterfall marked by orange buoys floating across the creek, just before the confluence of the two streams. These are signals to kayakers and canoeists not to float farther downstream.

You will likely see anglers along Hat Creek, particularly at the stretch by the county park where you started. The stream is famous for wild trout and is popular with fly fishers. People travel from all over the country to try their skills at this catch-and-release section of the creek. You won't see any frying pans. Then again, you're unlikely to see any fish get caught and released here, either. Hat Creek trout are notoriously wily.

Options
Several other trails lead from Hat Creek County Park, and all are worth exploring. For starters, try the path on Hat Creek's west side that leads northwest for 1.6 miles to Lake Britton.

Information and Contact
There is no fee. For more information, contact Shasta County Public Works, 1855 Placer Street, Redding, CA 96001, 530/225-5661, website: www.co.shasta.ca.us.

Directions

From Burney, drive 7.5 miles east on Highway 299, past the intersection of Highways 89 and 299, to just before the highway bridge over Hat Creek. It's five miles west of Fall River Mills. Turn left into Shasta-Hat Creek County Park just before the bridge; park, and then walk back to the road and across the bridge. The trailhead is a dirt road about 20 feet from the east end of the bridge.

🎱 LAKE SHASTA OVERLOOK TRAIL

Shasta-Trinity National Forest, off I-5 north of Redding

Total distance: 1.6 miles round-trip   **Hiking time:** 1 hour

Type of Trail: some steep terrain   **Best season:** October–May

---

Lake Shasta is the largest man-made reservoir in California, with statistics that rank with some of the greatest recreation lakes in America—370 miles of shoreline, more than 1,000 campsites, 29,000-plus acres of water, and nearly two dozen boat ramps. Anglers, boaters, water-skiers, houseboaters, sun worshipers—everybody loves Lake Shasta.

But most people don't think of it as a place to hike. For one thing, it's hot as Hades around here in the summer months, so you must confine your hiking to the cooler months of the year. And for another, with so many recreation enthusiasts out on the lake, it's hard to imagine that you could find any peace and quiet here. But you can, especially in the non-summer months.

The best way to hike at Lake Shasta is to climb above it all to get the big picture. The Lake Shasta Overlook Trail does just that. It ascends gently through a mixed conifer and oak forest, with the sound of a running creek serenading you as you walk.

From the trailhead, you climb just under a mile, slowly switchbacking up a ridge. At the top, you reach the first Shasta Lake overlook, which comes supplied with a wooden bench for enjoying the view. The trees have grown quite large here, framing the water vista. But this overlook is only a preview, so don't use up all your film taking pictures. Just 50 yards farther is the main overlook, with a wide-angle look at Packers Bay as it opens into the main body of the lake. Gaze over the water for a while and you might get lucky and see an eagle or an osprey go fishing. Beyond the overlook, the path makes a tiny loop around some huge manzanita bushes and then heads back downhill.

A few words of caution are in order. The paths around Lake Shasta have become the playground of mountain bikers in recent years. If you time your trip for the non-summer months, you are much less likely to share the trail with bikes. But in any season it is wise to pay strict attention to the sound of squealing brakes, and be sure to give the two-wheelers plenty of room. Many of them have a hard time controlling their speed on this trail.

Options
If you want to hike farther, go back to the parking area and pick up Waters Gulch Trail, which is another out-and-back trail but is about twice as long. This trail will lead you down to the water's edge rather than staying high above it.

Information and Contact
There is no fee. For more information, contact Shasta-Trinity National Forest, Shasta Lake Ranger District, 14225 Holiday Road, Redding, CA 96003, 530/275-1587, website: www.fs.fed.us/r5/shastatrinity.

Directions
From I-5 at Redding, drive north for 15 miles and take the O'Brien/Shasta Caverns exit. Cross the freeway and get back on I-5 heading south. Drive one mile and take the Packers Bay exit. Drive one mile to the trailhead, a dirt parking area on the right. (If you reach the boat ramp, you've gone too far.) Overlook Trail and Waters Gulch Trail both begin here.

9 MILL CREEK TRAIL
Whiskeytown National Recreation Area,
off Highway 299 west of Redding

Total distance: 4.0 miles round-trip   **Hiking time:** 2 hours

Type of trail: rolling terrain   **Best season:** April–October

The Mill Creek Trail is for people who prefer the Ferris wheel to the roller coaster at amusement parks. Going on the Ferris wheel makes you feel like you're having an adventure, when in fact you know you're perfectly safe. You can have all the fun you want without any nagging worries. Riding the roller coaster feels like an adventure, too, but you can't relax until it's over and you've survived. Somehow, that's not as much fun.

Clear Creek Bridge, Whiskeytown National Recreation Area

This out-and-back trail in the Whiskeytown National Recreation Area is for people who want to have an adventure—hiking in a dense forest, hopping from boulder to boulder across a stream more than two dozen times, taking a dip in a swimming hole—without any worries. The trail bounces back and forth across crystal-clear Mill Creek, but because the creek is rarely more than five feet wide and eight inches deep, a misstep is no big deal.

Hiking the entire length of the Mill Creek Trail is not for everybody, however. It continues for 2.5 miles one-way, ending in a climb to a dirt fire road, and looping back isn't possible. The trail also becomes more narrow and indistinct, and the stream crossings grow progressively more difficult. But you can simply travel as far as you like, weaving your way through the dense pine and fir forest and rock-hopping across Mill Creek, then turn around and head back. In summer, when the water level is low, most people hike about two miles out. You'll know it's time to head back when you start thinking, "Jeez, do I have to cross this creek again?"

The trail begins at the El Dorado Mine, which was built in the 1880s and was still in operation as late as 1967. Over the years, El Dorado and other mines in this area produced substantial gold profits. Recreational gold panning continues to this day. After you've visited the remaining mine buildings, continue past them on the signed trail that heads up the creek. At the first few trail intersections, you can choose to stay where you are or cross to the other side of the creek. Either direction is fine, as long as you keep heading upstream. But don't take the trail fork on the east side of the creek that connects to the Clear Creek Vista Trail, or you'll be heading downstream. Soon the choices cease and only one trail skips back and forth across Mill Creek, crossing some 20 times on the way out and 20 more on your return.

Depending on the season, the path can be somewhat indistinct in places, but the stream always keeps you on track. Be sure to pause for a rest break on a granite boulder, cool your feet in a pool, and take time to notice the flora and fauna in this riparian habitat. You'll see elephant ears (the big leafy plants alongside the stream), as well as vine maples growing underneath the shade of incense cedars and Ponderosa pines. The music of songbirds fills the air and, because this is a rock-hopping stream, frogs are ubiquitous.

Information and Contact
There is no fee. For more information and a free trail map, contact Whiskeytown National Recreation Area, P.O. Box 188, Whiskeytown, CA 96095, 530/246-1225 or 530/241-6584, website: www.nps.gov/whis.

Directions
From I-5 at Redding, take Highway 299 west for 16.5 miles, passing Whiskeytown Lake and turning left at the sign for "Towerhouse Historic District." Park in the lot, walk down the paved path, cross a wooden bridge, walk through a white picket gate, and cross a second bridge. A dirt road leads past a park residence to the El Dorado Mine and the trailhead.

🔟 CHAOS CRAGS & CRAGS LAKE
Lassen Volcanic National Park,
off Highway 44 east of Redding

Total distance: 3.6 miles round-trip   **Hiking time:** 2 hours

Type of trail: some steep terrain   **Best season:** June–August

---

When most of Lassen Volcanic National Park is still buried in snow, it can feel like summer in the Manzanita Lake area of the park. This early season is an excellent time to hike uphill to Crags Lake, and perhaps take a bracing swim before the long days of sunshine dry up the snow-fed lake. Crags Lake is a beauty, and the trail to reach it is an easy ascent of only 1.7 miles, followed by a short but steep drop to the water's edge.

Initially, the path climbs very gently through pine and fir forest. Many of the trees are stunted from the poor volcanic soil they grow in; some have a healthy quantity of bright green staghorn lichen coloring their trunks. The forest is situated along the edge of Chaos Jumbles, a two-mile-square rockslide caused by volcanic activity sometime around the year 1700.

The trees hide much of your view of the rockslide, but as you climb, you'll see other evidence of volcanism. A group of six plug domes called the Chaos Crags rise above the upper reaches of the trail. The Chaos Crags were formed by thick, viscous lava. The lava was so thick that it didn't flow outward; rather it squeezed upward through vents in the earth and then hardened in place. The Crags are esti-

Chaos Crags and Crags Lake

mated to be about 1,000 years old—much older than the Chaos Jumbles. A depression or small crater at the base of the Crags is what forms Crags Lake each year as the snow melts.

As you proceed uphill, the forest cover starts to thin and your views get wider. A few switchbacks take you up to the crest of a ridge—the high point on this trail. You are rewarded with a dramatic view of the Chaos Crags towering hundreds of feet above you. Below you is the steep bowl in which blue-green Crags Lake lies, and far off in the distance are the Chaos Jumbles and forested Hat Creek Valley.

Many people turn around at this point, but it's only a short descent of about 100 yards down to the lake's edge. If you go swimming, you'll find that the water temperature is comfortable near the shore, but it drops dramatically the deeper you go. If you don't want to swim, you can find a spot along the water's edge and have a picnic, admiring the ephemeral lake. By about September, its snow-fed waters will have dried up under the Lassen sun.

Options

Another easy hike in the same area of the park is the trail that loops around Manzanita Lake. Start this 1.6-mile loop from the boat ramp and picnic area at Manzanita Lake, which is located just beyond the Manzanita Lake store and off the road to the campground.

Information and Contact

There is a $10 entrance fee at Lassen Volcanic National Park (good for seven days). Free park maps are available at the entrance stations. For more information, contact Lassen Volcanic National Park, P.O. Box 100, Mineral, CA 96063, 530/595-4444, website: www.nps.gov/lavo.

Directions

From Redding, drive east on Highway 44 for 46 miles. Turn right on Highway 89 and drive .5 mile to the park's northwest entrance station. Continue southeast on Lassen Park Road for .5 mile to the right turnoff for Manzanita Lake Campground (just beyond the Loomis Museum). Turn right and drive 100 yards to the trailhead on the left.

11 KINGS CREEK FALLS
Lassen Volcanic National Park,
off Highway 36 east of Red Bluff

Total distance: 2.4 miles round-trip   **Hiking time:** 1.5 hours

Type of trail: some steep terrain   **Best season:** June–September

---

The waterfall on Kings Creek is pretty, not spectacular, but the beauty of the trail to reach it makes Kings Creek Falls one of the most visited attractions in Lassen Volcanic National Park. The hike is a downhill trek along Kings Creek, starting from a nondescript pullout along the park road. On weekdays, a yellow school bus is often parked in this pullout; Kings Creek Falls is a popular destination for visiting school classes.

The first part of the trail meanders under the shade of big fir trees, but at .25 mile, the trail leaves the forest for a pleasant traverse along the edge of Lower Meadow. The meadow is dark green and teeming with ebullient corn lilies in spring and early summer. It makes a perfect place to rest on the uphill hike back.

Beyond the meadow, you reach a fork and have two options: the Foot Trail or the Horse Trail. The Foot Trail is the most scenic choice. It leads

hiking alongside the stream above Kings Creek Falls

steeply downhill for .5 mile on stairsteps cut into the rock, just inches away from an area of Kings Creek called The Cascades. Hikers who have trekked the world-famous Mist Trail in Yosemite will find a kinship between that trail and the granite walkway to Kings Creek Falls, although the latter has much less of a grade.

Just before you step down the granite staircase, take a look ahead at the far-off valley vista. Once you're on the stairsteps, you must keep your eyes on your feet and their placement, because you're hiking only a few inches from the rushing cascade of white water. Some hikers mistake these cascades for Kings Creek Falls, and they unknowingly turn around before they reach the real thing. Keep going until you come to a fenced overlook area.

Kings Creek Falls are about 50 feet high and split by a rock outcrop into two main cascades, which make a steep and narrow drop into the canyon. The fence surrounding the waterfall keeps hikers out of trouble on the unstable canyon slopes. If you want to take pictures, arrive here in the morning, when the cataract is evenly lit.

For your return trip, you can retrace your steps on the spectacular Foot Trail back uphill along Kings Creek, or you can take the easier Horse Trail, which connects back with the main trail near Lower Meadow.

Options
You can add on a side trip to Sifford Lakes and then loop back to the trailhead for a total round-trip of 5.2 miles. Look for the right turnoff to

Sifford Lakes about 100 yards before the waterfall overlook. Make sure you carry a trail map with you; there are several junctions to negotiate in order to stay on the loop.

Information and Contact
There is a $10 entrance fee at Lassen Volcanic National Park (good for seven days). Free park maps are available at the entrance stations. For more information, contact Lassen Volcanic National Park, P.O. Box 100, Mineral, CA 96063, 530/595-4444, website: www.nps.gov/lavo.

Directions
From Red Bluff on I-5, turn east on Highway 36 and drive 45 miles. Turn north on Highway 89 and drive 4.5 miles to the park's southwest entrance station. Continue north on Lassen Park Road for 12 miles to the Kings Creek Falls pullouts on both sides of the road. The trail begins on the right side of the road.

12 TERRACE, SHADOW, & CLIFF LAKES
Lassen Volcanic National Park,
off Highway 36 east of Red Bluff

Total distance: 3.4 miles round-trip   **Hiking time:** 2 hours

Type of trail: some steep terrain   **Best season:** June–September

There are many, many lakes in Lassen Volcanic National Park, resulting in a fair amount of debate over which one is the best, the prettiest, and/or the most suitable for swimming. It's hard to make a definitive choice on the matter, but certainly this hike to Terrace, Shadow, and Cliff Lakes takes you to three lakes that qualify for the park's Top 10 list. Surprisingly, all three are remarkably different, although they lie only one mile apart.

Although some hikers trek to the lakes the long way, starting from Hat Lake in the north part of the park, the more common route is a short downhill hike from the park road two miles east of the Lassen Peak Trailhead. Following this path, you'll reach Terrace Lake in .5 mile, Shadow Lake in .8 mile, and Cliff Lake in 1.7 miles. Of the three lakes, Shadow Lake is the largest and is best for swimming. If you hike only to Shadow Lake, you'll have a mere 1.6-mile round-trip. Remember that no matter how far you go, it's downhill on the way in, and uphill on the return.

Although many lakes in Lassen are a disappointment for swimmers, due to shallow waters, forested or grassy shorelines, and too many tree snags in the water, these three lakes are exceptions. You'll reach the first lake, Terrace, in about 15 minutes of hiking. Terrace Lake is long and narrow, with a cliff forming its back wall and trees and rocks surrounding the rest of it. The trail leads closely along its south side. At the far end of the lake, you can look back and see the pointy tip of Lassen Peak peeking up. Hike a few yards farther on the trail and you'll peer down on Shadow Lake, remarkably close by.

The trail drops to Shadow Lake, which is huge and round—at least double the size of Terrace Lake. Like Terrace, it has a rocky shoreline and some trees, but overall it is much more open and exposed. Conveniently, the trail clings to the lake's southeast shore, so at any point, you can kick off your shoes and wade in. It takes another 10 minutes to hike to the far side of Shadow Lake, but when you get there, look back over your shoulder for a fine view of Lassen Peak in the background.

Shadow Lake makes a fine destination by itself, but it would be a shame to turn around here, because the trail just keeps getting more scenic. It descends again, then crosses a stream and passes a small pond in a meadow. Again, look over your shoulder for admirable views of Lassen Peak—the best of the entire trip. The trail then re-enters the forest. Watch for a fork and a spur leading to the right; this is the path to Cliff Lake. Hike through the trees to the small lake, which does indeed have a cliff, plus an impressive talus rockslide of white rocks on its southwest perimeter. Reading Peak rises to the south; the rockslide began on its slopes.

Cliff Lake's waters are shallow, clear, and green. The lake's most intriguing element is a small, tree-lined island on the west end. Walk to your right along the shoreline until you reach the lake's

Shadow Lake with Lassen Peak in the background

inlet, where you'll find an abundance of wildflowers, including wandering daisies, lupine, heather, and corn lilies.

Information and Contact

There is a $10 entrance fee at Lassen Volcanic National Park (good for seven days). Free park maps are available at the entrance stations. For more information, contact Lassen Volcanic National Park, P.O. Box 100, Mineral, CA 96063, 530/595-4444, website: www.nps.gov/lavo.

Directions

From Red Bluff on I-5, turn east on Highway 36 and drive 45 miles. Turn north on Highway 89 and drive 4.5 miles to the park's Southwest entrance station. Continue north on Lassen Park Road for 8.8 miles to the pullout area on the left. A small trail sign indicates the path to Terrace, Shadow, and Cliff Lakes.

13 BUMPASS HELL TRAIL
Lassen Volcanic National Park,
off Highway 36 east of Red Bluff

Total distance: 3.0 miles round-trip   **Hiking time:** 1.5 hours

Type of trail: mostly level terrain   **Best season:** June–September

If you travel Lassen Volcanic National Park with children, you will quickly learn that Bumpass Hell is their favorite trail destination because it has the distinction of having not one but two foul words in its name. When you explain that "Bumpass" was the name of the man who discovered this strange geologic area, this distinction may be lessened somewhat, but then again, maybe not.

The "Hell" in Bumpass Hell is easy to recognize. Bumpass Hell is an active hydrothermal area, part of the Lassen Geothermal System, which encompasses Bumpass Hell, Sulphur Works, Boiling Springs Lake, Little Hot Springs Valley, Morgan Springs, and Terminal Geyser. Bumpass Hell is geology in action—16 acres of boiling springs, hissing steam vents, noisy fumaroles, and bubbling mud pots.

All this geologic commotion is the result of crack-like fissures in the earth that penetrate deeply enough to tap into volcanic heat (or with a little imagination, into the searing hot landscape of Hades). Surface water from rain and snowmelt seeps into these fissures and travels downward until it touches volcanically heated rock. This creates steam, which rises back up to the surface. As a result, pools of water in the Bumpass Hell area can reach temperatures of 200°F. Kendall Vonhook Bumpass, who discovered Bumpass Hell in the 1860s, lost one of his legs when he stepped into one of these boiling, acidic pools.

Fortunately, today, hikers have a trail to follow in Bumpass Hell, and a plethora of signs to remind us to stay on the boardwalk and off the unstable soil. The hike is an easy stroll with a gradual elevation change, and it's a popular route for families. In addition to its fascinating geology, the Bumpass Hell Trail features wide views of surrounding peaks in its initial stretch. A half mile from the trailhead a spur trail on the right leads to an overlook of Mount Conard, Diamond Peak, Brokeoff Mountain, Mount Diller, and Pilot Pinnacle. These mountains were parts of the ancient volcano Mount Tehama, which stood on this spot in eons past. Long since collapsed and eroded, Mount Tehama once soared to an elevation of 11,500 feet. Lassen Peak may have been formed from lava that flowed from Mount Tehama's side vents.

As you round a curve and reach the highest point in the trail, you find an interpretive sign explaining the wonders of Bumpass Hell, which is now directly below you. You also hear the strange ruckus caused by all the hydrothermal activity—sounds variously described as steam engines, trucks speeding by, or turbine motors. The smell of sulfur is ubiquitous. A short

hiker at Bumpass Hell

descent takes you into the hydrothermal area, and boardwalks lead you over and around the various hot pools, steam vents, and mud pots. Even the stream that flows through Bumpass Hell is odd looking—its water is milky gray instead of clear. Bring color film for capturing the scene in photographs: Most of the hot pools are a striking gray green to turquoise blue in color.

Options

From Bumpass Hell, you can continue another 1.5 miles to Cold Boiling Lake, then turn around and retrace your steps for a six-mile round-trip. The "boiling" feature of this small pond occurs as gases continually bubble up through the surface of the water.

Information and Contact

There is a $10 entrance fee at Lassen Volcanic National Park (good for seven days). Free park maps are available at the entrance stations. For more information, contact Lassen Volcanic National Park, P.O. Box 100, Mineral, CA 96063, 530/595-4444, website: www.nps.gov/lavo.

Directions

From Red Bluff on I-5, turn east on Highway 36 and drive 45 miles. Turn north on Highway 89 and drive 4.5 miles to the park's Southwest entrance station. Continue north on Lassen Park Road for 5.8 miles to the Bumpass Hell Trailhead on the right.

Mendocino and Wine Country

Mendocino and Wine Country

The Mendocino and Wine Country region encompasses a vast and diverse landscape ranging from wave-swept beaches, rugged cliffs, and rolling sand dunes to vineyard-covered hills and valleys. Despite the technological advances of our modern 21st century, this area has retained its pastoral character more than perhaps anywhere else in California. Highway 1 winds up the rocky Pacific coast past seaside villages with population counts lower than their elevation—which is close to sea level. In the grassland-covered hills east of the Sonoma and Mendocino coast, you're likely to see more sheep and cows than people. The talk in the towns is about the crab harvest, or how many head of cattle are grazing in what plot of land, or what kind of grapes can grow in the coastal hills.

This peaceful, rural countryside is a marvelous setting for a hiking excursion, and fortunately the area is blessed with an abundance of parks. Within a few miles of the Mendocino town limits are four state parks with easy hiking trails—Russian Gulch, Jug Handle, Van Damme, and MacKerricher. In the redwood forests east of Mendocino lie more parks to explore, including the vast acreage of Jackson

State Forest and the intimate beauty of Hendy Woods State Park. And if you're clamoring for a fine meal or a cozy bed-and-breakfast to ease you off the trail at the end of the day, visitors are always welcome at the charming shops and business establishments in downtown Mendocino.

Like the Mendocino coast, the neighboring Sonoma coast is also blessed with unforgettable coastal scenery. Rugged headlands, rocky promontories, and sandy coves offer breathtaking panoramas. Trails at Salt Point State Park and Fort Ross State Historic Park give hikers the opportunity to partake in the seaside drama, by following nearly level trails that skirt the edge of the coastal bluffs.

Unforgettable too are the inland valleys in and around Santa Rosa and the Napa and Sonoma Wine Country. Several of the Wine Country's parklands offer easy hiking trails for visitors seeking a little fresh air and exercise: Bothe-Napa Valley State Park, Bale Grist Mill State Historic Park, and Sugarloaf Ridge State Park, among others. For a perfect day trip, plan on a morning hike topped off by an afternoon of wine tasting.

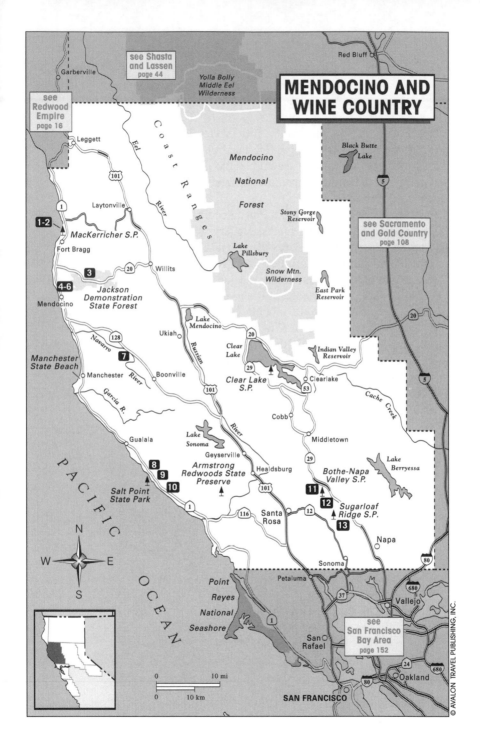

MENDOCINO AND WINE COUNTRY

see Shasta and Lassen page 44

see Redwood Empire page 16

see Sacramento and Gold Country page 108

see San Francisco Bay Area page 152

Red Bluff

Garberville

Yolla Bolly Middle Eel Wilderness

Black Butte Lake

Leggett

101

Mendocino

National

Forest

Stony Gorge Reservoir

1

Laytonville

Coast Ranges

Eel River

1-2

MacKerricher S.P.

Fort Bragg

Lake Pillsbury

20

Willits

Snow Mtn. Wilderness

3

Jackson Demonstration State Forest

East Park Reservoir

20

4-6

Mendocino

Lake Mendocino

Navarro River

128

Ukiah

Russian River

Clear Lake

Indian Valley Reservoir

7

20

Manchester State Beach

Manchester

Boonville

29

Clear Lake S.P.

Clearlake

53

Cache Creek

5

Garcia R.

101

Cobb

Gualala

Lake Sonoma

River

Geyserville

Middletown

29

Lake Berryessa

8

9

Armstrong Redwoods State Preserve

Healdsburg

Bothe-Napa Valley S.P.

10

Salt Point State Park

1

101

11

12

Sugarloaf Ridge S.P.

116

Santa Rosa

12

13

PACIFIC

Napa

80

Sonoma

Point Reyes National Seashore

Petaluma

37

680

Vallejo

OCEAN

1

San Rafael

24

0   10 mi
0   10 km

SAN FRANCISCO

80

Oakland

680

© AVALON TRAVEL PUBLISHING, INC.

N W E S

Contents

1. La Laguna Trail 78
2. Headlands Trail 80
3. Chamberlain Creek Falls 82
4. Ecological Staircase Nature Trail 84
5. Headlands & Devil's Punchbowl Trails 86
6. Fern Canyon & Falls Loop Trails 88
7. Big Hendy Grove & Hermit Hut Trails 90
8. Chinese Gulch & Phillips Gulch Trails 91
9. Bluff Trail 93
10. Fort Ross Cove Trail 96
11. Ritchey Canyon & Coyote Peak 97
12. History Trail to Bale Grist Mill 100
13. Canyon Trail 101

1 LA LAGUNA TRAIL

MacKerricher State Park, off Highway 1 near Fort Bragg

Total distance: 1.1 mile round-trip

Type of trail: mostly level terrain

Hiking time: 45 minutes

Best season: year-round

MacKerricher State Park is a rare find in the California state park system for two reasons: It's free, and its trails have excellent wheelchair-accessibility. In addition, MacKerricher is a coastal park with a freshwater lake just a few hundred yards from the ocean, with a great easy hiking trail on the lake's perimeter.

It comes as a bit of a shock not to hand over five bucks as you drive through the state park entrance station. Apparently, the guy who donated all this land to the California State Parks system insisted that day use at MacKerricher must always be free. Just wave and smile at the park rangers and they'll even give you a free map as you drive in. Then head for the parking area by Lake Cleone, a striking circle of freshwater blue just a short walk from the ocean beach.

Start this walk on the ocean side of the parking lot, where you'll find restrooms and a billboard describing some of the birds you may see on the lake: mallards, surf scooters, sanderlings, and avocets. More than 90 bird

La Laguna Trail, MacKerricher State Park

species live near or visit here. Follow the dirt path parallel to the paved access road for about 75 yards until you reach the La Laguna Trail on your left. The path leads away from the road and into thick vegetation along the lake's southwest side. The only distraction is the faint sound of Highway 1, which soon fades away as you head deeper into the dense thicket. A couple of cutoff trails lead to campgrounds and the ranger's residence, but just stay on the main trail as it circles the lake.

Bird viewing is excellent on this trail, even for novices. We saw a great blue heron and a great egret, as well as several types of smaller birds. We were close enough to see the egret catch a small fish and swallow it, leaving a telltale lump in its long neck. The Department of Fish and Game stocks the lake with trout every few weeks in summer, so you may see a few anglers trying their luck from shore, or plying the waters in small rafts and kayaks.

At the east end of the lake, where the route traverses a marsh, the trail is set on a .5-mile-long raised boardwalk, which serves the dual purpose of making this stretch completely wheelchair-accessible and also keeping foot traffic off the fragile wetlands.

As you finish the loop on the north side of Lake Cleone, you'll leave the marsh and come close to the lake's edge again, where the shoreline is bordered by big Monterey cypress trees, poised to withstand the coastal winds. Picnic tables are located at the end of the trail, near the boat ramp, although a better choice for a picnic would be right along the trail on the more secluded south side of the lake.

Options
Combine this walk with a stroll on the Old Haul Road, which runs along the beach directly across the parking lot from Lake Cleone. This old railroad trail, which is also called the Ten Mile Coastal Trail, runs north for 1.2 miles and south for 2.0 miles along the coast. It provides non-stop views of wide-open beaches, sand dunes, and crashing waves, and it is completely level.

Information and Contact
There is no fee. A free trail map/brochure is available at the entrance station. For more information, contact MacKerricher State Park, P.O. Box 440, Mendocino, CA 95460, 707/964-9112 or 707/937-5804, website: www.parks.ca.gov.

Directions
From Mendocino, drive 11.7 miles north on Highway 1 to the signed entrance to MacKerricher State Park; it's on the left (three miles north of

Fort Bragg). Turn left into the park, drive past the ranger kiosk, and turn left again, heading toward the camping areas. In .5 mile, you'll see Lake Cleone on your left. Park in the parking lot right next to the lake, and begin hiking from the trail near the restrooms.

2 HEADLANDS TRAIL
MacKerricher State Park, off Highway 1 near Fort Bragg

Total distance: 1.0 mile round-trip

Hiking time: 30 minutes

Type of trail: mostly level terrain

Best season: year-round

The Headlands Trail at MacKerricher State Park offers something for everybody. Families can take their kids to explore the tidepools along the shore, lovers can hike off on side trails to secluded bluffs where they can hold hands and gaze out to sea, and everyone, including wheelchair users, can make the trip to the Laguna Point Seal Watching Station to watch those beloved sea mammals sunbathe on the rocks.

Although the trail is only one mile in length, the sights along the way are sure to slow you down. The trail is on a raised, wheelchair-accessible boardwalk that loops around Laguna Point, a small peninsula on the headlands overlooking a rocky stretch of Mendocino coast.

Laguna Point was the site of a Pomo American Indian village for thousands of years until the early 20th century, when it saw duty as a loading chute for big schooners sailing in to load lumber. Today, Laguna Point is inhabited by a 200-plus resident population of harbor seals, along with the thousands of visitors who come to see them.

A number of dirt trails break off from the main wooden walkway and explore around the neighboring bluffs and rocky tidepools. If you take your children tidepooling, be sure to explain to them that all the sea animals and plants in the tidepool areas are protected by law and should not be taken from their native habitat.

The best way to hike the Headlands Trail is to start on the left side of the loop, which cuts across the center of Laguna Point's land mass and leads directly to the seal-watching station, .5 mile away. There you can see dozens of seals and sea lions snoozing on offshore rocks. It is biology and not slothfulness that drives the pinnipeds' languid behavior: While body fat keeps most of the seal's body warm in the frigid ocean water, its flippers have little body fat and must be exposed to the sun for hours a day to retain heat.

From the overlook, most people climb down from the boardwalk to get a closer look at the rocky tidepools just below. You can explore this area for hours, finding sea anemones, starfish, limpets, and the usual cabal of tide-pool creatures. Bird-watching is also excellent here, with ocean birds such as seagulls and scooters hanging around in hope of finding a good catch.

If it's privacy you seek, take any of the dirt cutoff trails to the left of the seal-watching station and its boardwalk. These informal paths crisscross over the blufftops for more ocean vistas. It's a little quieter out on this side of the point, although you may meet up with equestrians. Most of these dirt trails were built for horseback riding, a popular activity at MacKerricher.

The return loop on the boardwalk from the Laguna Point Seal Watching Station back to the parking area takes you along the edge of the bluffs, past more tidepools and offshore rocks, where you might see abalone divers taking the plunge. The hike ends at the wide sandy beach that fronts the trailhead parking lot, which makes an excellent picnic destination.

Options
Combine this hike with the previous hike at Lake Cleone in MacKerricher State Park, or a stroll on the park's Old Haul Road, an old railroad trail that runs along the coast (see Options for the previous hike).

Information and Contact
There is no fee. A free trail map/brochure is available at the entrance station. For more information, contact MacKerricher State Park, P.O. Box 440, Mendocino, CA 95460, 707/964-9112 or 707/937-5804, website: www.parks.ca.gov.

Directions
From Mendocino, drive 11.7 miles north on Highway 1 to the signed entrance to MacKerricher State Park on the left (three miles north of Fort Bragg). Turn left into the park, drive past the ranger kiosk and turn left again, heading toward the camping areas. Drive .5 mile past Lake Cleone and turn right, continuing .2 mile farther to the parking lot at the beach near Laguna Point. Begin hiking at the wooden walkway that leads from the west side of the parking lot.

3 CHAMBERLAIN CREEK FALLS

Jackson Demonstration State Forest,
off Highway 20 east of Fort Bragg

Total distance: 0.5 mile round-trip

Type of trail: mostly level terrain

Hiking time: 30 minutes

Best season: December–May

A trip to Mendocino means seeing spectacular ocean vistas, visiting rocky coves laden with tidepools, and watching the sun set over the ocean whenever the fog rolls out to sea. For most people, Mendocino is thought of as the quintessential place for a Northern California coastal experience.

But there's another, lesser-known face to the Mendocino landscape, and a short drive inland on Highway 20 unveils it. Jackson Demonstation State Forest, approximately 20 miles northeast of Mendocino, is comprised of 48,000 acres of big trees, mostly redwoods and Douglas firs. Much of the land is used for logging, but plenty more is available for public recreation, including the trail to 50-foot-tall Chamberlain Creek Falls.

The drive to the waterfall trailhead includes four miles of narrow, unpaved road, with the possibility of logging trucks bearing down on you at any time, so go slowly. In good weather, passenger cars can make the trip without incident, but when the roads are wet and muddy, four-wheel drive is more than a good idea.

After parking your car alongside the road at the trailhead, walk down the steep wooden steps into the canyon, then continue downhill on the dirt trail. If the weather is wet when you

Chamberlain Creek Falls

visit, be wary both on the steps and on the trail, as the fallen oak leaves underfoot can be slippery.

Chamberlain Creek's canyon is dense with foliage, including old-growth Douglas firs, redwoods, ferns, and sorrel. After 10–15 minutes of descent through this enchanting forest canopy, you'll catch your first glimpse of Chamberlain Creek Falls and then proceed right to its base. The waterfall's setting is stunningly simple—just a huge piece of black rock jutting out of the forest wall, forcing Chamberlain Creek to tumble over its bulk before the stream can continue on its way. In winter, the entire rock face is covered with rushing water, while in summer, the stream diminishes to less than a foot wide. In July and August, the water is usually warm and tame enough for you to stand beneath its spray and take a shower.

There are many fallen logs on which you can sit and admire Chamberlain Falls, or you can continue hiking on the Chamberlain Creek Trail by crossing the waterfall's stream. Just around the bend is a pristine stand of old-growth redwoods. It's a good place to ponder your relatively short existence on the planet.

Options

You can continue hiking past the waterfall as far as you wish. Beyond the old-growth grove, the trail begins to climb steadily out of the canyon, heading northward for one mile to its end.

Information and Contact

There is no fee. A free trail map is available by mail. For more information, contact Jackson Demonstration State Forest, 802 N. Main Street, Fort Bragg, CA 95437, 707/964-5674, website: www.fire.ca.gov/php/.

Directions

From Fort Bragg, drive south on Highway 1 for one mile to the turnoff for Highway 20. Turn east on Highway 20 and drive 17 miles. Turn left on Road 200, an unsigned dirt road immediately after the Chamberlain Creek bridge. Drive one mile on Road 200 until it forks, then bear left and drive 3.5 miles. Look for a wooden railing on the left side of the road; this is the trailhead. Park in the dirt pullouts alongside the road. (Road 200 can also be reached from Willits by driving 17 miles west on Highway 20 to just before the Chamberlain Creek bridge.)

4 ECOLOGICAL STAIRCASE NATURE TRAIL
Jug Handle State Reserve, off Highway 1 near Mendocino

Total distance: 5.0 miles round-trip

Type of trail: rolling terrain

Hiking time: 2 hours

Best season: year-round

The Ecological Staircase Nature Trail is a great five-mile hike featuring all kinds of interesting natural phenomena, from rocky ocean coastline to dry grasslands to dense green forest. But the name is a little misleading. The trail is like a staircase only in theory, not in practice, so don't start envisioning a continually elevating trail that climbs to some final destination. In fact, the trail climbs only 200 feet the whole way, and it does so almost imperceptibly, making for a gentle walk through a variety of natural terrain.

So why is it called the Ecological Staircase? Jug Handle State Reserve consists of a series of marine terraces, carved by ocean waves and other forces of nature over the course of half a million years or more. Each terrace is 100 feet higher in elevation and 100,000 years older than the one below, with very different and distinct soil and plant life. The geological evolution continues to this day, with future terraces still under water. Although marine terraces are common along the California coast, they are rarely as well preserved and distinguishable as they are here.

The trail starts off with stunning coastal scenery as it heads out from the parking area for a short half-mile walk around the Jug Handle Bay headlands, with access to and views of beautiful white sand beaches. April through June are the best wildflower months along this stretch of coast, when the bluffs are peppered with colorful golden poppies, Indian paintbrush, coastal lupine, seaside daisies, and wild strawberries. Summer is occasionally blessed with fog-free days, and at these times the beach life here is as good as anywhere on the California coast.

After exploring the blufftops, head inland underneath the freeway bridge and along the streambed of Jug Handle Creek. You'll have to tolerate a certain amount of road noise for about 15 minutes while you walk up the creek canyon, but it will soon fade away as you enter the first terrace, a grassland environment dotted with bishop and Monterey pines. Although the bishop pines are natives to the area, the Monterey pines are not, and the park is making efforts to remove them.

Another .75 mile of hiking brings you to the second terrace, a mixed conifer forest of bishop pine, Douglas fir, Sitka spruce, and western hemlock. The Sitka spruce, found along the Pacific coast all the way to Alaska, are at the far southern end of their range here. Farther along the trail on

Jug Handle State Reserve's wide beach

the second terrace is a combination redwood and Douglas fir grove. These tall trees tower over the shade-loving ferns and sorrel growing at their base.

The third terrace, nearly two miles in, is composed of hardpan soil, sand dunes, and pygmy trees. Soil and drainage are so poor here that trees and shrubs grow only in stunted sizes. If you pay close attention, you can see the warning signs of the approaching third terrace as you near it: The tall trees of the conifer forest begin to thin out and diminish in size. The soil in the pygmy forest is 300 feet higher in elevation than that at the nearby beach, but 300,000 years older.

The trail, which is now a logging road, makes a loop around the pygmy forest. At this point you've officially left Jug Handle State Reserve and are within the boundary of Jackson Demonstration State Forest. You can choose to either walk the entire loop around the pygmy forest, or hike a short way in and out. When you're ready to return to the trailhead, just turn around, head back to the redwood forest, and hike downhill.

Information and Contact

There is no fee. A map and trail guide is available at the building on the southwest side of the parking lot. For more information, contact Jug Handle State Reserve, P.O. Box 440, Mendocino, CA 95460, 707/937-5804, website: www.parks.ca.gov.

Directions

From Mendocino, drive four miles north on Highway 1 to the entrance to Jug Handle State Reserve on the left. Turn left and park in the parking area. The Ecological Staircase Nature Trail begins on the southwest side of the parking lot. A more direct trail, which bypasses the coastal headlands, begins on the northwest side of the parking lot.

5 HEADLANDS &
DEVIL'S PUNCHBOWL TRAILS
Russian Gulch State Park, off Highway 1 near Mendocino

Total distance: 1.0 mile round-trip   **Hiking time:** 30 minutes

Type of trail: mostly level terrain   **Best season:** year-round

There's something so compelling about the Mendocino coast that it draws millions of visitors every year. Many of them are hoping for little more than the chance to walk on an uncrowded coastal bluff and watch the sun go down. One of the best places to do just that is at Russian Gulch State Park, or more specifically at a small stretch of the park west of Highway 1 and east of the ocean breakers.

The trail on the ocean side of Russian Gulch is so informal that it doesn't even have a proper name, but everyone knows it as the place to see the Devil's Punchbowl. That's the rather imaginative name for a "blowhole" in the headlands, a geyser-like hole in the middle of soft bedrock, where ocean waves push up underneath the rock and then burst, spouting and splashing, through the top of the hole. The Devil's Punchbowl is one of the Mendocino coast's most famous blowholes.

At first glance, the Devil's Punchbowl looks like little more than a large hole in the ground that is surrounded by a wooden fence. A closer look at the hole—which is more than 100 feet in diameter and 60 feet deep—reveals that its bottom is a tidepool, with the rhythm of ocean waves continually moving water in and out. That means the land you're standing on, which seems firm and sturdy enough, is actually "land" for only about 30 feet down—its base is carved out by the pounding of the sea. You are actually standing on a ledge, the roof of a giant sea cave.

Although the park brochure describes the Devil's Punchbowl as "geyser-like," don't come here expecting to see Old Faithful. The blowhole is so large and wide-open that the geyser effect is greatly diminished except during big storms and very high tides. Most of the time waves just roll in through the sea cave, then retreat back out to sea.

Keep your eyes and ears on alert for big spouts and splashes, however, although not necessarily from the Devil's Punchbowl. Friendly gray whales frequent this area of the coast from December until April. We saw one about 200 yards offshore, spouting and flopping about like he or she was having a fine time.

From the parking area, the hike begins at the wooden fence by a signboard explaining how erosion creates the sea caves and other formations. Start hiking on either of two trails; the trail on the right takes you more directly to the fenced-in Devil's Punchbowl. After that, you're on your own. A series of paths cross the blufftop and all of them lead to dramatic views of the rocky shoreline and azure ocean. If you keep heading to your right along the bluffs and then circle back along the coast to your left, you can make a loop out of the trip.

The best times to take this walk are in the early morning or just about sunset, when the coastal wind diminishes. Always bring a jacket and be prepared for either heavy fog or brilliant sunshine and wind.

Options
Combine this trip with the following hike in Fern Canyon on the inland side of Russian Gulch State Park.

Information and Contact
A $6 day-use fee is charged per vehicle. A free map is available at the entrance kiosk. For more information, contact Russian Gulch State Park, P.O. Box 440, Mendocino, CA 95460, 707/937-5804, website: www.parks.ca.gov.

Directions
From Mendocino, drive two miles north on Highway 1 to the entrance sign for Russian Gulch State Park on the left. Turn left and then left again immediately to reach the entrance kiosk at the park. After paying, drive past the kiosk and turn right at the sign for the picnic area. Drive past the picnic area to where the road ends at the parking area for the Blowhole and Devil's Punchbowl. The trailhead is at the fence directly in front of you.

6 FERN CANYON & FALLS LOOP TRAILS

Russian Gulch State Park, off Highway 1 near Mendocino

Total distance: 4.6 miles round-trip

Type of trail: rolling terrain

Hiking time: 2 hours

Best season: December–May

There comes a time when you just have to stretch the rules a little. For me, the time came when I hiked the Fern Canyon Trail to the waterfall at Russian Gulch State Park. My cardinal rule was "never hike on pavement," and I was fairly self-righteous about it. But the lure of a waterfall in a fern-filled canyon was too good to pass up, even though it required walking on an old paved trail for two thirds of the total 4.6-mile round-trip.

The paved Fern Canyon Trail may not be completely au naturel, but it is rutted, cracked, and covered with leaves and fir needles. The route is almost completely level, making for a gentle, easy hike accompanied by the sound of water from Russian Gulch, which accompanies you the whole way. A dense forest, filled with second-growth redwoods, hemlocks, Douglas firs, big leaf maples, alders, and tons of ferns, borders the trail on both sides. In late summer, trailside blackberry bushes provide nourishment for hungry hikers. Stinging nettles and poison oak are also prevalent, so watch where you tread if you stray off the pavement.

The trail directions are simple: you follow Fern Canyon Trail to its intersection with the Falls Loop Trail, where the pavement ends. Here you'll see a few picnic tables and a bike rack, as well as a junction with the North Trail for those who choose to hike the longer path (see Options, below). The Falls Loop Trail gives you the choice of going left or right; both paths even-

Russian Gulch Falls

© ANN MARIE BROWN

tually join at the waterfall, but the left trail is much shorter (.7 mile to the waterfall versus 2.3 miles), so that's our choice for a 4.6-mile round-trip. The unpaved stretch has a few more ups and downs than the paved trail, including some wooden stairsteps. In .7 mile, a glimpse of Russian Gulch Falls comes into view just before the trail heads downhill to its base.

The falls at Russian Gulch prove the adage that when it comes to waterfalls, setting rather than size is what counts. At a mere 36 feet, Russian Gulch Falls is no record setter, but it drops over a huge slab of rock into a verdant grotto so beautiful that it makes a lasting impression. In winter, the waterfall can be a rushing torrent that spills over the huge boulder at its base, while in summer, it is reduced to one main cascade and a smaller, thinner stream that pours down the left side of the rock. Broken tree trunks and branches are jammed around the base of the falls, having fallen and tumbled over its lip. Some have been there so long that plants are growing on top of them, creating a lush green frame for the falling water. One tree trunk, leaning vertically against the waterfall's boulder, is completely lined with dense thriving ferns.

It isn't easy to leave this special place, and so often you will find hikers picnicking or just hanging out at the footbridge near the base of the falls. Chances are good that you will probably decide to join them.

Options

Purists can get around the pavement problem by taking the alternate, unpaved North Trail. For hikers only, it connects to the Falls Loop Trail but adds two miles to your hike, making a 6.6-mile round-trip. Another way to extend the hike is to follow the paved Fern Canyon Trail, but then hike the entire Falls Loop Trail instead of just the .7-mile out-and-back to the falls. This makes a 6.9-mile round-trip.

Information and Contact

A $6 day-use fee is charged per vehicle. A free map is available at the entrance kiosk. For more information, contact Russian Gulch State Park, P.O. Box 440, Mendocino, CA 95460, 707/937-5804, website: www.parks.ca.gov.

Directions

From Mendocino, drive two miles north on Highway 1 to the entrance sign for Russian Gulch State Park on the left. Turn left and then immediately left again to reach the entrance kiosk. After paying, drive past the kiosk and continue straight, crossing back under the highway, to the eastern side of the park. Drive past the recreation hall and all of the campsites to the parking area for the Fern Canyon Trail. Start hiking from the trailhead at the east side of the parking area.

7 BIG HENDY GROVE & HERMIT HUT TRAILS
Hendy Woods State Park, off Highway 128 near Philo

Total distance: 2.0 miles round-trip

Type of trail: rolling terrain

Hiking time: 1 hour

Best season: year-round

As you drive on Highway 128 from Cloverdale to Mendocino, you notice through your car windows that the landscape changes from dry oak grasslands to dense, deep redwood forest. Would-be hikers may be tempted by the sight of hiking paths leading from the roadside into the redwoods. Who could resist a walk among big trees paralleling the Navarro River?

If you decide to pull over, you may be disappointed. None of these trails go farther than a few hundred yards, ending at swimming and fishing holes. If it's a more lengthy hike in the redwoods that you desire, the best place in the neighborhood is at Hendy Woods State Park, a little visited preserve that features many beautiful trees, plus an unusual twist—a story that will add an unexpected dimension to your trip.

From the park's day-use parking area, start hiking on the wheelchair-accessible All-Access Trail, turning left and following the trail signs for the Discovery Trail and Big Hendy Grove. You'll pass tall standing redwoods as well as several downed trees, where children love to play on the huge horizontal trunks and gnarled root balls. The farther you walk from the parking area, the more peaceful and quiet this old forest becomes. Patches of sorrel form soft green clouds on the ground. Black-tailed deer can be seen munching on the greenery. Sunlight filters through the tall trees, softly illuminating the scene.

After looping around the Big Hendy Grove, walk a little farther south on the All-Access Trail (away from the parking area) until you come to the trail marker for the Hermit Hut Trail on your left. The Hermit Hut Trail climbs steadily up from the redwood-lined valley floor through a drier forest of oaks and madrones. You'll feel the temperature rise as you ascend out of the redwoods' dense shade. After crossing a fire road, you'll climb another 100 yards until you reach an unmarked intersection. Continue straight to a billboard displaying newspaper clippings about the Hermit Hut Trail's hermit, a Russian immigrant named Petrov, who lived for 18 years in these woods, building huts out of branches and tree stumps.

The display serves as a memorial to Petrov, who died in the early 1980s. He lived out his days eating food he gathered from the forest and neighboring gardens; wearing patched-together, discarded clothing from campers and park visitors; and living in the huts he built that still stand on these trails. One is located right behind the billboard. A ramshackle batch of branches serves as a roof over a large, hollowed-out tree stump. Another of Petrov's huts is found a few yards away near the unmarked intersection you just passed.

Not surprisingly, children are mesmerized by the story of Petrov and the sight of his primitive huts. Maybe it's the immensity of the redwood trees in this area, or maybe it's the way the light filters through the forest, but it isn't hard to imagine him here, living his simple life in the woods.

Options

You can park your car near the ranger station and visitors center and hike to the Little Hendy Grove of redwoods, which is smaller in size but no less impressive than the Big Hendy Grove.

Information and Contact

A $6 day-use fee is charged per vehicle. A free map is available at the entrance station. For more information, contact Hendy Woods State Park, P.O. Box 440, Mendocino, CA 95460, 707/895-3141 or 707/937-5804, website: www.parks.ca.gov.

Directions

From Mendocino, drive south on Highway 1 for approximately 10 miles to the Highway 128 turnoff. Head east on Highway 128 for 18 miles to the directional sign for Hendy Woods State Park at Greenwood Road. Turn right on Greenwood Road and drive to the park entrance on the left. Follow the park road to the day-use parking area. The trailhead is on the east (right) side of the parking area.

8 CHINESE GULCH & PHILLIPS GULCH TRAILS
Kruse Rhododendron State Reserve,
off Highway 1 near Jenner

Total distance: 2.8 miles round-trip   **Hiking time:** 1 hour

Type of trail: rolling terrain   **Best season:** April–June

You've made the long trip to the Sonoma Coast on Memorial Day weekend and the beaches and parks are packed with people. On top of that, the sun hasn't shown itself for days, so you're not exactly enjoying stellar coastal views. Well, cheer up, because this is a peaceful coastal hike that's enjoyable even in the densest fog.

© ANN MARIE BROWN

a showy rhododendron at Kruse Rhododendron State Reserve

The Chinese Gulch and Phillips Gulch trails in Kruse Rhododendron State Reserve combine to provide a pleasant woodland hike with many opportunities to view the park's featured species—the coast rhododendron (rhododendron macrophylum). You have to show up in the right season, through. From April–June, these tree-like shrubs have large clusters of pinkish-purple flowers, with each showy cluster about the size of a nosegay or small bouquet. But in the non-blooming months, the rhododendrons blend into the forest backdrop and you might not even notice they are there.

The rhododendrons thrive because of a fire that burned through this area many years ago, causing a succession of plant regeneration that will eventually lead to a completely reforested second-growth redwood and fir grove. The showy shrubs are slowly losing their hold in the forest as the trees grow up and around them, blocking out their light.

If it's the regal rhododendron that you've come to see, make your first trip on the .25-mile Rhododendron Trail Loop that starts right at the parking lot. That's where you'll find the most flowers. But the longer Chinese Gulch and Phillips Gulch trails offer charms of their own, including plentiful ferns and a dense redwood and fir forest, plus tiny grasses and wildflowers growing up and out of dying redwood stumps—new life literally springing from the old. Both Chinese and Phillips gulches are good-sized streams flowing under rustic wooden bridges. Whimsically built of rough-hewn logs with branches for railings, some of the bridges have large mushrooms growing on them.

The loop route is well marked. At several points, the trail junctions with paths that lead to "County Road" (the dirt and gravel road you drove in on), but stay on the gulch trails unless you want to take a shortcut back. At about 1.5 miles, you cross the road to transfer from the Chinese Gulch Trail to the Phillips Gulch Trail. The hiking is generally easier on the

Phillips Gulch Trail, the second half of your loop. The pathway climbs and descends a considerable amount, but redwood logs along the way make comfortable benches. This is a path for taking your time and stopping to enjoy the forest as you go.

Your final stream crossing is at Chinese Gulch, which flows all the way to the Pacific Ocean. From there you begin a short but steep climb back up to the parking lot. It's less than a quarter mile of climbing, but it's just enough to make you feel like you got a workout right at the end of the trip.

Options
Neighboring Salt Point State Park has many excellent hiking trails; see the Bluff Trail description and its accompanying Options.

Information and Contact
There is no fee. For more information on Kruse Rhododendron State Reserve, contact Salt Point State Park, 25050 Coast Highway 1, Jenner, CA 95450, 707/847-3221 or 707/865-2391, website: www.parks.ca.gov.

Directions
From U.S. 101 at Santa Rosa, drive west on Highway 116 for 33 miles, through Sebastopol and Guerneville, to Highway 116's intersection with Highway 1 near Jenner. Continue north on Highway 1 for 24 miles, passing several Salt Point State Park entrances. Turn right on Kruse Ranch Road, 100 yards north of the Fisk Mill Cove parking area. Drive .5 mile on Kruse Ranch Road to the small dirt parking area at the trailhead. Begin hiking on the north side of the parking lot at the wooden steps on the left that lead to Chinese Gulch.

9 BLUFF TRAIL
Salt Point State Park, off Highway 1 near Jenner

Total distance: 1.75 miles round-trip   **Hiking time:** 1 hour

Type of trail: rolling terrain   **Best season:** year-round

Salt Point State Park is blessed with a long stretch of pristine Sonoma coastline, rich tidepools and kelp beds teeming with sea life, and plentiful hiking trails. One of the easiest and most rewarding is the Bluff Trail that begins at Fisk Mill Cove, a few miles north of the main park entrance and campground.

The trail is good from the get-go. As you start down the dirt path, you'll see a trail marker that points you to the left to South Cove (.1 mile away), or to the right to Sentinel Rock and Fisk Mill Cove. If you're visiting in winter or early spring, this signpost is a good place to get a view of a seasonal waterfall that plunges from the bluffs down to the sea. Head left to South Cove, ending up right on top of this small waterfall. Continue a short distance to the bluffs beyond the cove, gaining more coastal views before the path dissipates in the coastal scrub. Then simply turn around and hike back, keeping the ocean on your left. When you reach the trail sign again, continue past it toward Sentinel Rock and Fisk Mill Cove.

This is not a hike where you'll mind retracing your steps. While wandering on the Bluff Trail, you're never more than 50 feet from the land's edge and the crashing shoreline (and often tantalizingly closer). Your path is a nearly level walkway through a forest of ferns, rhododendrons, and stands of cypress and bishop pines. Even while you're enveloped in the shade of this peaceful woodland, you're given peek-a-boo views of rocky pocket beaches with crashing waves, playful seals swimming in the surf, and abalone divers plying their trade.

The trail crosses three wooden footbridges, spanning streams that carry runoff from the hills down to the ocean. A highlight is a large sandstone formation with tiny hollowed caves begging for exploration. Perhaps most enticing is a lovely trailside meadow, protected from the wind on three

a winding path along the blufftops, Salt Point State Park

sides. During one late April visit, this meadow was completely covered with purple Douglas irises.

The Bluff Trail is fairly level, with many short spurs that lead to vistas of the ocean and coves below. The spurs either dead end or rejoin the main trail, so it's impossible to stray too far. The only major ascent occurs on the stairstepped path to the viewing platform atop Sentinel Rock, a dramatic coastal overlook. You'll find that the climb is worth the effort for the expansive view, and a bench on top of the rock invites you to stay a while.

After descending from Sentinel Rock, finish out your trip by following the short path that leads down to rocky Fisk Mill Cove, a picturesque beach and popular spot for abalone diving. Then make the one-mile return walk to your car. Picnic tables and fire grills are situated right at the trailhead, so you might cap off your hike with a spot of lunch.

Options

Proceed to the main park entrance and turn into the inland side of the park, which is signed for Woodside Campground. From the parking area just beyond the kiosk you can take a steep one-mile hike to see the park's pygmy forest of stunted cypress and pine trees.

Information and Contact

A $3 day-use fee is charged per vehicle at Fisk Mill Cove. (Pay at the "iron ranger," a metal box in which you deposit your money and keep a receipt.) At the main park entrance the day-use fee is $6. Trail maps are available at the ranger kiosk or visitors center. For more information, contact Salt Point State Park, 25050 Coast Highway 1, Jenner, CA 95450, 707/847-3221 or 707/865-2391, website: www.parks.ca.gov.

Directions

From U.S. 101 at Santa Rosa, drive west on Highway 116 for 33 miles, through Sebastopol and Guerneville, to Highway 116's intersection with Highway 1 near Jenner. Continue north on Highway 1 for approximately 24 miles. Bypass the main Salt Point State Park entrance at Gerstle Cove and turn left at the Fisk Mill Cove parking area, located 2.6 miles north of Gerstle Cove. Park in the parking lot on the left, then find the trailhead on the ocean side of the lot. The trail is not signed but it is the only trail, with picnic tables and fire grills nearby.

🔟 FORT ROSS COVE TRAIL

Fort Ross State Historic Park, off Highway 1 near Jenner

Total distance: 2.0 miles round-trip

Type of trail: rolling terrain

Hiking time: 1 hour

Best season: year-round

If you're traveling along the Sonoma Coast, stop the car, put on a jacket, and take this hike at Fort Ross State Historic Park. Not only will you have the chance to learn a little history and explore an old Russian colonial fort, but you'll also get to stroll along the scenic Sonoma coastline.

The Fort Ross Cove Trail is not an official designated trail, but rather a wander-as-you-please meander through Fort Ross's stockade walls and then along the top of steep bluffs that drop 100 feet into the sea. You can choose your own route, stopping to enjoy the history or the scenery as you wish.

The old Russian fort, with its huge barracks area and two-story block-houses complete with cannons, is an intriguing sight. Fort Ross was built in 1812 in only a few weeks by Russian colonists who were eager for eastern expansion. It was occupied until 1841. The smell of the wood in the old buildings evokes images of those earlier times, when colonists tried to develop an economy here based first on sea otter pelts and later on agriculture. Neither led to substantial profits.

When you've seen enough of the fort, follow the gravel road that leads out the main gate toward the ocean. The road circles down into Fort Ross Cove, which was the first shipyard in California, established by the Russians for their pelt-trading business. Today you'll find a few picnic tables here.

You can explore the tiny cove, which is covered with odd-shaped driftwood and wave-smoothed rocks. A small, shallow stream must be crossed in springtime—a little strategic foot placement on rocks should work, although some hikers prefer the leap-and-pray method of stream crossing. On the far side, look for the closest point on the bluffs across from you. Here, about 30 yards from the stream, you'll find an indistinct trail that leads up the bluffs.

Follow this faint path to get a true taste of what the Sonoma Coast is all about. If it's a clear day, the wind will likely blow with near-gale force. In spring, you'll see the usual cabal of coastal wildflowers—lupine, paintbrush, and Douglas irises. Raptors and gulls soar overhead. You can peek over the edge of the bluffs to watch the waves crash against the rocky shoreline.

The trail soon descends to a gravel road where you'll find restrooms and a 20-site campground. A path leads off to the right, down to the beach.

Two tiny streams join together here on their way to the ocean, with horse-tail ferns growing along their banks. Pick your way among the rocks down to the beach.

Information and Contact
A $6 day-use fee is charged per vehicle. A park brochure is available at the visitors center. For more information, contact Fort Ross State Historic Park, 19005 Coast Highway 1, Jenner, CA 95450, 707/847-3286 or 707/865-2391, website: www.parks.ca.gov.

Directions
From U.S. 101 at Santa Rosa, drive west on Highway 116 for 33 miles, through Sebastopol and Guerneville, to Highway 116's intersection with Highway 1 near Jenner. Continue north on Highway 1 for approximately 15 miles to the entrance to Fort Ross State Historic Park.

⬛11 RITCHEY CANYON & COYOTE PEAK
Bothe-Napa Valley State Park,
off Highway 29/128 near St. Helena

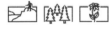

Total distance: 4.6 miles round-trip

Type of trail: rolling terrain

Hiking time: 2 hours

Best season: year-round

Even the most devoted and enthusiastic Napa Valley wine tasters eventually tire of their task. If it's a hot summer day, perhaps they start to day dream of a shady redwood forest where they could walk for a while or sit by a stream. Such musing might seem preposterous: Where in the midst of the sun-baked vineyards could a redwood tree possibly grow?

At Bothe-Napa Valley State Park, that's where. Ritchey Canyon and Redwood trails take you through a delightful stand of them, one of the most eastern groves of coastal redwoods in California. Paired with a visit to the summit of Coyote Peak, this loop trip will leave you even more intoxicated with Napa Valley's wine country.

Joining the redwoods are plenty of Douglas firs, buckeyes, and big-leaf maples, plus ferns galore. Look carefully among the branches of the trees: five different kinds of woodpeckers dwell within the park's borders. I was lucky enough to see the largest of these, the pileated woodpecker, on a tree right by the picnic area. He was working his way up and down a big Douglas fir like a telephone lineman on triple overtime.

Start your hike by heading up Ritchey Canyon Trail from the horse trailer parking lot. (You can also start by the small bridge near the visitors center, or access the trail from the park campground if you are camping there.) The first .5 mile is somewhat noisy due to the proximity of the highway and campground, but soon you leave those distractions behind. Ferns, wild grape, and spice bush line the path. Second-growth redwoods are mixed in with Douglas firs. Black oaks and big-leaf maples form a canopy over the trail and also Ritchey Creek, which runs dependably year-round. (The oaks and maples wear bright yellow coats in autumn.) Keep the creek on your right; the trail narrows and meets up with Redwood Trail, which you then follow. Ritchey Canyon Trail crosses to the north side of the stream.

Three-quarters of a mile from the start, reach a junction with Coyote Peak Trail and bear left. The trail doles out a fair climb but remains shaded most of the way. Soon you leave the conifers and enter drier slopes and a bay and live oak forest. In short order the oaks give way to low-growing chaparral and scattered rock outcrops. Wide views open up on your right of conifer-covered Ritchey Canyon below.

Near the top of the climb you reach a junction; the right fork will be your return. Bear left and make a short but steep ascent to a knoll just below Coyote Peak's summit. You're rewarded with a pastoral view of the vineyards and valley far below—the best view of the day. The summit is a short

boulder-laden Ritchey Creek

distance farther, but its vista is somewhat obstructed by trees. Peering through the branches, you can make out Mount St. Helena to the northwest.

Return to the junction with the western leg of Coyote Peak Trail and follow it steeply down the opposite side of the mountain. You'll soon leave toyon, chemise, and ceanothus in favor of shady redwoods. At a junction with South Fork Trail, turn right. Follow a concrete apron across Ritchey Creek, then turn right on Redwood Trail and cross the creek again. The next half mile on Redwood Trail is the loveliest of the trip, featuring the densest redwoods and ferns.

If Ritchey Creek isn't running too full and wide, you can cross it at an obvious (but unbridged) spur, then follow Ritchey Canyon Trail for part of your return. On the opposite bank of Ritchey Creek, Ritchey Canyon Trail passes the old Hitchcock home site, where Lillie Hitchcock Coit and her parents spent their summers in the 1870s. Lillie Coit is best known for lending her name and money to Coit Tower on Telegraph Hill in San Francisco.

Spring is the best season to hike at Bothe-Napa. In April and May, the buckeyes are in fragrant bloom and the creek is running strong. Wildflowers, including solomon's seal and redwood orchids, bloom in the cool shade in February and March. Park volunteers manage a small Native American plant garden near the visitors center, where you can learn about the local native flora and how it was used by the people who once lived here.

Options

To extend your trip, combine this hike with the following hike, which leads from Bothe-Napa Valley State Park to Bale Grist Mill State Historic Park. To shorten it, skip the ascent to the top of Coyote Peak and instead just hike out-and-back on Ritchey Canyon and Redwood Trails.

Information and Contact

A $6 day-use fee is charged per vehicle. Trail maps are available at the ranger kiosk. For more information, contact Bothe-Napa Valley State Park, 3801 St. Helena Highway North, Calistoga, CA 94515, 707/942-4575 or 707/938-1519, website: www.parks.ca.gov.

Directions

From Highway 29/128 in St. Helena, drive north on Highway 29/128 for five miles to the entrance to Bothe-Napa Valley State Park; it's on the left side of the highway. (It's 3.5 miles south of Calistoga.) Turn left and drive .25 mile to the entrance kiosk, then continue past the visitors center to the horse trailer parking lot on the right. The trail begins on the right side of the horse trailer parking lot.

12 HISTORY TRAIL TO BALE GRIST MILL

Bothe-Napa Valley State Park,
off Highway 29/128 near St. Helena

Total distance: 2.4 miles round-trip

Type of trail: rolling terrain

Hiking time: 1.5 hours

Best season: November–May

You may have seen the sign for Bale Grist Mill while driving through the Napa wine country and wondered what the heck it was. Most likely you never found the time to check it out. After all, a trip to a historical monument is a hard sell in Napa, considering the area's other attractions and diversions.

The best way to learn about the history of the Bale Grist Mill is to hike there from neighboring Bothe-Napa Valley State Park on the History Trail. The trail begins at a small pioneer cemetery near the highway, then slowly starts to climb, heading up a ridge. A canopy of hardwoods provides much-needed shade on hot days. Madrone trees with their shiny red trunks brighten the forest. In spring, the woodland wildflowers put on a show, including waxy yellow fairy lanterns and purple, vine-like spring vetch. Also in spring, the buckeye trees blossom, with their banana-shaped flower clusters and sweet lilac aroma. Although non-native in Northern California, the buckeye tends to grow in places formerly inhabited by Native Americans, who apparently carried the buckeye seeds with them to plant.

The scenery changes as the History Trail nears the Bale Grist Mill. In contrast to the dry, wooded slopes you've been walking on, the terrain here includes a stream and water—enough to drive the big water wheel that ran Edward Bale's flour mill in the 1840s and 1850s.

Still in operating condition, Bale Grist Mill's water wheel is 36 feet tall and has several large millstones, which were used to convert grains grown in the Napa Valley to usable flour. Water was diverted from Mill Creek into a millpond and several ditches, where it was transported to the top of the waterwheel via a wooden flume. The water turned the wheel and generated power, which in turn ran the millstones that ground the grains.

After your visit to this interesting piece of machinery and a significant part of Napa's history, you might consider a picnic near the waters of Mill Creek. Pack your lunch before you go, and keep in mind that the History Trail is best walked on cool spring days, before Napa's summer temperatures heat up. Avoid midday walks when it's warm, because the trail climbs a few hundred feet before dropping into Bale Grist Mill State Park.

Options
You can drive to Bale Grist Mill State Park and walk around the mill area from the parking lot. The entrance to Bale Grist Mill State Park is 1.5 miles south of Bothe-Napa Valley State Park on Highway 29/128.

Information and Contact
A $6 day-use fee is charged per vehicle. Trail maps are available at the ranger kiosk. For more information, contact Bothe-Napa Valley State Park, 3801 St. Helena Highway North, Calistoga, CA 94515, 707/942-4575 or 707/938-1519, website: www.parks.ca.gov.

Directions
From Highway 29/128 in St. Helena, drive north on Highway 29/128 for five miles to the entrance to Bothe-Napa Valley State Park, which is on the left side of the highway. (It's 3.5 miles south of Calistoga.) Turn left, drive .25 mile to the entrance kiosk, and then go straight past the swimming pool and restrooms to where the road ends at the picnic area and trailhead for the History Trail.

13 CANYON TRAIL
Sugarloaf Ridge State Park, off Highway 12 near Kenwood

Total distance: 1.0 mile round-trip   **Hiking time:** 45 minutes

Type of trail: rolling terrain   **Best season:** December–May

---

You want a short, pretty trail in a shady forest? You got it. You want to see a 25-foot waterfall cascading down over rocks, surrounded by big-leaf maples and ferns? Here it is. You want to walk downhill all the way to reach it? No problem. You get all of this on the Canyon Trail in Sugarloaf Ridge State Park when you pay a visit to Sonoma Creek's tumbling waterfall.

The fall is surprising not just because it exists in notoriously dry and warm Sonoma County, but also because it's hidden just off the road, less than a half-mile walk from where you leave your car. The path is short enough so that almost anyone, even very small children, can hike it. And the trail is such a lovely shaded route that you'll find plenty of reason to go slow, enjoying the sounds of gurgling Sonoma Creek, and the sight and texture of the many trees, plants, and mossy rocks along the way.

Start walking downhill at the Canyon Trail sign from near the entrance kiosk, dropping a steep 300 feet in .4 mile. Descend through a dense and shady forest of hardwoods—oaks, bays, madrones, and alders. When you reach the falls after about 15 minutes of walking, you enter a lush, wet grotto that is piled with huge, rounded, moss-covered boulders. Many of them are more slippery than they look, so use caution. The trail runs along the edge of the creek. You can climb on the rocks and explore quite close to the cascading water.

on top of the waterfall at Sugarloaf Ridge State Park

Huge boulders have tumbled down the canyon to create Sonoma Creek Falls, a stairstepped cascade about 25 feet high. Big-leaf maple vines and plentiful ferns thrive at the water's edge, providing a leafy green contrast to the dark, jagged rock. Although Sonoma Creek Falls is best seen right after a period of rain, this shady glen remains a cool respite even in the summer heat, when the waterfall is nearly dry. Downstream of the falls the maples give way to a fine grove of tall redwood trees.

A caveat: It gets hot at this park in summer, with temperatures in the 90s almost every day, so Sonoma Creek often dwindles by June or July. The best time to see the waterfall is shortly after winter and early spring rains.

Options

If you want to hike farther, continue downstream from the falls into the grove of redwoods along Sonoma Creek. When the trail meets up with Adobe Canyon Road, cross the road and follow Pony Gate Trail back to the parking lot where you left your car. This makes a 3.5-mile loop.

Information and Contact

A $6 day-use fee is charged per vehicle. A trail map is available from the ranger kiosk. For more information, contact Sugarloaf Ridge State Park, 2605 Adobe Canyon Road, Kenwood, CA 95452-9004, 707/833-5712 or 707/938-1519, website: www.parks.ca.gov.

Directions

From U.S. 101 in Santa Rosa, turn east on Highway 12 and continue for 11 miles to Adobe Canyon Road. Turn left and drive 3.5 miles to the park entrance kiosk. Pay the entrance fee, then turn around and head back down the road for about 100 yards to the gravel parking area on your right and the trailhead for the Pony Gate Trail. (Don't park anywhere in the park without a permit from the kiosk.) Cross the road to reach the trailhead for the Canyon Trail.

© ANN MARIE BROWN

Sacramento and Gold Country

Chapter 4

Sacramento and Gold Country

The Sierra Nevada foothills region surrounding the north-south corridor of Highway 49 is known as the Gold Country or the Mother Lode. It's the place where James Marshall discovered gold in January 1848, sparking a huge and frenzied migration westward. When it became known that a rich vein of gold ran underground from Mariposa to Downieville, the history of California was forever changed.

Evidence of the area's mining past is obvious, from historic brick and wooden buildings to old bridges, mines, water ditches, and an abundance of antique shops. Many of the region's towns have barely changed since their heydays: Streets are just wide enough for two stagecoaches to pass, buildings are constructed of stone from local rivers and streams, and storefronts look like they are right out of a movie set. You can travel for many miles in the Gold Country without ever seeing a traffic light. There's a whole lot of California here just waiting to be rediscovered.

The landscape of the Gold Country is made up of low-elevation foothills studded with oaks and pines, and deeply carved, roaring river canyons. Hot weather is to be expected in summer, which means the area's hiking trails are best explored in the autumn, winter, and spring months.

Also, a part of this region is the Central Valley, with its endless acres of cotton, orchards, and grazing lands, and its famous rivers: the Sacramento, American, and Feather, among others. Extending for hundreds of miles from these rivers are marshy wetlands that attract ducks and waterfowl. The Central Valley, which may seem like an empty wasteland to hurried drivers on I-5 or Highway 99, is a place of critical refuge for millions of birds on the Pacific Flyway. While following a hiking trail under the much slower speed of your own leg power, you may develop a new appreciation for this vast landscape of grasslands and waterways. After all, that much wildlife just can't be wrong.

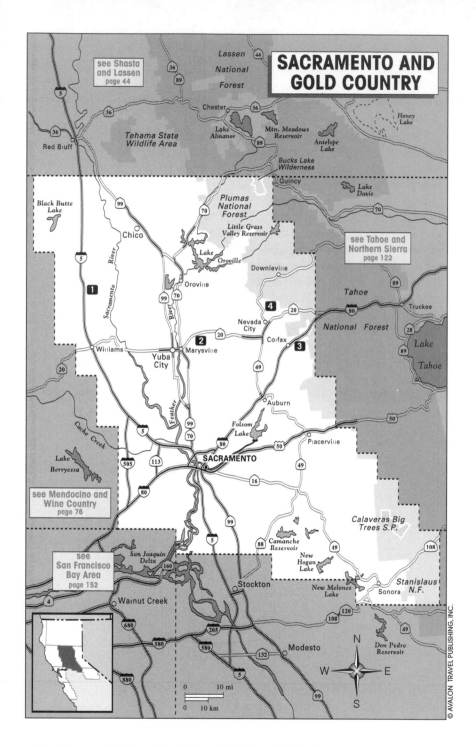

SACRAMENTO AND GOLD COUNTRY

see Shasta
and Lassen
page 44

Lassen
National
Forest

Honey
Lake

Chester

Tehama State
Wildlife Area

Lake
Almanor

Mtn. Meadows
Reservoir

Antelope
Lake

Red Bluff

Bucks Lake
Wilderness

Quincy

Lake
Davis

Black Butte
Lake

Plumas
National
Forest

Little Grass
Valley Reservoir

see Tahoe and
Northern Sierra
page 122

Chico

Lake
Oroville

Downieville

Tahoe

Truckee

Oroville

4

Nevada
City

National Forest

Lake

Williams

2

Marysville

Colfax

3

Tahoe

Yuba
City

Auburn

Cache Creek

Folsom
Lake

Placerville

Lake
Berryessa

SACRAMENTO

see Mendocino and
Wine Country
page 76

Calaveras Big
Trees S.P.

see
San Francisco
Bay Area
page 152

San Joaquin
Delta

Camanche
Reservoir

New
Hogan
Lake

Stanislaus
N.F.

Walnut Creek

Stockton

New Melones
Lake

Sonora

Modesto

Don Pedro
Reservoir

N
W   E
S

0   10 mi
0   10 km

© AVALON TRAVEL PUBLISHING, INC.

Contents

1. Wetlands Walk. 110
2. Dry Creek Falls. 111
3. Stevens Creek Trail 114
4. South Yuba Independence Trail 116

1 WETLANDS WALK
Sacramento National Wildlife Refuge, off I-5 near Willows

Total distance: 2.0 miles round-trip

Type of trail: mostly level terrain

Hiking time: 1 hour

Best season: November–May

This trail may require a leap of faith to get you hiking on it. Not because it's steep, dangerous, or patrolled by a pack of hungry wolves, but because this peaceful little path in Sacramento National Wildlife Refuge is situated smack in the middle of the Central Valley, only about a mile from the endless noise and exhaust of I-5. This place probably would win the award for Least Likely Place for a Nature Preserve. Or maybe Most Likely Place to Experience Car Fumes.

But don't let the miles of asphalt highway fool you. The area surrounding this part of I-5 is prime farmland, mostly for rice and other grains. That's why the Sacramento National Wildlife Refuge is positioned here. Long before modern farmers moved in to the area, the Central Valley was a key stop for birds on the Pacific Flyway. Even today, an estimated 60 percent of all ducks, geese, swans, and other birds on the Flyway spend part of each year in the Central Valley.

It turns out the birds and the farmers all want the same thing—the valley's huge expanses of marshes and wetlands, which are created by seasonal flooding of the Sacramento River. The problem is, when man and birds covet the same resources, man usually wins. In the Central Valley and most of California, agricultural needs combined with the encroachment of urbanization and industry have led to the destruction of more than 90 percent of the wetlands—prime bird territory—that once existed.

But the birds don't give up easily. In the Central Valley, they tried using farm fields for their habitat, much to the chagrin of the farmers. So as early as the 1950s the federal government smartened up and opened three wildlife refuges in the Central Valley. Now the birds are happy, the farmers are happy, and people who love easy wildlife walks are especially happy.

When you visit, you have to overcome a little culture shock: Moments before you were passing trucks going 70 mph on the freeway, but now you are walking through peaceful seasonal marshes, gazing at placid ponds and vernal pools, and seeing an incredible amount of wildlife. I saw more jackrabbits along the refuge's two-mile loop trail than I saw collectively in a year of hiking. You may also see raccoons, deer, squirrels, frogs, and lizards, plus more birds than you can imagine. Be on the lookout for migrating ducks and geese, plus resident great blue herons, great egrets, pheasants, hawks, harriers, coots, avocets, sandpipers, owls, woodpeckers, and songbirds.

The trail is a breeze to follow, completely level, and well signed. From the parking area, the path crosses the entrance road, then makes two connected loops, forming a figure eight. Winter is the prime season to see wildlife (particularly migratory waterfowl). But even in June, there is much life in these marshes. Time your trip so that you arrive in the morning or late afternoon—the best times for wildlife watching.

Information and Contact

There is no fee. A free trail map/brochure is available at the trailhead or refuge visitors center. For more information, contact the Sacramento National Wildlife Refuge, Route 1, Box 311, Willows, CA 95988, 916/934-2801, website: http://pacific.fws.gov/sacramento.

Directions

Traveling north on I-5 from Sacramento, take the Norman Road/Princeton exit, 18 miles north of Williams and Highway 20. (It is signed for the Sacramento National Wildlife Refuge. If you're driving south on I-5, the exit is seven miles south of Willows.) At the first intersection, turn left on County Road 99W and drive one mile, then turn right into the refuge. The trail begins at the parking area. You can walk the loop in either direction.

2 DRY CREEK FALLS

Spenceville Wildlife Area, off Highway 20 near Marysville

Total distance: 5.0 miles round-trip

Hiking time: 1 hour

Type of trail: mostly level terrain

Best season: November–May

From the first autumn rain until midsummer, Dry Creek is anything but dry. Because the creek is located in the middle of arid oak-and-grassland country in the Central Valley, it's surprising that Dry Creek keeps a steady flow of water year-round, but Dry Creek is fed by perennial springs. An even greater surprise is that although the terrain it traverses is mostly level, the creek possesses a steep and narrow rock gorge, which forms two sizable cataracts.

Dry Creek Falls is known by two other names, Shingle Falls or Fairy Falls. The source of the latter name is unknown, but may be related to the wildflowers—commonly called fairy lanterns—that bloom in the grasslands near the falls. Shingle was the name of a retired military officer from nearby Beale Air Force Base.

Access to Dry Creek Falls is through Spenceville Wildlife Area, an 11,000-acre wildlife preserve that is seldom visited by hikers but frequently visited by hunters and equestrians. Leashed dogs are allowed in the refuge, and horses and bikes are allowed on the fire roads. A small campground is located near the end of Spenceville Road, shortly before the start of the trail to the falls.

Don't be put off by Dry Creek Falls' trailhead, which is a blocked-off, old concrete bridge at the end of Spenceville Road. Although it's

Dry Creek Falls

only an eyesore now, at one time, you could drive across this bridge over Dry Creek. When you walk across it, watch out for gaping holes that have been burned through some of the planks.

Turn right on the dirt road immediately following the bridge (Old Spenceville Road Trail) and hike eastward. Dry Creek is on your right, gurgling over rounded rocks. The route is wide, level, and easy, winding through open grasslands and stands of white, valley, and canyon oaks. When the white oaks' leaves drop in winter, you see that their branches are completely shrouded with lime-colored lichens. Spring wildflowers can be fantastic in these oak grasslands. April and early May are usually the best months to see California poppies, blue gilias, Chinese houses, many species of brodiaea, and other colorful blooms.

Keep on the lookout for wild turkeys. We saw a large flock of them, as well as a couple of handsome ring-necked pheasants, scurrying across the trail. The plentiful turkeys invite plentiful hunters during turkey season; you would be wise to avoid this trail during the weekends of turkey season (late March and April).

Stay on this main road, ignoring any side trails, for just shy of a mile, then turn right and hike south where the left fork is gated off. Shortly beyond a cattle guard, two trails take off on your left, the Upper and Lower Loop Trails, open to hikers only. Either of these will take you to the falls, but a better choice is to stay on the main path, which becomes Fairy Falls Trail. This trail brings you alongside Dry Creek, then heads upstream to Dry Creek Falls (or Fairy Falls, Shingle Falls, or whatever you prefer to call it). The first waterfall you reach is about 30 feet tall, pouring through a notch in the rounded rock. It's somewhat difficult to get a full-length view of it. If you scramble around, you can find some good picnicking spots on the rocky, serpentine outcrops above the creek.

A more impressive fall awaits about 100 yards upstream, this one dropping 50 feet into an immense pool. It free-falls, then hits a slanted ledge, then free-falls again. The trailside of the cliff is barricaded with a 50-yard-long chain-link fence so you can view the fall without plummeting over the edge. A sign warns against diving off the cliffs but it's hard to believe that anyone would try it. It's a long, scary drop to the pool.

Options

From the upper fall, you can choose to simply backtrack for your homeward trip, or follow the Upper or Lower Loop Trails back to the cattle guard and Old Spenceville Road Trail.

Information and Contact

There is no fee. Free maps of Spenceville Wildlife Area are available at information signposts in the refuge. For more information, contact Spenceville Wildlife Area, c/o Oroville Wildlife Area, California Department of Fish and Game, 945 Oro Dam Boulevard West, Oroville, CA 95965, 530/538-2236, website: www.dfg.ca.gov. Or contact Friends of Spenceville, P.O. Box 1408, Wheatland, CA 95692.

Directions

From Marysville, drive east on Highway 20 for approximately 14 miles, then turn right (south) on Smartville Road. Drive .9 mile and bear left at the fork to stay on Smartville Road. Continue another 3.8 miles to Waldo Road and bear left on the gravel road. Follow Waldo Road 1.9 miles to the Waldo Bridge. Cross it and turn left on Spenceville Road, then drive 2.2 miles to the end of the road at an old, blocked-off bridge. Park by the bridge and walk across.

If you are coming from Grass Valley, drive 12.5 miles west on Highway 20 to Smartville Road, then turn left (south) and continue as above.

3 STEVENS CREEK TRAIL

BLM Folsom Resource Area, off I-80 in Colfax

Total distance: 3.0 miles round-trip

Hiking time: 1.5 hours

Type of trail: some steep terrain

Best season: January–June

Most people need a darn good reason to get out of their air-conditioned cars when driving east of Sacramento on I-80 in the summer heat. Like maybe because a UFO has landed on the freeway in front of them, or Elvis is selling lemonade and signing autographs at a rest stop.

The Stevens Creek Trail, managed by the Bureau of Land Management, is a good reason to pull off the road and challenge the heat. The trail tunnels through a lovely mixed forest graced with abundant wildflowers, crosses multiple streams, and travels past a small waterfall to spectacular views of the South Fork of the American River. Just remember these tips: Don't hike here in the middle of the day, and try to time your trip for sometime between January and June. By midsummer, it's uncomfortably hot and dry.

At the trailhead, you can hear the near-deafening sound of cars whizzing by on the freeway, but don't be discouraged. In 10 minutes of walking, you will have descended far enough into the canyon to be completely free of

flowering buckeye trees on the Stevens Creek Trail

any noise except the enchanting sounds of nature. The path cuts through a tranquil oak, pine, fir, and dogwood woodland. Spring months bring plentiful flowers, including poppies, lupine, and monkeyflower.

The trail is well signed the entire way, which is fortunate because you need to negotiate a few turns. In some seasons the vegetation may grow so thick that it obscures the trail signs, so pay careful attention at junctions. After about 15 minutes of downhill walking through a shady forest canopy, you reach a dirt road where you turn left and head out into the sunlight. Shortly thereafter, you reach an intersection of four dirt roads and turn right. Then, after a 250-yard stretch on open road bordered by numerous buckeye trees and a coursing stream, you'll head back into dense woodland again on your final descent to the waterfall.

The waterfall, like almost everything else on this trail, comes as a surprise. It's hard to believe how much water runs through here in the spring. The trail crosses the stream on granite slabs near the fall. It consists of two cascades, one that you walk right over and one that is about 30 yards upstream, hidden by dense vines and branches. On one June trip, the stream crossing was easy because the lower cascade was dry, but I followed a short spur trail upstream a few yards and was amazed at how much water still poured in the larger cascade. With a little scrambling over rocks, you can find a few shallow pools to dunk your feet in. You'll probably want to cool off before heading back uphill to your car.

Oh, and when you get back to the trailhead, I hope Elvis is around somewhere selling lemonade. It sure tastes good after hiking on a warm day.

Options
The entire Stevens Creek Trail is 4.5 miles in length (nine miles round-trip), leading all the way to the edge of the American River's South Fork. You can hike as much of this as you please, but keep in mind that your return trip will be all uphill. Make sure you have plenty of water with you.

Information and Contact
There is no fee. For more information, contact the Bureau of Land Management, Folsom Resource Area, 63 Natoma Street, Folsom, CA 95630, 916/985-4474, website: www.ca.blm.gov/folsom.

Directions
From Sacramento, drive east on I-80 for approximately 50 miles to Colfax. Take the Colfax exit, turn left at the stop sign, and drive east on the frontage road (North Canyon Way) for .7 mile to the trailhead. The trail and parking area are clearly marked.

4 SOUTH YUBA INDEPENDENCE TRAIL
South Yuba River State Park, off Highway 49 near Nevada City

Total distance: 2.0 miles round-trip

Type of trail: mostly level terrain

Hiking time: 1 hour

Best season: February–June

The problem with most wheelchair-accessible trails is that they are paved. Although pavement is certainly practical for wheelchair travel, wheelchair users often say that the pavement takes away from the experience of being in nature. After all, most people head outdoors to get away from such man-made materials.

So for wheelchair-users, the South Yuba Independence Trail is a stroke of genius and a blessing. It's the first identified wheelchair wilderness trail in the United States, and it is blissfully free of pavement. It leads a total of six miles on hard-packed dirt and wooden flumes along the Yuba River canyon.

A nonprofit group called Sequoya Challenge looks after the trail in partnership with California State Parks. The path was originally built in 1859, not as a hiking trail but as a canal to carry water from the South Yuba River to a hydraulic mining site in Smartville, 25 miles downstream. Consisting of rock-lined ditches with adjacent paths for ditch tenders, plus wooden flumes (bridges) allowing passage over creeks, the canal followed a nearly level contour along the steep hillsides above the South Yuba River.

Since 1970, the abandoned water canal underwent a major transformation. The old flumes were upgraded and rebuilt, and new sections of trail were opened up for all-access hiking. In many places, two trails run parallel, one for wheelchairs and one for hiking legs. Outhouses built for wheelchair users are positioned along the trail, as well as accessible platforms for picnicking and fishing on Rush Creek.

At the trailhead, you have a choice of hiking east or west. (The trail does not loop; if you want to walk the whole route, you must go out-and-back in both directions.) To see one of the trail's main highlights, a waterfall on Rush Creek, head to the right (west) for one mile. In the first 100 yards from the parking area, you must duck your head and pass through a tunnel under Highway 49. Beyond it, you walk through a densely wooded area and pass a roofed platform with a scenic overlook of the South Yuba River.

In short order you leave the forest and come out to an amazing cliff-hanging flume, its wooden boards making a horseshoe-shaped turn around the back of a canyon. Above and below it, Rush Creek Falls flows in multiple tiers over polished granite. The best place to see its lower cascades is from the eastern edge of the flume, before you reach the creek itself. The flume forms a bridge just above the tallest drop of the falls, a double tier that is 50 feet tall. This trail section is called the Rush Creek Ramp at Flume 28. Volunteers built an intricate wooden ramp which circles down from the flume to the edge of Rush Creek, above the main drop of the fall. It's a fine place for both wheelchair users and hikers on two legs to picnic, fish, or just admire the flow of water.

Options

If you wish to continue beyond the falls, you can go another mile to Jones Bar Road, then turn around and hike back, making a four-mile round-trip. You can also hike the eastern section of trail from the parking area, a five-mile round-trip that includes more flumes, views of the river and foothills, and springtime wildflowers.

Information and Contact

There is no fee. For more information and a map/brochure, contact South Yuba River State Park, Bridgeport Visitor Center and Ranger Station, 17660 Pleasant Valley Road, Penn Valley, CA 95946, 530/432-2546, website: www.parks.ca.gov.

Directions

From I-80 at Auburn, drive north on Highway 49 for 27 miles to Nevada City. Continue on Highway 49 for eight miles past Nevada City to the trailhead parking area along the highway (just before the South Yuba River bridge). Park at the large paved pullout.

Tahoe and Northern Sierra

Tahoe and Northern Sierra

For most visitors, the Tahoe region is clearly defined by its 22-mile-long, azure lake—"a noble sheet of blue water lifted six thousand three hundred feet above the level of the sea, and walled in by a rim of snow-clad mountain peaks," in the eloquent words of Mark Twain. The 10th deepest lake in the world (1,645 feet at its deepest point) and with remarkable water clarity, it is among the most notable features in the landscape of North America.

Easy hikers in the Tahoe region will note two other outstanding features besides the mammoth lake: steep hills and high elevation. There is no getting around it: This spectacular Sierra scenery can only be seen by breathing in the high mountain air. For lowlanders, it takes a few days to get acclimated. Even a relatively level trail can seem more challenging when its trailhead is situated at 7,000 feet. Be sure to take it slow when setting out on Tahoe's trails, especially if you just drove up from your home on the coast the day before.

But that's not to say you won't find easy hiking. This chapter describes more than a dozen hikes to high mountain lakes, shimmering creeks, and granite-lined waterfalls that are suitable even for families with young children to accomplish.

The trails detailed in this chapter also encompass a somewhat lesser traveled region north of Lake Tahoe, the outdoor recreation playground of Plumas National Forest and the Gold Lakes Basin. A sparsely inhabited land with numerous mountain lodges, cabin resorts, and abundant hiking and biking trails, the Plumas area has long been known as the Tahoe vacation alternative, offering similar scenic beauty but without the crowds who flock to the world-famous lake.

The only disappointing fact about hiking in the Tahoe and Northern Sierra region is that the season is so short. Snow can fall as early as mid-October, and the spring melt can hold off till mid-June. Because of the brief season, thousands of hikers take to the trails of Tahoe each year in only a few months' time period. To avoid the crowds, the best time to hike is usually September and October, when most of the summer visitors have gone home. And how fortunate, because that's when Tahoe's famous fall-color show occurs. It's worth waiting for.

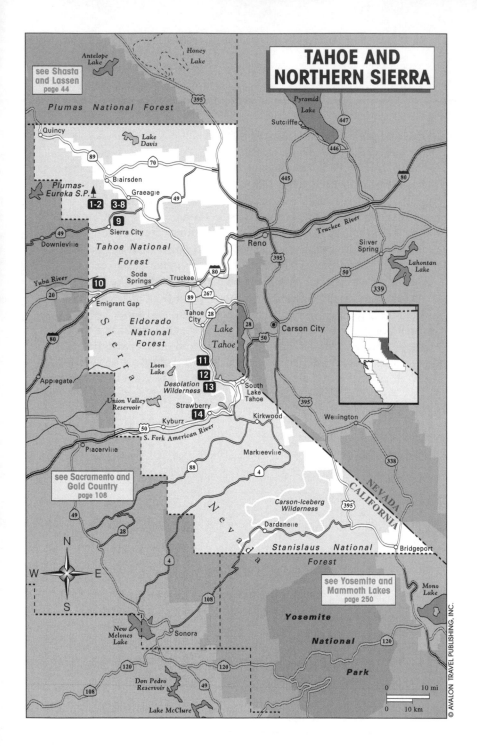

Contents

1. Grass Lake Trail. 124
2. Madora Lake Trail 126
3. Halsey Falls Trail 127
4. Smith Lake Trail. 129
5. Lily Lake & Fern Falls Trails 131
6. Frazier Falls Trail 132
7. Sand Pond Interpretive Trail 134
8. Sardine Lakes Trail 136
9. Wild Plum Loop 138
10. Fuller Lake Trail 139
11. Rubicon Trail 141
12. Cascade Falls Trail. 143
13. Angora Lakes Trail 145
14. Horsetail Falls Trail 147

1 GRASS LAKE TRAIL
Plumas-Eureka State Park, off Highway 89 near Graeagle

Total distance: 3.6 miles round-trip

Type of trail: some steep terrain

Hiking time: 2 hours

Best season: June–October

Every summer weekend, backpackers head for Rock, Jamison, and Wades Lake in Plumas National Forest, hoping for a secluded overnight spot and maybe a chance to catch a few fish for dinner. In the process, they walk right past Grass Lake and don't even give it a second look, since it is only a mere 1.8 miles from the trailhead. But this is exactly why Grass Lake is a perfect destination for easy hikers: A trek of less than an hour will get you there, and you probably won't have to share the lakeshore with too many others. Most people will be pushing ahead on the trail, schlepping their packs to the upper lakes.

You pick up the trail at the old Jamison Mine buildings in Plumas-Eureka State Park. (Although the trail begins in the state park, the lakes are located outside the state park border in national forest land.) The Jamison Mine was in operation from 1887–1919, producing gold for the Sierra Buttes Mining Company. Evidence of mining operations can be seen here and elsewhere along Jamison Creek.

The trail is well signed and easy to follow. With a left turn at the Jamison Mine buildings, you'll climb up, up, and up on a steep and rocky path until you reach the left spur trail for Smith Lake. Ignore this trail; it climbs even more steeply and then makes a mean descent to Smith Lake. Instead, continue straight to Grass Lake, now a level .5-mile away. A

Jamison Creek on the trail to Grass Lake

sign tells you when you've left the state park and entered Plumas National Forest, but there are more obvious clues: You'll start to notice felled trees and stumps, which tells you a thing or two about the different mandates of a state park and a national forest.

Listen for the sound of running water .2 mile beyond the state park boundary. A trail spur on the right leads you to Little Jamison Creek's edge and an overlook of 40-foot-high Jamison Falls. After snowmelt in spring the cascade is quite impressive. Back on the main trail, five more minutes of level walking brings you to Grass Lake at elevation 5,842 feet, a lovely circle of blue surrounded by Jeffrey pine, lodgepole pine, and huge red firs. You'll see plenty of gnawed-off trees, the evidence of beavers living near Grass Lake. Although beavers are rarely seen in the daytime, they make their whereabouts plain by leaving chewed stumps wherever they go.

The trail continues along the east side of Grass Lake before heading farther to Rock, Wades, and Jamison lakes. Circle around to the west side of Grass Lake for an awesome view of the craggy ridge that forms a backdrop on the lake's east side. A few trail camps are located here, and it's not hard to imagine how fine it would be to wake up in the morning, rub your eyes, and see that view.

Options

The ambitious can continue on the trail past Grass Lake for another two miles to Rock Lake, Jamison Lake, and Wades Lake. On the other hand, if you are looking for something easier, another trail leads from the same parking lot. This level path travels through pine and fir forest and along Little Jamison Creek to the state park campground. It's a perfect short walk for young children.

Information and Contact

There is no fee. A trail map is available at the state park museum and office, which is .5 mile past the trailhead access road on County Road A-14. For more information, contact Plumas-Eureka State Park, 310 Johnsville Road, Blairsden, CA 96103, 530/836-2380 or 530/525-7232, website: www.parks.ca.gov.

Directions

From Truckee, head north on Highway 89 for about 50 miles to Graeagle. At Graeagle, drive west on County Road A-14 for 4.5 miles to the Jamison Mine/Grass Lake access road on the left. Turn left and drive one mile, past Camp Lisa, to the trailhead parking area. The trailhead is on the far side of the lot, signed for Grass, Smith, Rock, Wades, and Jamison Lakes.

2 MADORA LAKE TRAIL

Plumas-Eureka State Park, off Highway 89 near Graeagle

Total distance: 1.5 miles round-trip

Hiking time: 45 minutes

Type of trail: mostly level terrain

Best season: June–October

Even though hiking on this state park trail doesn't require a day-use fee, I'd be willing to plunk down some change just to experience what can only be described as the "primordial" environment of the place. That word kept running through my mind as I circled around the marshy pond that is Madora Lake. This must have been the kind of spot where life as we know it first crawled its way out of the ooze.

Hike this trail in the quiet of the morning or evening and you'll see what I mean. The Madora Lake Trail seems like a throwback to a more primitive time when the earth was younger. The small lake (really a pond) is remarkably still and peaceful, and the surrounding area is abundant with wildlife.

The completely level trail begins conventionally enough near some pic-

nic tables and restrooms at the trailhead. A few hundred yards of walking leads you to a stream and the beginning of the trail loop. Set out on the streamside path, make a left turn at the footbridge, and head through the dense conifer forest. The stream provides the ideal soggy environment for a veritable forest of ferns. Pine and fir trees towering above them form a shady canopy over the soft dirt trail.

Soon you'll see what looks like a stagnant pond on your right. It may seem disappointing if you were expecting Madora Lake to be a big, dramatic alpine lake, but don't judge too quickly. As you approach you will

© ANN MARIE BROWN

Madora Lake

begin to notice that this body of water is teeming with life. Water birds—ducks, coots, and geese—as well as land birds such as pileated woodpeckers, hummingbirds, and saw-whet owls live on and around the lake. Choruses of frogs call to each other from across the water.

A picnic table on the far side of the lake provides the perfect spot to sit and contemplate a cluster of dead tree snags protruding from the water. The snags look like an eerie ghost forest, but they provide important habitat for birds and other creatures. Have a seat for a while, listen and look, and notice what the creatures of the forest are doing today. This is a great place to teach kids about the joys of quiet observation and nature study.

When you are ready to head back from this special place, stay on the main path until you circle all the way around the lake. (Ignore the dirt roads that intersect the trail.) You'll wind up back at the short connector trail to the parking lot.

Information and Contact

There is no fee. A trail map is available at the state park museum and office, which is 2.3 miles farther up the road from this trailhead. For more information, contact Plumas-Eureka State Park, 310 Johnsville Road, Blairsden, CA 96103, 530/836-2380 or 530/525-7232, website: www.parks.ca.gov.

Directions

From Truckee, drive north on Highway 89 for about 50 miles to Graeagle. Turn west on County Road A-14 and drive three miles to the Madora Lake Trailhead on the right.

3 HALSEY FALLS TRAIL

Plumas National Forest, off Highway 89 near Graeagle

Total distance: 2.0 miles round-trip   **Hiking time:** 1 hour

Type of trail: rolling terrain   **Best season:** June–October

People who stay at Gray Eagle Lodge in the Lakes Basin have a sweet deal. Like most of the lodges that are sprinkled throughout the Lakes Basin area, Gray Eagle Lodge has cozy cabins, a good restaurant, and access to all the hiking and fishing that anybody could want. But day visitors who don't have a hard-to-come-by reservation at the lodge can get a piece of the action by accessing the Forest Service trailhead located just .25 mile away. From this single trailhead in the Lakes Basin, you can hike to several lakes, a mountain summit, and two waterfalls.

Of the many good options from the Gray Eagle trailhead the easiest and perhaps most rewarding trail is the one-mile path to Halsey Falls. Because it's nearly level and easy to walk, even a two-year-old can make the trip. All you have to do is layer on the bug repellent and go. That's the only drawback to the Lakes Basin area—the abundant standing water in the numerous lakes and ponds means there are tons of mosquitoes in midsummer, kind of like a miniature Minnesota.

Halsey Falls

Besides the insect pests, another thing to be wary of are the trails signs, which tend to disagree with each other about mileage and make oblique references to nonexistent trails. Luckily, trail markers are nearly superfluous for the trip to Halsey Falls. The path follows the creek for the entire route; your ears guide you to the sound of rushing water at the end.

Along the way, shady pine and fir forest alternates with open views of surrounding ridgelines. One brief ascent takes you to the top of a low ridge directly behind Gray Eagle Lodge, but the rest of the hike is completely level. You'll cross two small streams that feed into Gray Eagle Creek, the source of flow for Halsey Falls. The roar of water gets louder and the air gets cooler as you approach the waterfall. Standing near its base in early summer, you can feel a breeze from the wide, 20-foot-high cascade. If you want to cool off, you can climb on rocks and fallen trees until you're right beneath its spray.

Options

Intrepid hikers can continue from Halsey Falls for another mile southeast to Grassy Lake or west to the northern edge of Long Lake. Both are good trout fishing lakes, but their trails are only passable well after snowmelt.

Information and Contact

There is no fee. For more information, contact Plumas National Forest, Beckwourth Ranger District, P.O. Box 7, Mohawk Road, Blairsden, CA 96103, 530/836-2575, website: www.fs.fed.us/r5/plumas.

Directions

From Truckee, drive north on Highway 89 for about 50 miles to Forest Service Road 24 (Gold Lake Highway), and turn left. (Forest Service Road 24 is 1.4 miles south of the town of Graeagle on Highway 89). Drive five miles south on Road 24 until you see the sign for Gray Eagle Lodge. Turn right and drive .3 mile to the trailhead for Smith Lake and Halsey Falls (.25 mile before the lodge). The trailhead for Halsey Falls is on the left side of the parking lot.

4 SMITH LAKE TRAIL

Plumas National Forest, off Highway 89 near Graeagle

Total distance: 2.0 miles round-trip

Hiking time: 1 hour

Type of trail: some steep terrain

Best season: June–October

Smith Lake beckoned, and I followed its call. The only problem was that I followed it on the most difficult trail available, and when I arrived I was so tuckered out that I had to take a nap. It's impossible to fully appreciate an alpine lake with your eyes closed, so I vowed to return another time. Luckily, on my second trip, I followed a much tamer trail, which left me with plenty of enthusiasm to explore Smith Lake and its surroundings.

"Tamer" is a relative term, of course. In this case, the tamer route to Smith Lake still requires a heart-pumping ascent over a dry, manzanita-covered ridge. But it's worth the effort to access this classic glacial lake, which is set just above 6,000 feet in a rocky bowl that forms a rough and jagged shoreline. If you can stand the extra weight on your back, you might even want to carry your fishing tackle with you.

The climb starts right from the parking area and is completely exposed, with no shade. But the ridge above looks more difficult to conquer than it actually is, thanks to multiple switchbacks. In 15 minutes or so, you'll be at the top, marveling at how high you've climbed in such a short time and looking across at the parallel ridge to your right.

A shady pine and fir forest on the ridge top is the reward for the ascent. The trail tunnels through a sea of conifers before descending to a

glant red firs at Smith Lake

lush meadow, then crossing a creek. Here you'll find a trail marker pointing left to Smith Lake in .25 mile. In short order you'll arrive at the lake,
which is surrounded by an incredible old-growth fir forest. The trees in
this grove are so big, there is almost no undergrowth. Staghorn moss (really a lichen) covers the firs' trunks. A few fallen giants lay prone, and for
many hikers this sight evokes images of the old-growth redwood forests of
northwest California. The terrain seems oddly barren except for these
huge, imposing trees.

Walk to the left around the lakeshore and you'll see that Smith Lake is
really two lakes (one very small) that merge during spring run off. A creek
separates the lakes the rest of the year. Follow the trail as far as you like
along the water's edge. You'll probably want to turn around when the path
begins to climb out of the lake bowl and up a steep ridge, heading back toward Plumas-Eureka State Park.

Parts of the trail around the lake's southern edge are submerged by
water after snowmelt, so only go as far as you can without getting soaked
feet. The trail doesn't make a complete circle around the lake because the
northern edge is a steep wall of granite. Retrace your steps when you're
ready to return.

Information and Contact

There is no fee. For more information, contact Plumas National Forest,

Beckwourth Ranger District, P.O. Box 7, Mohawk Road, Blairsden, CA 96103, 530/836-2575, website: www.fs.fed.us/r5/plumas.

Directions
From Truckee, drive north on Highway 89 for about 50 miles to Forest Service Road 24 (Gold Lake Highway), and turn left. (Forest Service Road 24 is 1.4 miles south of the town of Graeagle on Highway 89). Drive five miles south on Road 24 until you see the sign for Gray Eagle Lodge. Turn right and drive .3 mile to the trailhead for Smith Lake and Halsey Falls (.25 mile before the lodge). The trailhead for Smith Lake is on the right side of the parking lot.

5 LILY LAKE & FERN FALLS TRAILS
Plumas National Forest, off Highway 89 near Graeagle

Total distance: 1.0 mile round-trip   **Hiking time:** 30 minutes

Type of trail: mostly level terrain   **Best season:** June–August

---

The trail to Lily Lake may be the shortest walk in the entire Lakes Basin that leads to a pristine alpine lake. You park your car at the trailhead, walk for 10 minutes, and you're there. If wandering around the lake, having a picnic on a rock, or dropping a line in the water isn't enough to maintain your interest, you can get back in the car, drive .5 mile up the road, and hike to Fern Falls on what must be the shortest trail in the entire Lakes Basin that leads to a waterfall overlook.

That's two short walks, together totaling one mile in length, combined with a two-minute drive from trailhead to trailhead, resulting in access to a pretty little lake and a pretty little waterfall.

Lily Lake at 5,920 feet in elevation has a secluded feel to it, even though it is fairly close to the highway. It's a fine place for a picnic. The origin of the lake's name remains a question. One friend told me the lake is completely covered with water lilies in the summer. I saw no lilies in June, however, and was told by someone else that the lake's namesake was a pioneer gal named Lily, who made her way in these parts by participating in the world's oldest profession.

You can debate that little mystery on the .5-mile drive to the Fern Falls pullout, which is marked with a large sign that reads "Fern Falls Picnic Area and Vista Trail." The quarter-mile trail from the road takes you across a footbridge and up to the waterfall overlook, where you can climb on smooth granite rocks to get close to the stream. With a drop of just 15 feet, Fern Falls seems more like a billowing creek choked by big boulders than a true waterfall, but the sight and sound of cascading water is satisfying nonetheless.

If you plan to spend any time hanging around Lily Lake or Fern Falls, be sure to lather on the bug spray. The mosquitoes will generally leave you alone if you keep moving, but they flock to a sitting target. And remember, as my hiking partner always says, "God put mosquitoes in the Lakes Basin so we would know we are not yet in heaven."

Options
If you're in the mood for a little more exercise, you can walk halfway around Lily Lake and follow the trail that leads to the Gray Eagle trailhead, from which you can hike to Halsey Falls (see the Halsey Falls Trail hike in this chapter). That would add another three miles to your round-trip.

Information and Contact
There is no fee. For more information, contact Plumas National Forest, Beckwourth Ranger District, P.O. Box 7, Mohawk Road, Blairsden, CA 96103, 530/836-2575, website: www.fs.fed.us/r5/plumas.

Directions
From Truckee, head north on Highway 89 for about 50 miles to Forest Service Road 24 (Gold Lake Highway), and turn left. (Forest Service Road 24 is 1.4 miles south of the town of Graeagle on Highway 89). Drive 5.5 miles south on Road 24 to a pullout along the road marked for Lily Lake (it's .5 mile south of the turnoff for Gray Eagle Lodge). The pullout for Fern Falls is .5 mile farther south of Lily Lake on Road 24.

6 FRAZIER FALLS TRAIL
Plumas National Forest, off Highway 89 near Graeagle

Total distance: 1.0 mile round-trip

Type of trail: mostly level terrain

Hiking time: 30 minutes

Best season: May–July

Frazier Falls is one of the most famous landmarks in all of the Lakes Basin area, and deservedly so. In spring and early summer, the waterfall is a showstopper. It doesn't matter how jaded you are, Frazier Falls will give you a thrill.

© ANN MARIE BROWN

Frazier Falls

Reached via an easy, paved, wheelchair-accessible trail, Frazier is a 178-foot free fall with a total height of 248 feet if you include its lower cascade. The fall is big, but more importantly, it's dramatic. It has style. Frazier Creek is incredibly mild and tranquil both above and below the falls. As you hike along the trail, Frazier Creek seems to be just an average-sized stream channeling around and through granite. Then all of a sudden, its flow hits a big cliff and *whoosh!*—over it goes, creating a tremendous free fall.

In springtime, millions of gallons of water hurtle over Frazier Falls's granite lip, producing a convincing display of the power of melting snow. But by the Fourth of July, Frazier Falls is almost tame.

The walk to the fall's observation point is as delightful as the fall itself. The easy, nearly level path is popular with campers, and especially families, staying in the Lakes Basin. Even restless toddlers are momentarily impressed by the sight of the giant waterfall.

From the parking lot, head east on the well-marked trail, which is surrounded by shiny, polished granite, ponderosa and Jeffrey pines, and bunches of lupine and Indian paintbrush. Cross a footbridge over Frazier Creek and gaze downstream. You'll notice the water seems to disappear over the edge—you can't hear it yet but you're on top of the waterfall. The trail continues to circle around to Frazier Falls's overlook, a fenced-in platform across the creek canyon and about 200 yards from the fall. This is the best possible view of the waterfall's entire length. Check out the visitors' sign-in register to see how many people made the trek to Frazier Falls that day, or write in a few comments yourself. When we visited in May, an earlier visitor had simply scribbled, "Holy snowmelt."

One warning: Because Frazier Falls is so easy to reach and so dramatic, you can bet on having plenty of company at the waterfall overlook. The best way to see the falls is to visit early in the morning or late in the day, when the crowds are diminished and the sunlight on the rocks and ridges is spectacular.

Information and Contact
There is no fee. For more information, contact Plumas National Forest, Beckwourth Ranger District, P.O. Box 7, Mohawk Road, Blairsden, CA 96103, 530/836-2575, website: www.fs.fed.us/r5/plumas.

Directions
From Truckee, head north on Highway 89 for about 50 miles to Forest Service Road 24 (Gold Lake Highway), and turn left. (Forest Service Road 24 is 1.4 miles south of the town of Graeagle on Highway 89). Drive 8.4 miles south on Road 24 and turn left at the sign for Frazier Falls (on Old Gold Lake Road, directly across Road 24 from Gold Lake). Drive 1.8 miles north to the trailhead parking lot.

7 SAND POND INTERPRETIVE TRAIL
Tahoe National Forest, off Highway 49 near Bassetts

Total distance: 1.0 mile round-trip   **Hiking time:** 30 minutes

Type of trail: mostly level terrain   **Best season:** June–October

---

For people who are fascinated by cute, furry mammals, especially ones with large teeth that mow down trees for a living, the Sand Pond Interpretive Trail is a must-see. In a half hour of hiking you'll see so much beaver evidence that it will be impossible not to imagine seeing the little tree-chewers everywhere you go.

But "evidence" is the operative word. It's highly unlikely that you'll see any beavers, unless perhaps you walk the trail at midnight and do your best lodgepole pine imitation. Beavers are nocturnal creatures and shy besides, so it's rare that they are spotted in the daytime. But this trail will show you what happens to a forest and meadow area when a bevy of beavers moves in. This is a fascinating example of how one change in the order of things can drastically alter an ecosystem.

That one change occurred about 20 years ago. Several beaver families discovered Salmon Creek in the mid-1980s. Deciding the creek was a great place to live, they dammed it and flooded the surrounding forest. (The beavers move in and there goes the dam neighborhood!) Entire stands of

Sand Pond Interpretive Trail

lodgepole pines drowned as their roots became submerged in water, and this created a "ghost forest," an eerie-looking marsh with tall, dead tree trunks poking upward. Hikers follow a wooden boardwalk over the flooded area. With the snow-covered Sierra Buttes in the background the marsh is an unforgettable sight.

Beyond the ghost forest the trail leads into a conifer forest with signs identifying the different types of pines and firs. Most prevalent is the lodgepole pine, with scale-like bark and small, two-inch cones. Lodgepoles get their name from the Plains American Indians, who made teepees from them. You'll see many tall, sturdy lodgepoles along this trail—some that are healthy and growing, others a "ghost forest" of dead trees, and still more that are just beaver-chewed stumps.

The end of the Sand Pond Trail brings you to Sand Pond, a small, shallow lake that attracts anglers. Sand Pond, a man-made body of water, was formed by miners in the mid-1800s. The miners deposited tailings here from the nearby Young America mine, then removed the tailings to sift through them for valuable ore. The removal left a depression that is now filled with water and fish.

Options
You can extend your walk from Sand Pond to the dam at Lower Sardine Lake, just 100 yards farther. From Lower Sardine Lake, you can hike to Upper Sardine Lake (see the following trail description).

Information and Contact

There is no fee. For more information, contact Tahoe National Forest, Downieville Ranger District, 15924 Highway 49, Camptonville, CA 95922, 530/288-3231, website: www.fs.fed.us/r5/tahoe.

Directions

From Truckee, head north on Highway 89 for about 30 miles to Highway 49 heading west at Sattley. Turn west on Highway 49 and drive about 10 miles to the town of Bassetts, at the intersection of Highway 49 and Forest Service Road 24 (Gold Lake Highway). Drive 1.2 miles north on Road 24 to the turnoff for Sardine Lake and Packer Lake. Stay to the left and drive west on the Sardine Lake access road for .5 mile to the parking area for the Sand Pond Trail (before the lake and lodge).

8 SARDINE LAKES TRAIL

Tahoe National Forest, off Highway 49 near Bassetts

Total distance: 2.5 miles round-trip

Hiking time: 1.25 hours

Type of trail: rolling terrain

Best season: June–October

Upper and Lower Sardine Lakes are the raison d'être for Sardine Lake Lodge, a dream-like cabin resort where you can stay in a cabin with mountain and lake views from your front porch, eat gourmet meals prepared by the lodge's chef, have your own boat on Sardine Lake, and hike and fish to your heart's content.

That's the good news. The even better news is that you don't have to be a guest at the lodge to enjoy the hiking, shore fishing, and swimming at Sardine Lakes, because this land is national forest—open and free to the public—even though the lodge has a lease to operate on it.

Of all the lakes in the Lakes Basin, the Sardine Lakes are arguably the most scenic. Backed by the spectacularly jagged Sierra Buttes, an 8,500-foot range of peaks that towers imposingly above, this lakeside scene is as perfect as that of any jigsaw puzzle. A perfect easy trail leads from Lower Sardine Lake, right by the lodge, to Upper Sardine Lake about a mile away. The path, which is actually an old logging and mining road, heads straight for the upper lake, so you march headfirst toward the Sierra Buttes. The view gets better every step of the way.

Start your walk at the lodge parking lot. Take the gravel road (it's paved for the first few yards) on the right side of the lower lake. The trail climbs gently and offers no shade, so carry plenty of water with you. Keep looking to your left for increasingly broad views of the lower lake as you ascend above and beyond it. Watch for a huge boulder on your left, about two thirds of the way up the trail, which marks an informal spur trail that drops down over some rocks to wind up on top of a small waterfall on the upper lake's outlet stream. Even if the waterfall is running low when you visit, this is a great place to sit by the water and admire the views.

Lower Sardine Lake

At last you'll reach Upper Sardine Lake, a perfect alpine lake with a jagged, rocky shoreline and deep blue water. Clamber your way over rocks and boulders to find that perfect spot to sit, sunbathe, read a book, or drop a line in the water. On warm days, a swim in this lake is highly recommended. Some anglers pack along a float tube; fishing for trout is only fair. But the view of the dramatic Sierra Buttes can't be beat.

Information and Contact

There is no fee. For more information, contact Tahoe National Forest, Downieville Ranger District, 15924 Highway 49, Camptonville, CA 95922, 530/288-3231, website: www.fs.fed.us/r5/tahoe.

Directions

From Truckee, head north on Highway 89 for about 30 miles to Highway 49, heading west at Sattley. Turn west on Highway 49 and drive about 10 miles to the town of Bassetts at the intersection of Highway 49 and Forest Service Road 24 (Gold Lake Highway). Drive 1.2 miles north on Road 24 to the turnoff for Sardine Lake and Packer Lake. Stay to the left and drive west on the Sardine Lake access road for .5 mile to the parking area for the Sand Pond Trail (before the lake and lodge). Walk past the lodge and begin hiking on the fire road that leads from the far side of the lodge parking lot.

9 WILD PLUM LOOP

Tahoe National Forest, off Highway 49 near Sierra City

Total distance: 3.0 miles round-trip

Type of trail: some steep terrain

Hiking time: 1.5 hours

Best season: June–October

We came to the Wild Plum Loop Trail in search of waterfalls, but left empty-handed. We walked three miles and never found what we wanted. Were we disappointed? Frustrated? Ready to throw our map out the window? Not at all. In fact, the Wild Plum Loop turned out to be our favorite hike of the trip. Plenty of rewards are found along this trail: an unusual look at the southeast side of the steep and craggy Sierra Buttes, a walk alongside the steep-walled rock gorge of Haypress Creek, and a peaceful interlude in a dense forest of cedars and firs.

If you aren't camping at Wild Plum Campground, start your trip from the trailhead parking area, .25 mile before the camp. Hike the connector trail to the access road and bridge for the camp, where you'll see a sign that reads "Haypress Trail, Pacific Crest Trail, and Wild Plum Loop." This is your ticket. The trail stays level as it parallels Haypress Creek for .25 mile, then near a small hydroelectric building it starts to switchback up a ridge.

view of the back side of the Sierra Buttes from the Wild Plum Loop

This long series of zigzags will get your heart rate up. Console yourself with the thought of what this hill would be like without the switchbacks.

After about 15 minutes of climbing, you'll top the ridge. Any grumbling is sure to end when you see the fine view of the southeast side of the Sierra Buttes. At a small clearing, you can gaze in wonder at the canyon below and the mountains above while you pat yourself on the back for toughing out the ascent. When you have caught your breath, continue along the ridge. When you meet up with the Pacific Crest Trail, turn right. Your work is officially done and you'll start to descend; the remaining part of the loop is either level or slightly downhill.

After crossing the footbridge over Haypress Creek, turn right to leave the Pacific Crest Trail and head back on the last leg of your loop, tracing alongside Haypress Creek through dense conifers. This pretty, shaded stretch brings you to a logging road, which leads downhill to Wild Plum Campground. Finish out your walk on the connector trail to the day-use parking area and your car.

Information and Contact

There is no fee. For more information, contact Tahoe National Forest, Downieville Ranger District, 15924 Highway 49, Camptonville, CA 95922, 530/288-3231, website: www.fs.fed.us/r5/tahoe.

Directions

From Truckee, head north on Highway 89 for about 30 miles to Highway 49 heading west at Sattley. Turn west on Highway 49 and drive about 15 miles west toward Sierra City. Turn left on Wild Plum Road one mile before Sierra City. Drive 1.2 miles to the end of Wild Plum Road and the trailhead parking area. The last half mile is not paved. Begin hiking at the trail marker on the left side of the parking lot.

10 FULLER LAKE TRAIL

Tahoe National Forest, off Highway 20 near I-80

Total distance: 1.5 miles round-trip

Type of trail: mostly level terrain

Hiking time: 45 minutes

Best season: June–October

Dozens of lakes are located on Bowman Lake Road off Highway 20 in the Grouse Lakes area. But many of them require a 4WD vehicle to reach their shorelines or a long drive on rutted dirt and gravel roads. Even if you can gain access, the lakes' hiking trails can be buried under snow until late in the year, as I discovered one Fourth of July.

Fuller Lake is the exception to the rule in the Grouse Lakes area, and it's the perfect destination for an easy hiking trip. You don't have to drive for miles on Bowman Lake Road; it's the first lake you reach as you head north, just four miles in. There is no dirt-and-gravel access road; you just pull off the pavement into the lake's parking lot. Fuller Lake is set at 5,600 feet in elevation, so it is ice free long before the higher elevation lakes. Best of all, its shoreline trail is an easy, pleasant stroll just a few feet from the water's edge.

There may appear to be a good crowd at the lake when you visit, but few of them will be on the trail. Most people come here to fish, not hike, because Fuller Lake has an easy-access boat ramp and is generously stocked by the Department of Fish and Game. Anglers get so involved with fishing here that they miss out on this terrific short hiking trail.

Begin your walk by crossing the dam to the right of the parking area, then pick up the path on the far side. The trail and scenery improve as you hike farther from the dam; you'll leave the crowds and enter a mixed conifer forest. The trail is littered with soft needles; hundreds of cones lay at your feet. This is the perfect place to bring a child for a lesson about the different kinds of conifers and their cones. You'll find several varieties here—the Douglas fir with its brownish-red bark and three-inch cones with winged seeds; the ponderosa pine with its yellowish, jigsaw-puzzle bark and four-inch round cones; the white fir with its gray, furrowed bark and barrel-shaped cones; and the red fir with its reddish-brown bark and oblong, smooth cones.

Some of Fuller Lake's shoreline lies on private property, with posted signs telling you to keep away, but much of it is yours to explore at will. You can hike almost a mile from the boat ramp and dam before reaching the first "keep out" signs. Be sure to watch for wildlife as you stroll along the shoreline. A picnic or a fishing rod can make your trip even more enjoyable.

Information and Contact
There is no fee. For more information, contact Tahoe National Forest, Nevada City Ranger District, 631 Coyote Street, Nevada City, CA 95959, 530/265-4531, website: www.fs.fed.us/r5/tahoe.

Directions
From Auburn, drive east on I-80 for about 45 miles, past Emigrant Gap. Take the Highway 20 exit and drive west for 3.5 miles, then turn right on Bowman Lake Road (Forest Service Road 18). Drive north for four miles to Fuller Lake, on the right side of the road. The trail begins across the dam, to the right of the parking area.

11 RUBICON TRAIL

D. L. Bliss State Park,
off Highway 89 on Lake Tahoe's west shore

Total distance: 2.0 miles round-trip

Type of trail: rolling terrain

Hiking time: 1 hour

Best season: June–October

Two problems plague hikers in Tahoe: too many other hikers and too much private property surrounding the lake. Combine the two and you have lots of visitors trying to share a very small space. Add in the fact that the hiking season in Tahoe is only a few months of the year, and you have overload.

But if you want to hike and get an eyeful of azure Lake Tahoe, the Rubicon Trail is the only way to go, even if it means braving the crowds. Steel yourself, then drive to D. L. Bliss State Park and the trailhead at the Calawee Cove Beach parking lot. To increase your chance of peace and quiet, go as early in the morning as possible.

You should also steel yourself if you are afraid of heights. The path is on a mostly level grade, but it contours along a steep hillside that drops off more than 100 feet straight down to the water's edge. The park has put up safety cables in a few spots to keep hikers from falling off the trail.

hiker above the shores of Lake Tahoe on the Rubicon Trail

The Rubicon Trail is wildly popular for good reason. Plain and simple, it offers some of the best views of Lake Tahoe you'll find from public land. You can stare at all that blue H_2O and ponder this: At 22 miles long and 12 miles wide, Lake Tahoe holds more than 37 trillion gallons of water and is the largest alpine lake in North America. It's the 10th deepest lake in the world, with a greatest depth of 1,645 feet. From Rubicon Point, just .2 mile in on this trail, you can see several hundred feet down into the lake's depths.

If all that vastness is too overwhelming, focus on the close-up scenery, which includes plenty of chipmunks running along the path, and one spectacular curve in the trail where you get a sudden, breathtaking view of the often snow-capped mountains ahead of you.

At .5 mile, you'll see a right spur trail to the old lighthouse. The lighthouse no longer exists so the steep trip uphill to its former site has a disappointing conclusion. (You might want to pass by this spur and stick to the lake views.) The Coast Guard built a gas-powered lighthouse on Rubicon Point in 1916, but keeping the light supplied with fuel proved too difficult. Even when lit, the lighthouse was so high above the shoreline that it just confused everybody. It was shut down in 1919 and replaced by a newer lighthouse, which still stands at Sugar Pine Point.

Beyond the lighthouse spur, continue along the trail another .5 mile until you come to the next right turn, where you have three options: Turn around and go back the way you came for more gorgeous lake views, continue onward for more gorgeous lake views (see Options, below) or turn right and loop back for a change in scenery. To make a loop, turn right and you'll exit the forest at a parking lot. Turn right and walk about 30 yards until you see a sign for the Lighthouse Trail; take it. This alternate trail is higher on the hillside than the Rubicon Trail, and it heads through a thick stand of ponderosa and Jeffrey pines, firs, and cedars. A steep descent brings you back behind the old lighthouse site. Continue to the left, coasting downhill toward the start of the trail.

Options
You can continue hiking on the Rubicon for a total of 11 miles one-way. The trail ends at Emerald Bay, where you could plan to have a car shuttle waiting for you at the parking lot for Vikingsholm Castle.

Information and Contact
A $6 day-use fee is charged per vehicle. A trail map is available at the entrance station. For more information, contact D. L. Bliss State Park, P.O. Box 266, Tahoma, CA 96142, 530/525-7277 or 530/525-7232, website: www.parks.ca.gov.

Directions

From Tahoe City, drive south on Highway 89 for 15 miles and turn left at the sign for D. L. Bliss State Park. Drive .5 mile to the entrance station. Continue straight for .7 mile to a sign for Campsites 141–168 and Beach Area. Turn right and drive .7 mile to the Calawee Cove Beach parking lot. The Rubicon Trail begins on the far side of the lot.

12 CASCADE FALLS TRAIL

Lake Tahoe Basin Management Unit, off Highway 89 on Lake Tahoe's west shore

Total distance: 2.0 miles round-trip

Hiking time: 45 minutes

Type of trail: rolling terrain

Best season: June–August

The hike to Cascade Falls is far and away the best easy hike at Lake Tahoe. It's short and level enough for almost anybody to make the trip, including children. It has enough spectacular scenery to keep even the biggest whiners-in-the-outdoors from complaining. And the trail leads you right to the edge of a stunning 200-foot cascade that drops into the southwest end of Cascade Lake. What more could you ask for?

Cascade Falls has only one drawback—you have to see it early in the year. By August, the 100-yard-wide tower of water has become a thin, willowy stream, which greatly diminishes its dramatic effect. Plan your trip for sometime between the start of snowmelt and July, but no later.

From the trailhead parking lot at Bayview Campground, hike to your left on the well-signed trail. The route is a winner every step of the way. It meanders in and out of Jeffrey pine forest and open sunshine, alternately providing shade and views. After a mere five minutes of walking, you're rewarded with a tremendous vista of Cascade Lake, elevation 6,464 feet. The lake looks so large you may think it's part of Lake Tahoe, but with your bird's-eye view you can see that it's separated from Tahoe by a thin strip of forest and highway.

Moments later, the rumbling of the falls greets you as you break out of the forest and are given a clear view of the tumbling water. From here onward, the trail is out in the open on an exposed ledge trail with steep dropoffs. Watch your footing on the granite, and keep a firm handhold on small children. Watching your step is more difficult than you'd imagine, because the views of Cascade Lake and South Lake Tahoe will be vying for your attention.

© ANN MARIE BROWN

Cascade Falls plunges into Cascade Lake

The closer you get to the falls, the more the trail disintegrates, but numerous rock cairns show you the way. How far you go is up to you, but the best views of Cascade Falls are actually farther back on the trail. You lose sight of the falls in the last .25 mile of trail, and then if you walk right up to its edge, you can't see much of its 200-foot length. But upstream of the falls' lip are some lovely emerald green pools, and large shelves of granite where you can sit and picnic.

Cascade Falls was once known as White Cloud Falls. In the wind, it billows and scatters so much over its base of fractured granite that it creates a cloud of spray. Wildflowers enjoy all the water. Blue lupines and pink mountain pride present a superb springtime show as they cling to crevices in the rock.

Information and Contact

There is no fee. For more information, contact Lake Tahoe Basin Management Unit, 35 College Drive, South Lake Tahoe, CA 96150, 530/573-2600, website: www.fs.fed.us/r5/ltbmu.

Directions

From South Lake Tahoe, drive northwest on Highway 89 for 7.5 miles to the Bayview Campground and Trailhead. Turn left and drive to the far end of the campground to the trailhead parking area. If it's full, you can park across Highway 89 in the Inspiration Point parking lot.

13 ANGORA LAKES TRAIL
Lake Tahoe Basin Management Unit,
off Highway 89 south of Fallen Leaf Lake

Total distance: 1.0 mile round-trip   **Hiking time:** 30 minutes

Type of trail: rolling terrain   **Best season:** June–October

---

Warning: In the summer months, do not hike on the Angora Lakes Trail unless you are accompanied by a person under the age of seven. Well, okay, technically you can walk here without a child's supervision, but you'll feel like an outsider. That's because Angora Lakes is especially popular with children's day camps and groups.

The adventure begins with a scenic five-mile drive off Highway 89 near Fallen Leaf Lake. Much of the road is dirt, but it's easily navigated by passenger cars. Along the way, check out the far-and-away view from the Angora Fire Lookout. To your right and far below is Fallen Leaf Lake, to your left is a wide-open valley, and straight ahead is Angora Peak, elevation 8,588 feet. As you meander down this dirt road, you might feel like you are alone in the middle of nowhere, but surprise!—when you reach the Angora Lakes trailhead, it is usually packed with cars. The only way to avoid the crowd scenario is to wait to hike here until late September or October, when all the kiddies have gone back to school.

Angora Lakes Trail

But even if the trail and lakes are thronged with people, the trip is still worthwhile. Start hiking on the dirt road that climbs uphill from the upper parking lot's left side. In .3 mile, the wide road reaches the first lake, Lower Angora Lake. A few private houses are perched on the lake's far side, so most hikers just cruise past. The trail levels out now, and in another few minutes you reach Upper Angora Lake, where Angora Lakes Resort is located. The resort has been around since 1917 and has picturesque little cabins for rent. Not surprisingly, it is almost impossible to get a reservation to stay here. Upper Angora Lake at 7,280 feet in elevation is a perfectly bowl-shaped, glacial cirque lake. The granite wall on its far side is covered in snow most of the year, and in early summer a waterfall of snowmelt flows down its face. Some people paddle around the lake in rubber rafts. By late summer, swimmers will find the water warm enough to take a dip. Day visitors can take advantage of the lake's small beach, fish from shore for trout, or rent rowboats for a few bucks an hour.

No matter what other activities they choose to do at Upper Angora Lake, most everybody who visits here makes a stop at the resort's refreshment stand to buy a big glass of lemonade. Given the uphill walk to the lake, that lemonade stand is a gold mine.

Information and Contact
There is no fee. For more information, contact Lake Tahoe Basin Management Unit, 35 College Drive, South Lake Tahoe, CA 96150, 530/573-2600, website: www.fs.fed.us/r5/ltbmu.

Directions
From Lake Tahoe's Emerald Bay, drive south on Highway 89 for five miles to Fallen Leaf Lake Road and turn right. At .8 mile the road splits; stay to the left (do not head toward Fallen Leaf Lake) and continue .4 mile. At the junction, turn right on Forest Service Road 12N14, which alternates as paved and unpaved. Drive 2.3 miles, passing the Angora Fire Lookout, to the parking lot at the road's end. The trailhead is on the left side of the upper parking lot.

14 HORSETAIL FALLS TRAIL

Eldorado National Forest, off U.S. 50 west of Echo Lake

Total distance: 2.0 miles round-trip

Type of trail: some steep terrain

Hiking time: 1 hour

Best season: June–August

You'll know why they call it Horsetail Falls the minute you see it while cruising west on Highway 50. Straight and narrow at the top and fanning out to a wide inverted V at the bottom, Horsetail Falls swishes hundreds of feet down Pyramid Creek's glacier-carved canyon. Its powerful stream is reinforced by four lakes: Toem, Ropi, Pitt, and Avalanche.

Don't be put off by the crammed parking lot at Twin Bridges, the trailhead for the falls. Many of the cars belong to backpackers who are far off in the Desolation Wilderness on multi-day trips, and many more belong to people just milling around the trailhead, picnicking and admiring the falls from afar.

From the parking area at the highway bridge, pick up the trail at the large signboard. Hike through the dense cedar and pine forest, which smells like Grandma's cedar chest in the attic, only fresher and better. You leave most of your trail companions behind in the first .5 mile, as people drop off the route and choose their spots along Pyramid Creek. The trail continues into an exposed, rocky area—the glaciers paid a visit here—moving farther away from the creek and the cool shade of the forest.

About .5 mile in, you have a choice: continue straight toward Horsetail Falls and the Desolation Wilderness boundary, or veer off and follow the 1.5-mile Pyramid Creek Loop Trail. The latter

Horsetail Falls as seen from the Pyramid Creek Trail

© ANN MARIE BROWN

is a new trail that was built in 1999 specifically with day users in mind. This well-marked trail offers terrific long-distance views of Horsetail Falls and is routed past a beautiful stretch of Pyramid Creek called the Cascades. If you haven't obtained a wilderness permit and just want to day hike to a waterfall vista and swimming holes, this is your ticket.

If you choose to continue in the direction of the falls, in a short distance you may notice a bizarre phenomenon: arrows painted on the granite slabs pointing out the direction of the trail. Some ingrate vandalized this area in September 1995, spray-painting hundreds of green arrows on pristine granite. Apparently the culprit thought the trail was too difficult to follow and painted the arrows as some kind of a "service" to other hikers. (Go figure.) Eldorado National Forest rangers and various volunteer groups have made efforts to remove the graffiti, but it will take decades to get rid of it all.

Despite the controversy, Horsetail Falls is still a favorite hike around South Lake Tahoe. An estimated 15,000 people visit this trailhead and hike at least a portion of the trail each summer. Stay below the wilderness line and you're certain to stay out of trouble, although you'll have to be satisfied with long-distance views of Horsetail Falls. Aside from the beauty of Pyramid Creek and the falls, there is much more to see and enjoy. The up-close scenery includes ancient, twisted junipers and sturdy Jeffrey pines, and brightly colored lichens that coat the granite boulders. Bring a picnic with you, hike the Pyramid Creek Loop Trail, and then choose a spot along this granite-lined waterway to sit and relish the scenery.

Information and Contact
A $3 parking fee is charged per vehicle. A wilderness permit is necessary only if you are going to hike beyond the wilderness boundary (not for the trip described here). For more information, contact Eldorado National Forest, Pacific Ranger District, 7887 Highway 50, Pollock Pines, CA 95726, 530/644-2349, website: www.fs.fed.us/r5/eldorado.

Directions
From South Lake Tahoe, drive south on Highway 89 to Highway 50. Drive west on Highway 50 for about 15 miles to Twin Bridges, where there is a huge parking area on the north side of the highway just before the bridge. (It's .5 mile west of the turnoff for Camp Sacramento.) The trailhead is marked by a large signboard.

Chapter 6

© ANN MARIE BROWN

San Francisco Bay Area

San Francisco Bay Area

The San Francisco Bay Area is urban in nature. Or perhaps more accurately it is urban within nature. The Bay Area is a conglomeration of cities and suburbs that sit side by side, and is often enveloped by a ring of open space lands, parks, and preserves that beckon us to come and explore their open spaces.

It seems incongruous, but despite its six million human inhabitants, the San Francisco Bay Area is the most wild metropolitan area in the United States. Although grizzly bears no longer roam the Bay Area as they did 150 years ago, coyotes still gallop across the grasslands, herds of tule elk wander the coastal hills, and mountain lions and bobcats stalk their prey. Elephant seals still breed on the Bay Area's beaches, river otters ply the waterways, wild pigs root for acorns, and golden eagles and peregrine falcons soar overhead.

If you want to hit the trails, the Bay Area has the right ingredients for hiking nirvana: a mild climate that beckons us outdoors year-round, and an abundance of public land crisscrossed by trails. The Bay Area's mosaic of parklands includes federally designated parks such as Point Reyes National Seashore, Muir Woods National Monument, and the Golden Gate National Recreation Area, plus an incredible wealth of California state parks. Add to the mix an extensive system of county and regional parks and you have more trail choices than you could hike in a lifetime.

Then there is the landscape itself. If you hike much in the Bay Area, you will be in awe of the beauty and grace of centuries-old virgin redwoods. You'll wonder at the sight of rare and precious wildflowers, some of which grow here and nowhere else in the world. Your ears will be filled with the sound of crashing surf against miles of jagged coastal bluffs. You'll gaze at waterfalls coursing down basalt cliffs, pouring over sandstone precipices, and even dashing to the sea. You'll stand on summits and look down thousands of feet to the valleys below. In autumn, you'll watch black oaks and big leaf maples turn bright gold, and in winter, you'll see a dusting of snowfall on the Bay Area's high peaks and ridges.

This much is certain: Whenever and wherever you choose to hike in the Bay Area, you'll be witness to an urban wilderness like no other.

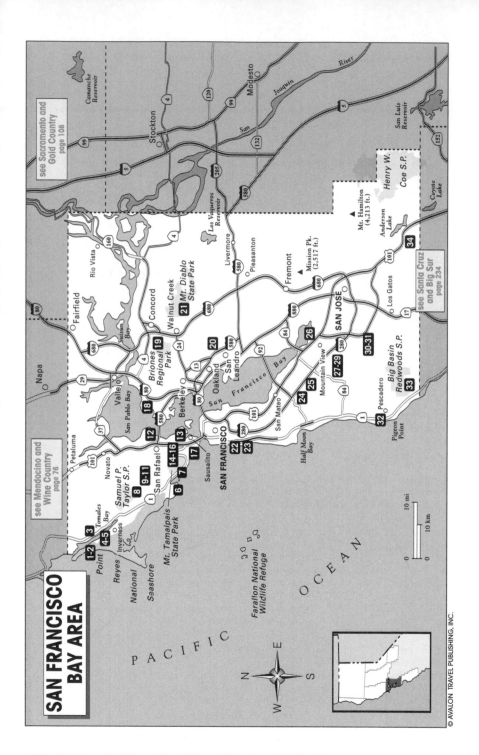

© AVALON TRAVEL PUBLISHING, INC.

Contents

1. Tomales Point Trail 154
2. Kehoe Beach Trail 156
3. Tomales Bay Trail 158
4. Marshall Beach Trail 160
5. Indian Nature Trail & Johnstone Trail 162
6. Fern Canyon Nature Trail 164
7. Kent, Griffin, & North Loop Trails 166
8. Stairstep Falls Trail 169
9. Bon Tempe Lake Loop 171
10. Cascade Falls Trail 174
11. Pine Mountain & Carson Falls Trails 176
12. Shoreline Trail 178
13. Phyllis Ellman Trail 181
14. Benstein, Mickey O'Brien, & Cataract Loop 184
15. Coastal & Matt Davis Trails 186
16. Ocean View, Lost Trail, & Fern Creek Loop 188
17. Lagoon Trail 191
18. Bay View Loop 193
19. Old Briones Road & Lagoon Trail Loop 196
20. Macdonald Trail 198
21. North Peak Trail to Prospectors Gap 200
22. Brooks Creek & Montara Mountain Trails 203
23. Valley View Trail 205
24. Whittemore Gulch Trail 207
25. Tafoni Trail 208
26. Palo Alto Baylands Nature Trail 210
27. Russian Ridge Loop 212
28. Horseshoe Lake Loop 214
29. Peter's Creek Trail & Long Ridge Road 216
30. Skyline Trail to Summit Rock 218
31. Saratoga Gap & Ridge Trail Loop 220
32. Sequoia Audubon Trail 223
33. Sequoia Trail 225
34. Waterfall Loop Trail 227

1 TOMALES POINT TRAIL

Point Reyes National Seashore, off Highway 1 near Olema

Total distance: 5.0 miles round-trip

Type of trail: rolling terrain

Hiking time: 2.5 hours

Best season: year-round

If seeing wildlife is one of the reasons you enjoy hiking, the Tomales Point Trail is sure to satisfy. You'll have a good chance at spotting big, furry animals before you even get out of your car (and not just the typical Point Reyes bovines).

The wildlife is plentiful because the Tomales Point Trail is located in Point Reyes National Seashore's tule elk preserve. Before 1860, thousands of native tule elk roamed Tomales Point, but in the late 19th century the animals were hunted out of existence. The creation of the preserve was the National Park Service's attempt to re-establish the elk in their native habitat. Their efforts have succeeded; today the herd is numbered at 450 and going strong.

Seeing the magnificent tule elk is almost a given. Frequently they're hanging out in large numbers near the trailhead parking lot, and often you can see them as you drive in on Pierce Point Road. Once you're out on the trail, you will probably see more elk as well as other wildlife. If you hike early in the morning before many other people have traipsed down the trail,

tule elk at Tomales Point

check the dirt path for footprints. I've seen mountain lion tracks as well as the more common raccoon and elk prints. While hiking, I've encountered large jackrabbits, various harmless snakes, big fuzzy caterpillars, and more birds than I could possibly remember. Once, I had to make a wide circle off the path to avoid a big skunk who insisted on walking down the trail ahead of me. He was just moseying along, indifferent to my presence.

It's 4.7 miles to the trail's end at the tip of Tomales Point, but you don't have to walk that far to have a great trip. Only a mile or two of hiking will provide you with splendid coastal and Tomales Bay views, plus a probable wildlife encounter. Set your own trail distance and turn around when you please. Just make sure you pick a clear day to take this trip. Although you may still see tule elk in the fog, you'll miss out on the trail's blue-water vistas. And be sure to carry a few extra layers. If the weather is clear, it is likely to be windy.

The Tomales Point Trail begins at Pierce Point Ranch, one of the oldest dairies in Point Reyes. The ranch manufactured milk and butter for San Francisco dinner tables in the 1850s. Begin by hiking around the western perimeter of the ranch, or take a few minutes to inspect its buildings. Interpretive signs describe the history of Pierce Point's dairy business.

The trail curves uphill around the ranch, then heads northwest along the blufftops toward Tomales Point, the northernmost tip of Point Reyes. The treadway is wide, smooth, and easy to hike from beginning to end. Wildflowers bloom profusely in the spring, especially poppies, gold fields, tidy tips, and bush lupine.

At .5 mile out, you reach the first short climb, in which you gain a mere 100 feet. Turn around and look behind you as you climb—you are bracketed by the ocean on one side and Tomales Bay on the other. On clear days, the water views are exquisite. Look for forested Hog Island in Tomales Bay, a popular pull-up spot for kayakers.

At 1.8 miles, the path starts to descend, offering a good view of Bird Rock jutting upward from the sea and the town and campground at Lawson's Landing across Tomales Bay. At 2.5 miles, the trail reaches its highest point. Views of Bodega Bay and the Sonoma Coast to the north are a standout. This high point makes an excellent turnaround spot for a five-mile round-trip. Although it may appear that the tip of Tomales Point is close at hand, don't be fooled—it is another two miles farther. Enjoy the vistas and then retrace your steps back to the trailhead.

Options

You can extend this hike by continuing the last two miles to Tomales Point, where the path disintegrates into sandy soil that is lined with fragrant yellow bush lupine in the spring. Alternatively, after you return to the parking lot at Pierce Point Ranch, you can drive or walk 100 yards to the McClures Beach trailhead (backtrack the way you came in), then hike the .5-mile path to McClures Beach. At low tide, you'll find good tidepooling at the south end of this beach.

Information and Contact
There is no fee. A free map of Point Reyes National Seashore is available at the Bear Valley Visitor Center on Bear Valley Road. For more information, contact Point Reyes National Seashore, Point Reyes, CA 94956, 415/464-5100, website: www.nps.gov/pore.

Directions
From San Francisco, cross the Golden Gate Bridge and drive north on U.S. 101 for 7.5 miles. Take the Sir Francis Drake Boulevard exit west toward San Anselmo and drive 20 miles to the town of Olema. At Olema, turn right (north) on Highway 1 for about 150 yards, then turn left on Bear Valley Road. Drive 2.2 miles on Bear Valley Road until it joins with Sir Francis Drake Highway. Bear left on Sir Francis Drake Highway and drive 5.6 miles, then take the right fork onto Pierce Point Road. Drive nine miles to the Pierce Point Ranch parking area.

2 KEHOE BEACH TRAIL
Point Reyes National Seashore, off Highway 1 near Olema

Total distance: 1.0 mile round-trip   **Hiking time:** 30 minutes

Type of trail: mostly level terrain   **Best season:** year-round

At most beaches in California, you just drive up, park your car in the paved parking lot, and then walk a few feet and plop down in the sand. Kehoe Beach beats that by a mile. Exactly a mile, in fact, because that's how far it is to hike there and back. The distance is long enough for a pleasant, level walk, and it can be combined with another mile or so of sauntering along the wide strip of beach.

The trail proves that the journey can be as good as the destination. The fun starts right where you park your car. In late spring and summer you'll find a huge patch of blackberries growing just across the road from the trailhead. If you're wearing long sleeves and long pants, you can pick enough berries to sustain you as you hike.

The trail is gravel, almost completely level, and wide enough for hand-

Wildflowers carpet the bluffs above Kehoe Beach.

holding. You walk alongside Kehoe Marsh, which provides excellent habitat for birds and bird-watchers. Songbirds are nearly as abundant as the non-native ice plant that weaves thick cushions of matted foliage alongside the trail. Grasses and vines also grow in profusion, encouraged by the proximity of the marshy creek and its underground spring. As you get closer to the ocean, the marshland transforms to sandy dunes, where you may see big jackrabbits hopping among the grasses.

Before you sprint down to Kehoe's brayed tan sands, take the spur trail that cuts off to the right and up the bluffs above the beach. In springtime, the bluffs are completely blue and gold with lupine and poppies—a glorious sight to behold. Once you've admired them, head to the beach for more walking or a picnic lunch. You'll return on the same trail.

Dogs are allowed on leash at Kehoe Beach, which is a great bonus for dog-lovers and their canine companions. There is little that makes a dog happier than going to a huge, wide-open beach, and there are only a few beaches in Point Reyes where dogs are permitted. Keep your canine friend leashed, though. The strict leash rules protect harbor seals that occasionally haul out on Kehoe Beach. Take care not to disturb them—they need to rest for an average of seven hours per day, and they nurse pups on land from late March–June.

Options
After exploring Kehoe Beach, get back in your car and backtrack 2.2 miles on Pierce Point Road to the trailhead for Abbotts Lagoon. This level, 2.4-mile round-trip is a bird-watcher's delight. It passes by protected lagoons teeming with bird life on the way to the windswept coast at Ten-Mile Beach.

Information and Contact

There is no fee. A free map of Point Reyes National Seashore is available at the Bear Valley Visitor Center on Bear Valley Road. For more information, contact Point Reyes National Seashore, Point Reyes, CA 94956, 415/464-5100, website: www.nps.gov/pore.

Directions

From San Francisco, cross the Golden Gate Bridge and drive north on U.S. 101 for 7.5 miles. Take the Sir Francis Drake Boulevard exit west toward San Anselmo and drive 20 miles to the town of Olema. At Olema, turn right (north) on Highway 1 for about 150 yards, then turn left on Bear Valley Road. Drive 2.2 miles on Bear Valley Road until it joins with Sir Francis Drake Highway. Bear left on Sir Francis Drake Highway and drive 5.6 miles, then take the right fork onto Pierce Point Road. Drive 5.5 miles to the Kehoe Beach Trailhead on your left. Park along either side of the road in the pullouts.

3 TOMALES BAY TRAIL
Point Reyes National Seashore,
off Highway 1 near Point Reyes Station

Total distance: 2.0 miles round-trip

Hiking time: 1 hour

Type of trail: rolling terrain

Best season: year-round

Now don't get the Tomales Bay Trail confused with the Tomales Point Trail, just because both are in Point Reyes. The Tomales Point Trail is the hike with the tule elk on the northern tip of Point Reyes. The Tomales Bay Trail is one of the few paths on the east side of Tomales Bay—not actually on the Point Reyes peninsula—that's administered by the park service. It gives you a unique view of the far southern end of Tomales Bay, just before the bay transitions into marshland.

A side attraction is that the hike leads right across the San Andreas Fault line, where the North American Plate and the Pacific Plate divide and conquer. The waters of Tomales Bay cover the northern end of the fault.

From the trailhead at Highway 1, you hike along rolling hills to the edge of the bay. This is an easy hike, and a good path for a contemplative walk on a foggy day—the norm in summer in Point Reyes. In the fog, the green hillsides and meandering waterways of the bay have a brooding, moody

The southern end of Tomales Bay transitions into marshland.

look to them, making you feel like you're hiking in Scotland's moors or the diked farmlands of the Netherlands.

Head straight west from the parking area on the only possible trail. At a few points, narrower spur trails branch off the Tomales Bay Trail, but stay on the main path and keep heading for the water. You'll walk downhill first, then uphill again to the top of a ridge with a wide view of Tomales Bay and the town of Inverness across the water.

Just after topping the ridge, you'll descend again and skirt a couple of small ponds. They're surrounded by tall reeds and cattails. Red-winged blackbirds can be seen here, as well as coots and mallards.

Make a final drop down to the bay's edge, where you'll find an old lock system on a levee that's no longer in use. In the early 1900s, the North Pacific Coast Railroad cut through this marsh. Its tracks were built around levees that channeled the flooded wetlands. The remains of the large trestles that once supported the tracks are still in place.

Walk to the north along the water's edge for a few hundred yards until you come to the trail's end at a fence. From this point, you can see how Tomales Bay divides into tiny shallow inlets here at its southern terminus, before draining into marshlands of willow, coyote brush, and grasslands.

Information and Contact

There is no fee. A free map of Point Reyes National Seashore is available at the Bear Valley Visitor Center on Bear Valley Road. For more information, contact Point Reyes National Seashore, Point Reyes, CA 94956, 415/464-5100, website: www.nps.gov/pore.

Directions
From San Francisco, cross the Golden Gate Bridge and drive north on U.S. 101 for 7.5 miles. Take the Sir Francis Drake Boulevard exit west toward San Anselmo and drive 20 miles to the town of Olema. At Olema, turn right and drive north on Highway 1 for four miles, passing through the town of Point Reyes Station, to the Tomales Bay Trail parking area on the left. (It is 1.8 miles beyond Point Reyes Station.)

4 MARSHALL BEACH TRAIL
Point Reyes National Seashore,
off Highway 1 near Point Reyes Station

Total distance: 2.4 miles round-trip   **Hiking time:** 1.5 hours

Type of trail: rolling terrain   **Best season:** year-round

The Marshall Beach Trail is one of the best kept secrets in Point Reyes. Few visitors know about Marshall Beach because the trailhead is situated on a dirt road to nowhere, at the northeastern tip of the Point Reyes peninsula. Although thousands of visitors pour into neighboring Tomales Bay State Park for its protected bay waters and stunning white beaches, few realize that right next door is Marshall Beach, with all the same advantages but none of the crowds and no entrance fee.

On your first trip to the Marshall Beach trailhead, you may question if you are going the right way, because the road leads through cow country with no beach in sight. The paved road turns to dirt and you keep driving along grassy coastal bluffs until you reach a nondescript trailhead sign. Then you start hiking through cow pastures. Be sure to keep a vigilant lookout for meadow muffins—the stuff can stay on your boot soles for days.

Why are there cow pastures in a national park? Cattle and dairy ranches have been operating in Point Reyes since the 1850s. The 1962 law that authorized Point Reyes National Seashore made allowances so that the original ranch owners could continue operating within the park's boundaries. Ranching is considered to be part of the "cultural history" of the park. Currently, there are seven viable dairies in the park, milking about 3,200 cows and producing over five million gallons of milk each year. Just wave and smile at Bessie as you walk to the beach.

hiking down to Marshall Beach

The hike is a simple out-and-back, with no trail junctions. Just amble down the wide ranch road, which curves around the hillside and descends to the water's edge. You'll find no shade along the route, except for at the edge of Marshall Beach's cove, where windswept cypress trees stand guard. Thick lichen hangs from their branches.

Marshall Beach is a nearly perfect beach, with coarse white sand bordering azure Tomales Bay water. It's a small slice of paradise overlooking the hamlet of Marshall on the other side of the bay. The most common visitors to the beach are kayakers who paddle over from Marshall, Inverness, or Tomales Bay State Park to the south. Other hikers are few. You can swim in the calm bay waters, which are protected from the wind by Inverness Ridge.

Essentials for this trip include a picnic, a bathing suit, a good book, and some binoculars for bird-watching. Settle in for a perfect afternoon, then drag yourself away—and back up the hill—when it's time to leave.

Information and Contact
There is no fee. A free map of Point Reyes National Seashore is available at the Bear Valley Visitor Center on Bear Valley Road. For more information, contact Point Reyes National Seashore, Point Reyes, CA 94956, 415/464-5100, website: www.nps.gov/pore.

Directions
From San Francisco, cross the Golden Gate Bridge and drive north on U.S. 101 for 7.5 miles. Take the Sir Francis Drake Boulevard exit west

toward San Anselmo and drive 20 miles to the town of Olema. At Olema, turn right (north) on Highway 1 for about 150 yards, then turn left on Bear Valley Road. Drive 2.2 miles on Bear Valley Road until it joins with Sir Francis Drake Highway. Bear left on Sir Francis Drake Highway and drive 5.6 miles, then take the right fork onto Pierce Point Road. In 1.2 miles you'll see the entrance road for Tomales Bay State Park. Drive just past it to Duck Cove/Marshall Beach Road; turn right and drive 2.6 miles. The road turns to gravel and dirt; stay to the left where it forks. Park in the gravel parking area, being careful not to block any of the dirt roads that connect here.

5 INDIAN NATURE TRAIL & JOHNSTONE TRAIL
Tomales Bay State Park, off Highway 1 near Inverness

Total distance: 2.0 miles round-trip

Type of trail: rolling terrain

Hiking time: 1.5 hours

Best season: year-round

In truth, the point of this trip is not really the hiking. The point is that Tomales Bay's beaches are so gorgeous, you simply have to come and explore them. You can swim, picnic, or just wander around for a while and then lay on the beach and take a nap. This is truly easy hiking.

Although it is quite large, Tomales Bay is shallow enough that its

Tomales Bay

water warms up to a tolerable swimming temperature. The bay is surf free for swimming—an activity that is nearly impossible at the turbulent beaches of neighboring Point Reyes. The water is nearly calm much of the time, and the bay is blessed with good weather. Protected by Inverness Ridge, Tomales Bay is often sunny and warm even when the nearby ocean coastline is fogged in or windy. Another bonus is that the water of Tomales Bay is a lovely light blue, making the white sand beaches look like a tropical paradise.

A perfect easy hike at Tomales Bay State Park is a start-in-the-middle and head-in-both-directions path on the Indian Nature Trail and Johnstone Trail. This provides a glimpse at some of the best features of this 2,200-acre park.

Begin on the north side of Heart's Desire Beach and take the Indian Nature Trail for .5 mile to Indian Beach. This interpretive trail is marked with signs identifying the park's plants and their uses by the coastal Miwok American Indians. Where the path divides, stay to the right (the left trail is the return loop). In about 15 minutes of walking, you'll descend to Indian Beach, a lovely strip of sand that extends from an inland marsh into Tomales Bay. Birds and wildlife are easily spotted here. On one trip, I stood on the footbridge by the marsh and watched a group of bat rays feeding in the ocean-bound stream. The rays hovered in the water, moving their fins just enough to hold their position in the current as they munched on tiny organisms being filtered out of the marsh and into the ocean.

To loop back to your starting point, you can take the bridge at the north end of the beach, but this path follows a dirt service road and isn't especially scenic. You're better off retracing your steps on the Indian Nature Trail, while quizzing your hiking partner about toyon, coffee berries, and bracken fern, which you learned about on the way in.

Back at Heart's Desire Beach, walk to the beach's south end and pick up the Johnstone Trail. You'll travel for .5 mile through a forest of oaks, bay, and madrone, gaining frequent views of Tomales Bay through the tree canopy. You will pass by a large picnic area, which might mar the solitude of your hike, but the area is generally deserted except on weekends.

At .5 mile from Heart's Desire, a short side trail descends to Pebble Beach, a gorgeous and secluded little beach composed of tiny—guess what?—pebbles. If you visit this park on a busy weekend and Heart's Desire and Indian Beaches are too crowded for your taste, Pebble Beach will be your chance to leave the crowds. Lay out a beach towel, pull your lunch out of your day pack, and settle in for a fine afternoon.

Options
You can loop back from Pebble Beach to Heart's Desire Beach by following Johnstone Trail for 1.4 miles to a junction with Jepson Trail. Turn

right on Jepson Trail, and you will return to the picnic area you passed on your way out. Turn left here to walk the last .25 mile to Heart's Desire Beach. This will add 2.2 miles to your day.

Information and Contact

A $6 day-use fee is charged per vehicle. A trail map/brochure is available at the park entrance. For more information, contact Tomales Bay State Park, Star Route, Inverness, CA 94937, 415/669-1140 or 415/898-4362, website: www.parks.ca.gov.

Directions

From San Francisco, cross the Golden Gate Bridge and drive north on U.S. 101 for 7.5 miles. Take the Sir Francis Drake Boulevard exit west toward San Anselmo and drive 20 miles to the town of Olema. At Olema, turn right (north) on Highway 1 for about 150 yards, then turn left on Bear Valley Road. Drive 2.2 miles on Bear Valley Road until it joins with Sir Francis Drake Highway. Bear left on Sir Francis Drake Highway and drive 5.6 miles, then take the right fork onto Pierce Point Road. Drive 1.2 miles to the access road for Tomales Bay State Park. Turn right and drive one mile down the park road. Turn left and park at the Heart's Desire Beach parking lot.

6 FERN CANYON NATURE TRAIL

Point Reyes Bird Observatory, off Highway 1 near Bolinas

Total distance: 0.75 mile round-trip   **Hiking time:** 30 minutes

Type of trail: some steep terrain   **Best season:** year-round

Many hikers make the journey to the Palomarin Trailhead near Bolinas to walk to Bass Lake or Pelican Lake, two classic Point Reyes destinations, or maybe to backpack to Wildcat Camp and see Alamere Falls, a spectacular waterfall dropping 50 feet from the blufftop to the sea. In the process, they drive right by the nondescript little building that is the Point Reyes Bird Observatory.

You'd never guess it, but this unassuming place is the center of some of the most important wildlife research happening in the United States. More than 100 biologists are studying birds here, in the interest of protecting and enhancing wildlife biodiversity. And the Observatory just happens to have a short and lovely nature trail that is used as a research area, where biologists and volunteers study breeding, territoriality, and habitat preferences of several resident bird species. Those of us who don't have PhDs are more than welcome to walk it, too.

The trail leads through a canyon that is located at the intersection of two distinct biological environments: coastal scrub on the open oceanside bluffs, and riparian forest in the deep shaded canyon. Where two types of habitat meet, animals and birds thrive, and wildlife-watching is at its best. The long list of birds studied in the canyon includes black-headed grosbeaks, bush tits, purple finches, red-tailed hawks, scrub jays, song sparrows, Swainson's thrushes, towhees, winter wrens, and wren tits.

The Fern Canyon Nature Trail departs the wide, open grasslands and coastal bluff territory you've been driving through and enters an unexpectedly lush, rain-forest-like canyon, filled with ferns, big trees, and deep green foliage. The walk begins on the bluffs above the sea, where the primary vegetation is coyote brush—a tough, leathery shrub with tiny leaves that thrives in harsh coastal scrub environments. In only about 100 yards, you'll reach the edge of the canyon, where you can look down between the trees and get a glimpse of the habitat change you'll soon witness. (It's easy to walk right past the canyon and miss it, because trails on the bluff travel in several directions. Keep watching on your left for the first spot where the trail turns and heads downhill.)

Follow the path as it descends quickly and steeply into the green, plant-filled ravine. If it has rained recently, hiking boots are a must or you may find yourself sliding all the way down. Go slowly, watch your footing, and notice all the ferns lining the canyon walls and the "old man's beard" draped over the bay trees. These lichens look like Spanish moss but are actually two different plants, an algae and a fungus, growing together.

At the bottom of the canyon, a small ladder carries you over the final descent to the streambed. Before crossing the stream and rejoining the trail on the other side, pause for a while to look around at all the different types of ferns growing on the canyon walls, nourished by underground seepage in the rock. This year-round stream is Arroyo Hondo Creek, the main drainage for the Bolinas watershed, which empties into the Pacific Ocean. Although the creek is fullest in winter and spring, the ravine stays wet enough year-round to supply water for numerous bird and plant species. Moist, thick air envelops the quiet of the canyon.

Continue up the path on the far side of the creek. A dozen wooden steps lead you up and out of the canyon, then a few switchbacks continue uphill to a large meadow, which was once the site of a Miwok village. With a turnaround here, you can retrace your steps through the fern-filled canyon and enjoy its wonders all over again. If you choose to remain on the loop instead, you'll have to walk back on the road for .5 mile.

Options

If you follow the loop trail out to the road, you can add on an out-and-back hike on the Arroyo Trail, which begins just across Mesa Road. Return to your car by retracing your steps through the fern canyon or walking .5 mile west on the road.

Information and Contact

There is no fee. For more information, contact Point Reyes Bird Observatory, 4990 Shoreline Highway, Stinson Beach, CA 94970, 415/868-1221, website: www.prbo.org.

Directions

From San Francisco, cross the Golden Gate Bridge and drive north on U.S. 101 for four miles. Take the Mill Valley/Stinson Beach/Highway 1 exit and continue straight for one mile to a stoplight at Shoreline Highway (Highway 1). Turn left on Shoreline Highway, drive to Stinson Beach, and then continue north on Highway 1 for another five miles to an unsigned road on the left, which is Olema-Bolinas Road. It's just beyond the Bolinas Lagoon. Follow Olema-Bolinas Road west for 2.1 miles to Mesa Road. Turn right and follow Mesa Road 3.8 miles (it's signed "Not a Through Road") to the Point Reyes Bird Observatory, just past the Coast Guard Station. The road turns to gravel. Park at the observatory lot, then take the Nature Trail that begins on the ocean side of the parking lot.

7 KENT, GRIFFIN, & NORTH LOOP TRAILS

Audubon Canyon Ranch/Bolinas Lagoon,
off Highway 1 near Stinson Beach

Total distance: 3.0 miles round-trip   **Hiking time:** 1.75 hours

Type of trail: some steep terrain   **Best season:** March–July

When I pulled into the parking lot at Audubon Canyon Ranch at Bolinas Lagoon, I thought I was in the midst of some major event. A row of cars lined the driveway, more cars kept pulling in, and somebody was trying to direct all the traffic. What was it—John Muir's birthday or something?

This was no special event, just a busy day at the ranch. The Bolinas Lagoon Preserve is one of three preserves in Marin and Sonoma counties run by Audubon Canyon Ranch. The preserve's chief attraction is the

Great egrets nest in the tall redwoods at Bolinas Lagoon Preserve.

Henderson Overlook, a hike-in bird-watching platform from which you can witness the miracle of great egrets and herons nesting in the tops of redwood trees.

The preserve is open only 10 A.M.–4 P.M. on Saturdays, Sundays, and holidays, between mid-March and mid-July. With visitation periods so limited, there's no way to avoid the crowds in the parking lot, except perhaps to show up on a rainy day. Fortunately, most visitors are either right by the parking lot or on their way to and from the egret overlook. If you're willing to hike a little farther, you can explore a beautiful protected wildlife preserve and find some solitude as well.

Start your trip with a visit to the Henderson Overlook. The Alice Kent Trail begins behind the preserve's buildings. It climbs moderately and pleasantly enough for .5 mile. About halfway up you'll get your first glimpse of snow-white great egrets, nesting in their treetop colony on the neighboring hillside. At the overlook platform there is a set of viewing benches, stacked like bleacher seats at a football game. Audubon volunteers set up sighting scopes; visitors take turns looking at the birds.

What you see through the scopes depends on what month it is. By May, the egret eggs have usually hatched. Looking through the scopes you can see the baby egrets in their nests. Typically you'll see two or three baby birds per nest, all clamoring for food. If you show up in late March or April, you'll see the adult birds (both male and female) incubating the eggs. In late June or July you may see young egrets learning to fly. In any month, the sighting scopes allow a beautiful magnified view of the adult egrets in their white-feathered finery. So large that they appear almost clumsy, the adult birds make the redwood branches sway and droop dramatically when they take off and land.

With luck, you may also get to see a great blue heron in its nest. There are presently only nine pairs of herons in the preserve, compared to about 100 egret pairs. The herons begin nesting a month earlier than the egrets.

The egret's delicate feathers were the reason for its near extinction. The birds were massively hunted in the early 1900s to provide plumage for ladies' hats. Efforts of the Audubon Society eventually resulted in legislation that protected the birds from hunting.

After you've marveled at the birds, continue beyond the overlook on Griffin Trail, which leads uphill through an oak and bay forest. The trail heads straight up with nary a switchback. This section of trail is only another .5 mile, but it's what gives this hike a resounding "steep" rating. Take it at your own pace, and conserve your energy by not grumbling under your breath. When you reach the marked intersection of Griffin Trail and North Loop Trail, follow North Loop Trail downhill into a fern-filled redwood forest along Garden Club Canyon's small stream. After about 10 minutes, you'll swing away from the creek and follow the ridge on a narrow path. Climbing ever so slightly, the trail tops out at a high, open bluff. Have a seat on the strategically placed wooden swing, which is wide enough for two or more, and enjoy the expansive view of Bolinas Lagoon. Sway back and forth to your heart's content as you review the day's wonders.

Finally, follow the trail downhill along the sloping hillside. The path curves gently all the way back to Audubon Ranch headquarters, providing sweeping coastal views all the way.

Options
Remain on the Griffin Loop Trail beyond the Henderson Overlook and hike a 2.7-mile loop around Picher Canyon. The Griffin Loop Trail leads through a mix of dense forests and open ridge tops with views of Stinson Beach, Bolinas Lagoon, and the coast.

Information and Contact
There is no fee, but donations are gratefully accepted. A trail map is available at the trailhead. Bolinas Lagoon Preserve is open 10 A.M.–4 P.M. weekends and holidays only, mid-Mar.–mid-July. For more information, contact Audubon Canyon Ranch Headquarters, 4900 Highway 1, Stinson Beach, CA 94970, 415/868-9244, website: www.egret.org.

Directions
From San Francisco, cross the Golden Gate Bridge and drive north on U.S. 101 for four miles. Take the Mill Valley/Stinson Beach/Highway 1 exit

and continue straight for one mile to a stoplight at Shoreline Highway (Highway 1). Turn left on Shoreline Highway and drive 12 miles to Stinson Beach, then continue north on Highway 1 for another 3.7 miles. Look for the entrance to Audubon Canyon Ranch on the right. (It's .5 mile beyond the entrance signed "Volunteer Canyon").

8 STAIRSTEP FALLS TRAIL
Samuel P. Taylor State Park,
off Sir Francis Drake Boulevard near Lagunitas

Total distance: 2.5 miles round-trip   **Hiking time:** 1.25 hours

Type of trail: rolling terrain   **Best season:** December–April

Samuel P. Taylor State Park gets somewhat overshadowed by its large and famous neighbor, Point Reyes National Seashore, but that's just fine with the people who know and love the place. Even when the state park campground is filled with campers on summer weekends, it's rare to find many people on Samuel P. Taylor's hiking trails. This means that Stairstep Falls has managed to remain something of a secret in Marin County. Tucked into the back of a shady redwood canyon, it's a tranquil spot where you can often find solitude at the base of a waterfall.

The trailhead isn't at the main Samuel P. Taylor park entrance; rather, it's a mile west on Sir Francis Drake Boulevard at Devil's Gulch Horse Camp. Park in the dirt pullout across the road from the camp, then walk up the paved camp road for about 150 yards until you see a trail leading off to the right along Devil's Gulch

Stairstep Falls drops in a steep canyon lined with ferns.

Creek, paralleling the road. Follow it and immediately you descend into a stream-fed canyon filled with Douglas firs, redwoods, oaks, bay laurel, and what seems like millions of ferns. By April, the ground near the stream is covered with forget-me-nots, buttercups, and milkmaids.

A few minutes of upstream walking brings you to a footbridge over Devil's Gulch. Just ahead is a huge, hollowed-out redwood tree—the only one of its kind along this stream. Go ahead, climb inside; everybody does it. The tree's charm is irresistible.

Turn right and cross the footbridge, then turn left on its far side, following the sign for "Bill's Trail to Barnabe Peak." You'll climb very gently above the creek, marveling at the walls of ferns and the long limbs of mossy oaks and bays, as you gain 350 feet over .75 mile. Soon you have a view of the bald, grassy ridge on the far side of the canyon.

After crossing a bridge over a feeder stream, look for the Stairstep Falls trail junction on your left. Bear left and in 10 minutes of walking, you'll reach the trail's end near the base of Stairstep Falls. True to its name, 40-foot-tall Stairstep Falls drops in three main cascades, with a rocky "staircase" producing dozens of rivulets of water. Trail maintenance crews try to keep the area cleared of fallen trees and branches so you can stand near the cascading flow. Some waterfall lover has fashioned a makeshift bench and carved the fall's name into a downed tree limb. It makes a lovely spot, perfect for quiet contemplation in the good company of ferns, forest, and water.

Options
If you're feeling energetic, you can retrace your steps from Stairstep Falls to Bill's Trail, then turn left and continue uphill through dozens of well-graded switchbacks. The path continues for another two miles through a dense forest of graceful bay laurel trees, immense Douglas firs, and prolific ferns, before topping out at a fire road just below Barnabe Peak, elevation 1,466 feet.

Information and Contact
If you park along the highway at legal turnouts, there is no fee. A $6 day-use fee is charged per vehicle if you park in the main paved parking areas. A trail map/brochure is available at the entrance kiosk at the main campground. For more information, contact Samuel P. Taylor State Park, P.O. Box 251, Lagunitas, CA 94938, 415/488-9897 or 415/898-4362, website: www.parks.ca.gov.

Directions
From San Francisco, cross the Golden Gate Bridge and drive north on U.S. 101 for 7.5 miles. Take the Sir Francis Drake Boulevard exit west to-

ward San Anselmo, then drive about 15 miles (through the towns of Ross, Fairfax, and Lagunitas) to the entrance to Samuel P. Taylor State Park's campground. Don't turn here; continue on Sir Francis Drake Boulevard for exactly one more mile. Park in the dirt pullout across the road from Devil's Gulch Horse Camp. Walk across the road and follow the paved road to the campground.

9 BON TEMPE LAKE LOOP
Marin Municipal Water District,
off Bolinas-Fairfax Road near Fairfax

Total distance: 3.0 miles round-trip

Hiking time: 1.5 hours

Type of trail: rolling terrain

Best season: year-round

When most people think of public parkland around Mount Tamalpais, they think of the towering redwoods of Muir Woods National Monument or the dense forests and stunning coastal views of Mount Tamalpais State Park. But fewer people know that five sparkling lakes are also part of the Mount Tam landscape. Located in the Mount Tamalpais Watershed on the northwest side of the mountain, the five lakes are Alpine, Bon Tempe,

© ANN MARIE BROWN

Bon Tempe Lake

Kent, Lagunitas, and Phoenix. Together they present five more reasons why the Mount Tamalpais area is so ideal for outdoor recreation.

The best lake for an easy hiking excursion is Bon Tempe. It is generally uncrowded, and it's closed to mountain bikers but open to dogs on leash. By linking together a couple of trails, you can walk all the way around the lake in about an hour and a half.

Start by parking near the dam at Bon Tempe. Walk uphill to the dam and cross it, and you'll gain immediate views of bright-blue Bon Tempe Lake on your left and the marshes and lowlands of Alpine Lake on your right. The unmistakable profile of Mount Tamalpais looms to the south. On the far side of the dam, pick up the single-track trail (signed as Shady Side Trail) that leads left around the lake. It climbs only slightly as it travels into a dense mixed forest of oaks, madrones, firs, and redwoods. The lake's edge is never more than a few dozen feet from where you walk, so you can listen to the water lapping on the shoreline as you travel.

About a mile down the trail, you leave the forest and enter a grassy area where you can look westward over the entire lake, all the way back to the dam where you started. This vista is particularly stunning if the sun is sinking low in the sky. The trail then heads back into the woods for a short distance until it reaches the parking lot for neighboring Lake Lagunitas. Cross a small footbridge just before the pavement, then walk to your left for a few feet across the parking lot and pick up the trail again on a dirt and gravel fire road.

Here and in several other places around Bon Tempe you'll find many trails crisscrossing and heading away from the lake. However, your mission is always to stay as close to the lakeshore as possible. When the fire road splits off with a single-track leading left along the lake, follow the single-track. Just ignore all trails that don't stay close to the water. There's only one short section on the lake's north side (about three-quarters of the way around the loop) where a feeder stream and marsh force the trail to move away from the lake. Here you must walk along the edge of paved Sky Oaks Road for 100 yards until you can pick up the single-track again.

If you enjoy seeing wildlife, rest assured that you're almost guaranteed to see deer on this trail. They've gotten used to human visitors in the watershed and are not particularly flighty. Often they'll stare you down for a while or move only a few feet away when you approach.

You're guaranteed to see anglers at the lake as well, because Bon Tempe is stocked with trout by the Department of Fish and Game from November–April. Even in summer, when the lake level drops and catch rates are much lower, some fishing enthusiasts persevere in their efforts along the shoreline. However, because Bon Tempe is a reservoir, no boating, swimming, or wading is allowed on the lake. Even your dog must be kept leashed and out of the water.

Late winter and spring are the best seasons to visit Bon Tempe, when the lake is brimming full and the hillsides are covered with wildflowers, particularly Douglas irises. The best times of day for hiking are early in the morning or just before sunset, when the crowds are down and the animals show themselves. For many Marin County locals, this is a favorite after-work walk, a way of regaining perspective after a hectic day.

Options
Add on to this hike a short loop around Lake Lagunitas. Just before reaching the pavement of Lagunitas's parking lot, turn right on the wide fire road that leads uphill to the lake's earthen dam. Follow this wide road all the way around the perimeter of the lake. You'll wind up back on the far side of the parking lot. From there, reconnect to the loop around Bon Tempe Lake. This will add about two miles to your day.

Information and Contact
A $5 day-use fee is charged per vehicle. For more information and a map, contact the Marin Municipal Water District, 220 Nellen Avenue, Corte Madera, CA 94925, 415/945-1195, website: www.marinwater.org. Or phone Sky Oaks Ranger Station at 415/945-1181.

Directions
From San Francisco, cross the Golden Gate Bridge and drive north on U.S. 101 for 7.5 miles. Take the Sir Francis Drake Boulevard exit west toward San Anselmo, then drive six miles to the town of Fairfax. Turn left by the "Fairfax" sign (on Pacheco Avenue), then turn right immediately on Broadway. In one block, turn left on Bolinas Road. Drive 1.5 miles on Bolinas Road to Sky Oaks Road, where you bear left. Drive straight for .4 mile to the ranger station and entrance kiosk, then continue .3 mile to a fork in the road. Bear right on the gravel road. Drive .4 mile until you reach another fork, then bear left and park in the gravel parking area next to a gated fire road. Start hiking at the gate, heading uphill to Bon Tempe Dam.

10 CASCADE FALLS TRAIL

Marin County Open Space District,
off Bolinas-Fairfax Road, near Fairfax

Total distance: 2.0 miles round-trip   **Hiking time:** 1 hour

Type of trail: rolling terrain   **Best season:** December–April

---

Here's proof that the true measure of a waterfall is not how big it is or how much water flows over it, but the overall impression it creates. Little Cascade Falls in Fairfax is no Niagara, but it's perfectly framed in a hidden rock grotto. It features a single cascade that drops about 15 feet from the edge of a boulder to a small pool, which is surrounded by large and small moss-covered rocks that are perfectly situated for watching waterfalls.

At its start, the Cascade Falls Trail doesn't seem like it could possibly lead to a waterfall. To get to the trailhead, you drive through a suburban

ANN MARIE BROWN

Cascade Falls pours over a dark rock face.

neighborhood. When you start hiking, you head out on an often dry and dusty fire road. The only water you'll see at the beginning of the trail looks stagnant, except during the heaviest rains. Things don't look promising.

But they get better. Stay close to San Anselmo Creek as you hike, avoiding the wide fire roads wherever you can and following the single-track hiking paths. Cross a wooden footbridge about a quarter-mile in and head to your right into a lovely oak and laurel forest, walking right beside the creek. The stream flow picks up, and is laden with many quiet pools.

In less than a mile from the trailhead you'll round a bend and hear the sound of falling water, then get your first glimpse of the waterfall. In winter or early spring, Cascade Falls flows with enthusiasm, but it dwindles to a trickle in summer.

On my first visit, I was pleasantly surprised by the beauty of the little waterfall, but even more surprised to find two musicians at its base, sitting cross-legged on a big boulder, playing a duet on the violin and guitar. I stayed and listened to their music, combined with the music of the falls, for more than an hour.

While I can't promise you'll be serenaded when you hike to Cascade Falls, I can tell you that this is a perfect short walk for after work or a midday stroll. You can even bring your four-legged friend, because leashed dogs are allowed in Cascade Canyon.

You might want to follow the trail up to the top of the waterfall. You'll find rocks to sit on above and alongside the falls, as well as others down below, surrounding the waterfall pool. Any of these spots would be perfect for picnicking.

Options
Beyond the waterfall, the trail continues for miles, connecting with Repack Fire Road and eventually San Geronimo Ridge Fire Foad. Hike out and back as far as you like.

Information and Contact
There is no fee. For more information, contact the Marin County Open Space District, 3501 Civic Center Drive, Room 415, San Rafael, CA 94903, 415/499-6387, website: www.marinopenspace.org.

Directions
From San Francisco, cross the Golden Gate Bridge and drive north on U.S. 101 for 7.5 miles. Take the Sir Francis Drake Boulevard exit west toward San Anselmo, then drive six miles to the town of Fairfax. Turn left by the "Fairfax" sign (on Pacheco Avenue), then turn right immediately on Broadway. In one block, turn left on Bolinas Road. Follow Bolinas Road for .3 mile to a three-road intersection. Bear right on Cascade Drive (the middle road) and continue for 1.5 miles. The road becomes very narrow and ends at Elliott Nature Preserve. Park alongside the road; be sure to avoid blocking driveways and obey the "No Parking" signs in the last 100 feet before the trailhead. Begin hiking at the gate.

11 PINE MOUNTAIN & CARSON FALLS TRAILS

Marin Municipal Water District,
off Bolinas-Fairfax Road near Fairfax

Total distance: 3.4 miles round-trip   **Hiking time:** 1.5 hours

Type of trail: some steep terrain   **Best season:** December–April

---

Quiz question: Name three waterfalls located on or nearby Mount Tamalpais, all within six miles of each other, that begin with the letter C.

Answer: Cascade Falls in Marin County Open Space lands near Fairfax, Cataract Falls near Mount Tamalpais State Park, and Carson Falls in the Marin Municipal Water District.

It's a good idea to learn them all and know which is which, because it saves a lot of confusion when you tell your co-workers about the great waterfall you saw. Carson Falls? Isn't that the one with the trail that starts at Alpine Dam and climbs the whole way? No, that's Cataract. Cataract Falls? Isn't that the one that falls in a long, stairstepped plunge through a steep, rocky canyon? Sorry, that's Carson. Cascade Falls? Isn't that the one that's just outside the Fairfax suburbs? Well, you got one right.

To set the record straight, Carson Falls is an unusual waterfall found in the middle of a dry grassland canyon in Marin Municipal Water District lands, high above Alpine and Kent lakes on the northwest slope of Mount Tamalpais. It's a long chain of four pool-and-drop cataracts that pour into rock-lined pools. The trail to reach the waterfall is not signed, so it gets less traffic than other waterfalls in Marin County.

Carson Falls's main trailhead is located along Bolinas-Fairfax Road at 1,078 feet in elevation. From the parking area, you cross Bolinas Road and pick up Pine Mountain Fire Road. Climb uphill for one mile, gaining more than 300 feet in elevation. Be sure to pause and look over your right shoulder as you ascend. Check out the sweeping view of Mount Diablo, San Pablo Bay, Marin County, the East Bay, and even the Richmond Bridge. The climb will get your heart pumping, but the views are more than fair compensation for your efforts.

Keep your eyes and ears attuned for mountain bikers on this fire road. They sometimes come flying downhill at breakneck speed, most often after experiencing the agony and ecstasy of climbing nearby Pine Mountain.

After a mile of climbing, you reach a high point on the ridge and a junction. Look due north for a surprising view of Mount St. Helena in Napa, 45 miles distant, then turn left on Oat Hill Road, also a fire road. As you descend on Oat Hill Road, pay attention to the telephone lines strung up above your head. These will indicate the turnoff for Carson Falls's watershed. Where the telephone lines turn right, you should, too. (The utility pole at the turnoff is posted with a "no bikes" sign.) Leave the fire road and begin walking downhill on a steep single-track path into the Carson Creek drainage. Watch your footing, especially if it's wet.

After dropping a couple hundred feet in elevation, you'll notice a change in the landscape. Although you're still in wide-open grasslands with no hint of a waterfall nearby, you'll notice some trees growing in a little slot in the hillside—evidence of an underground spring. Get closer and you'll see these are buckeye trees, which flower exuberantly in early summer and go dormant in

© ANN MARIE BROWN

Carson Falls

late summer. Buckeye trees are a dead giveaway that water is close at hand. Now you're in the watershed, and within moments you're right on top of the falls.

Don't expect that usual thunderous moment of "Wow! A waterfall!" Carson Falls is more subtle and mysterious than that. This waterfall reveals its pleasures slowly, one pool at a time. To see it in its entirety, descend carefully along the rough trail that parallels its cascades, dropping in elevation along with the stream. The waterfall pours in four tiers, but the lowest one is quite difficult to reach. Use extreme caution heading down the steep, rocky path. Carson Falls's green-gray rock looks like serpentine, but it's actually a type of greenstone basalt.

After your exploration, choose a rock near one of the waterfall pools, have a seat, and listen to the water music for a while. Even in summer, when Carson Falls is reduced to a mere trickle, a visit to it feels restorative, like resting in a Zen garden with the sound of the wind and the tinkling of water as your only companions.

Options

Another unusual sight in the region of Carson Falls is a stand of dwarf Sargent cypress trees off San Geronimo Ridge Fire Road. The Sargent cypress is a rare evergreen that grows in scattered groves in the region surrounding Mount Tamalpais. It is usually stunted in size when rooted in serpentine soil, which is the case here. Cypress trees that are more than 100-years-old may be only a few feet tall. To see them, continue straight on Pine Mountain Road at its junction with Oat Hill Road (the route is mostly level from here). In just under a half mile, you'll come to a junction of roads; the 1,762-foot summit of Pine Mountain is off to the left. Go straight on San Geronimo Ridge Road and reach the miniature Sargent cypress forest in .6 mile.

Information and Contact

There is no fee. For more information and a map, contact Marin Municipal Water District, 220 Nellen Avenue, Corte Madera, CA 94925, 415/945-1195, website: www.marinwater.org. Or phone Sky Oaks Ranger Station at 415/945-1181.

Directions

From San Francisco, cross the Golden Gate Bridge and drive north on U.S. 101 for 7.5 miles. Take the Sir Francis Drake Boulevard exit west toward San Anselmo, then drive six miles to the town of Fairfax. Turn left at the first gas station in Fairfax (by the "Fairfax" sign on unsigned Pacheco Road), then turn right immediately on Broadway. In one block, turn left on Bolinas Road. Drive 3.8 miles on Bolinas Road, past the golf course, to the trailhead parking on the left side of the road. Park and walk across the road to the trailhead.

12 SHORELINE TRAIL

China Camp State Park, off U.S. 101 near San Rafael

Total distance: 3.0 miles round-trip

Hiking time: 1.5 hours

Type of trail: mostly level terrain

Best season: year-round

Most people know China Camp State Park as a historic park that showcases the remains of a Chinese shrimp fishing village from the 19th century. It's the kind of place that's popular for school field trips. But don't forget about China Camp's scenic location on San Pablo Bay, which allows blue-water vistas at every turn of the park's Shoreline Trail. With more than 1,500 shoreline acres, plus a dense forest of oaks, bays, and madrones, the park is an island of natural beauty just outside the busy city of San Rafael.

China Camp is also a rare animal in the California State Park system. It's one of the few state parks that allows bike riders on its single-track trails. The park is rarely too crowded, and most bikers and hikers mind their manners and get along fine. Just be forewarned that if you don't like sharing the trail with bikes, avoid hiking here on weekends when the park is heavily used.

The park's Shoreline Trail shows off many of the park's best features, but you don't have to march the entire trail to enjoy the scenery. Instead, start at two different trailheads and, with two short and very special walks, see many of the highlights of China Camp.

Begin on the Shoreline Trail from the Back Ranch Meadows Campground parking area. You'll walk past a cattail-filled marsh and have immediate views of the tranquil blue waters of San Pablo Bay. The open grasslands are punctuated by a few spreading valley oaks. In only .25 mile, cross San Pedro Road and take Turtle Back Nature Trail. When bay waters were higher, Turtle Back was an island, but now it's a shoreline hill surrounded by saltwater marsh. In late autumn, the marsh's pickleweed turns a brilliant red color, accenting wide views of San Pablo Bay. Ancient duck blinds dot the water's edge. From Turtle Back, you can see Jake's Island to the north, another shoreline hill that was once an island. Two other such hills exist to the east—Bullet Hill and Chicken Coop Hill.

marsh and bay views from China Camp State Park

For your second short walk, drive back to North San Pedro Road, and follow the road east (to your right) for slightly over a mile to the Bullhead Flat parking area on the left. Cross the road and walk up the service road to the China Camp State Park office (a trailer). Take the Shoreline Trail to your left and hike .7 mile to China Camp Village.

The well-preserved remains of a 19th-century Chinese fishing village, China Camp Village was one of more than 30 such villages that sprung up on the shores of San Francisco and San Pablo bays. The people who lived in the village would fish for plentiful grass shrimp in spring, summer, and fall, and in winter, they would mend their nets and work on their boats. Some of the shrimp were sold at local markets, but most were exported to China, because Chinese people would eat dried shrimp while Americans only liked it cooked fresh. Eventually laws were passed that forbid the Chinese method of fishing for shrimp with bag nets. In 1905, the export of dried shrimp was banned, and this village, along with others like it, was slowly deserted.

A pier and four buildings, some partly furnished, are all that remain of the village. You can tour around the old camp, then follow the Rat Rock Cove Trail from the China Camp Point parking lot for 200 feet to a quiet little beach that is popular with great egrets. You'll probably see more of these graceful white birds out on Rat Rock, a few hundred yards offshore. The water in this shallow part of the bay is relatively warm, and children will enjoy playing on the beach.

Depending on the tide, you can sometimes walk around a small marshy pond and down the beach to Five Pine Point. Your return from the beach to Bullhead Flat and your car is less than a half mile, either following the Shoreline Trail or walking along the road.

Options
You can remain on Shoreline Trail and hike the entire distance from Back Ranch Meadows to China Camp Village. An out-and-back trip is a nearly level seven miles.

Information and Contact
A $6 day-use fee is charged per vehicle. A trail map is available at park headquarters, across from the Bullhead Flat parking area. For more information, contact China Camp State Park, 1455A East Francisco Boulevard, San Rafael, CA 94901, 415/456-0766 or 415/898-4362, website: www.parks.ca.gov.

Directions
From San Francisco, cross the Golden Gate Bridge and drive north on U.S. 101 for 11 miles to San Rafael. Take the North San Pedro Road exit

and drive east for four miles. Park at the Back Ranch Meadows Campground parking area on your right. The trailhead for the Shoreline Trail is on the bay side of the parking lot.

13 PHYLLIS ELLMAN TRAIL
Ring Mountain Preserve, off U.S. 101 near Corte Madera

Total distance: 3.0 miles round-trip

Type of trail: rolling terrain

Hiking time: 1.5 hours

Best season: March–May

The Nature Conservancy's Ring Mountain Preserve is located smack in the middle of the Corte Madera suburbs, not far from Paradise Drive's paradise of shopping malls. But while all the surrounding development may seem discouraging, Ring Mountain Preserve is a little paradise of open space. It features a wealth of grassland wildflowers, fascinating rock outcrops, and outstanding views.

The Nature Conservancy acquired this hillside land tucked between neighborhood developments in order to protect the Tiburon mariposa lily, which grows nowhere else in the world. Six other species of Ring Mountain wildflowers grow in few other areas, landing them a spot on the rare plant list. These special flora share Ring Mountain with many

© ANN MARIE BROWN

on top of Turtle Rock at Ring Mountain Preserve

more common wildflowers and grasses, as well as bay trees, live oaks, deer, gray fox, rabbits, quail, and songbirds. To see the preserve at its best, you must visit in spring when the grasslands are in bloom, and preferably on a clear day.

Phyllis Ellman Trail, combined with a path named Loop Trail, circles the preserve. From the trailhead, take the left side of the loop first, saving the right side for your return. Things don't look all that promising at first, but just be patient. Ignore the neighboring houses and the busy road behind you, start climbing, and take your time—there's nowhere to go but up.

As you ascend, be sure to turn around every few minutes to check out the view at your back. You gain elevation quickly, and with every few footsteps your vista will expand to include more of the North and East bays. Ring Mountain is situated directly across the bay from two easy landmarks: the Larkspur Ferry Terminal and San Quentin Prison. As you scan the horizon, you'll see the East and West Brothers Islands near Richmond, the East and West Marin Islands near San Rafael, Point San Pedro, the Richmond Bridge, and parts of the East Bay. The islands are perhaps the most intriguing sight. This is the only park in Marin where you can simultaneously see the Marin Islands, which are state owned and unoccupied, and the East and West Brothers Islands, which feature a lighthouse and tiny inn.

There's plenty to see right by your feet, also. Large and small rock outcrops jut out from the hillside, adding contrast to the grasslands. Flower lovers should watch for sky lupine with clusters of dark blue flowers, blue-eyed grass, western larkspur, Douglas iris, light blue flax, pink onions, tarweed, yarrow, owl's clover, and the yellow spikes of false lupine. California poppies are the most prevalent bloomers. If you want to see the rare Tiburon mariposa lily, you must show up in late May, after many of the other wildflowers have finished their bloom. Even then, you must look carefully for this precious plant. Its mottled flowers are camouflaged against the surrounding grasses.

You'll be in open sunshine for most of this walk, but as you gain the ridge the trail passes through small groves of live oaks. The trees create a surprisingly dense canopy of branches and leaves, shading the sky as you pass through.

Near the top of the ridge (at interpretive post number 11), the trail meets up with a wide fire road. You'll see a large water tank and a handful of immense houses to your left and a prominent serpentine outcrop straight ahead. This is known as Turtle Rock, although from here it's difficult to see why—the top of the rock resembles a turtle, but only when seen from the west. Climb on top of Turtle Rock for a fabulous view to the south of San Francisco, Angel Island, Alcatraz, Tiburon, and Sausalito. The whole of the

East and North bays remain visible in the opposite direction. You can see both San Francisco Bay and San Pablo Bay at the same time.

After enjoying the view from the big rock overlook, head west (right) on the fire road for a short distance to a junction of trails near interpretive post number 12. Walk to the south for a few yards to examine Petroglyph Rock, another large serpentine outcrop. The rock was carved by Native Americans approximately 3,000 years ago. The carvings are oval in shape and quite deep. (Unfortunately, the rock has been carved by vandals in more recent years.) Additional carvings are found on at least 30 other outcrops in the preserve. A midden on the lower part of the mountain suggests that Miwok people were living on Ring Mountain as early as 370 B.C.

Finally, return to the junction and take the signed Phyllis Ellman Trail back downhill for the return leg of your loop. The vistas should continue to inspire you all the way downhill.

Options
Continue past this trailhead for just under a mile, then turn right on Taylor Drive and drive to its end. This is the trailhead for Taylor Ridge Fire Road, which connects to Phyllis Ellman Trail along the ridge top. For a view-filled trip without a lot of effort, start your hike here and follow the ridgeline out-and-back as far as you please.

Information and Contact
There is no fee. For more information, contact Marin County Open Space District, 3501 Civic Center Drive, Room 415, San Rafael, CA 94903, 415/499-6387, website: www.marinopenspace.org. Or contact The Nature Conservancy at 415/435-6465 or 415/777-0487.

Directions
From San Francisco, cross the Golden Gate Bridge and drive north on U.S. 101 for seven miles. Take the Paradise Drive exit in Corte Madera. Follow Paradise Drive east for 1.6 miles through a residential neighborhood to the preserve entrance on the right. Park in the gravel pullout on the side of the road.

14 BENSTEIN, MICKEY O'BRIEN, & CATARACT LOOP

Marin Municipal Water District,
off Panoramic Highway near Mill Valley

Total distance: 4.0 miles round-trip

Type of trail: rolling terrain

Hiking time: 2 hours

Best season: year-round

If you just want a quiet walk in the woods, maybe with a little picnicking or a nature lesson along the way, here's a trail loop that's just right. Lots of people come to Mount Tamalpais to see the tall coastal redwoods or take in the sweeping coastal views, but there's much to be said for a simple woodland hike offering a little exercise, some solitude, and the comforting sounds of the birds and your own breathing.

The plethora of cars parked at Rock Spring parking area on the weekends might concern you, but fear not. Rock Spring is a major hub of trails; most hikers have set out on other paths to the scenic lookout at O'Rourke's Bench or the historic Mountain Theater. On one weekend trip, the only people I saw on this trail were a group of senior hikers who looked to be in their 70s. They were speeding up Benstein Trail as if they were going to a fire, arguing all the way about what species of oriole they had just seen. They passed me near Potrero Meadow and I never caught up with them.

Start by walking north from the parking area, traveling on Cataract Trail until it splits—Cataract to the left and Benstein to the right. Take Benstein Trail northeast, heading immediately into a tanoak and Douglas fir forest where you'll likely be greeted by the drumming of woodpeckers.

Trail markers point you toward Potrero Meadow. Benstein Trail ascends steadily until it reaches a junction with Rock Spring and Lagunitas Fire Road. Take the fire road left for only a few dozen yards. Join Benstein Trail again where it veers off to the left, back on single-track.

Prepare for a sudden scenery change as you come out of the hardwoods and on to the rocky back side of this ridge. You'll enter a contrasting world of manzanita, chemise, small Sargent cypress trees, and serpentine rock. Serpentine, California's state rock, is formed when water mixes with peridotite. It's a pretty grayish-green on Mount Tamalpais, although in other areas it's mostly gray. Spend some time examining the foliage growing here; it consists of plants that require few nutrients and are often dwarfed in size, which is typical of a serpentine environment. The most fascinating flora are the miniature cypress trees, which mature when they are only a few feet tall. Ironically, two of the world's largest Sargent cypress trees—over 80 feet tall—grow near here on the Mickey O'Brien Trail.

Descending from this gravelly, exposed ridge, follow Benstein Trail north for .25 mile until you reach Laurel Dell Fire Road. (A picnic area can be found across the road at Potrero Meadow if anyone in your group is getting hungry.) Turn left on the fire road and hike .125 mile. You'll gain a brief view of Bon Tempe Lake and the Marin watershed to the north.

Turn left on another fire road at a trail sign for Barth's Retreat. Barth's Retreat is an old camp that was built by poet, musician, and hiker Emil Barth in the 1920s. He was an avid Mount Tamalpais trail builder. Turn right and cross a bridge, pass by yet another picnic area, then continue straight. You are now on Mickey O'Brien Trail heading west along Barth's Creek in a thick forest of oak, bay, and Douglas fir. This is one of the best sections of the loop, especially when the stream is running strong, creating an enchanting melody of water sounds. Mickey O'Brien Trail, named for the 1920s president of the Tamalpais Conservation Corps, leads you gently downhill toward Laurel Dell, a grassy meadow.

Just before the meadowy dell, Mickey O'Brien Trail ends at an intersection with Cataract Trail. The latter is your ticket back to Rock Spring. Turn left on Cataract; it's just over a mile to the parking lot. If you want to make a side trip to picnic at Laurel Dell, go right for 150 yards, have your lunch, then follow Cataract home.

Options

In winter and spring, you can add on a visit to Cataract Falls from Laurel Dell. Just follow Cataract Trail northwest from the far end of the dell, then begin a steep descent through redwoods and Douglas firs. Watch for an intersection with High Marsh Trail on the right; continue straight, and shortly you'll reach the uppermost cascade of Cataract Falls. Cataract Trail curves in tightly, bringing you right alongside the stream. Water tumbles over huge boulders as it rushes downhill. Pick a rock and watch the show. If you like, you can continue downhill along Cataract Trail, visiting as many of the trail's cascades as you wish. Remember that the return trip to Laurel Dell is all uphill.

Information and Contact

There is no fee. For more information and a map, contact Marin Municipal Water District, 220 Nellen Avenue, Corte Madera, CA 94925, 415/945-1195, website: www.marinwater.org. Or phone Sky Oaks Ranger Station at 415/945-1181. You can also contact Mount Tamalpais State Park, 801 Panoramic Highway, Mill Valley, CA 94941, 415/388-2070, website: www.parks.ca.gov.

Directions

From San Francisco, cross the Golden Gate Bridge and drive north on U.S. 101 for four miles. Take the Mill Valley/Stinson Beach/Highway 1 exit and continue straight for one mile to a stoplight at Shoreline Highway (Highway 1). Turn left on Shoreline Highway and drive 2.5 miles, then turn right on Panoramic Highway. Drive 0.9 mile to a four-way intersection. Take the middle road (straight), continuing on Panoramic Highway for 4.3 more miles to Pantoll Road. Turn right on Pantoll Road and drive 1.4 miles to its intersection with Ridgecrest Boulevard, where there is a large parking area called Rock Spring. Park there and take the signed Cataract Trail from the north side of the lot.

15 COASTAL & MATT DAVIS TRAILS

Mount Tamalpais State Park,
off Panoramic Highway near Mill Valley

Total distance: 3.2 miles round-trip

Hiking time: 1.5 hours

Type of trail: rolling terrain

Best season: year-round

Is it a clear spring day in the San Francisco Bay Area? If so, then there's only one thing to do: Lace up your hiking boots and head for the Coastal Trail in Mount Tamalpais State Park.

The clear-day views from the Coastal and Matt Davis trails on Mount Tamalpais are truly jaw droppers, even for those whose jaws are not dropped by your average stunning view. The trick is to pick a day when the fog is either nonexistent or hovering far out to sea, when visibility is at its best. Then just follow the trail, which meanders in and out of the trees, providing the best of both worlds—secluded forest groves laced with small, coursing streams, and wide open grasslands covered with lupine and poppies in the spring.

There is some confusion about this trail's name. Both Coastal and Matt Davis are two lengthy trails that traverse Mount Tam. For the duration of the route described here, they are the same trail. Matt Davis Trail splits off from this route and descends to the ocean, while Coastal Trail continues straight and eventually ends at the intersection of Ridgecrest Boulevard and Bolinas-Fairfax Road.

After an initial glimpse at the ocean near the start of the trail, you'll head into a dense mixed hardwood forest and remain there for just shy of a mile. The beauty is close at hand—thick moss growing like fur on the bay

Coastal Trail at Mount Tamalpais State Park

laurel trees, dense ferns clustered around seasonal streams, and dappled sunlight filtering through the canopy of leaves.

Just as your eyes grow accustomed to the low light of the forest, the trail suddenly opens out to wide, sloping grasslands and bright sunshine. In spring, the mountain's wildflowers burst into colorful display, spurred on by cooling fog and plentiful sunlight. Because you can see so far and wide along the grassy slopes of Mount Tamalpais, you may spot deer as much as a mile away, or a couple of miniature hikers having lunch on a rock, looking like pieces out of a model train set. This trail is an incredible place for getting an idea of how small we are in the big scheme of things.

From where you stand, the mountain slopes drop more than 1,000 feet to the ocean. The farther you walk, the wider your view becomes, until it finally extends from the San Francisco skyline to Stinson Beach and Bolinas, then north to Point Reyes. If you ever wanted to explain to somebody how large the ocean is in relation to the size of the land, this would be the place to do it.

The best turnaround spot is 1.6 miles in, at a small unmarked spur trail to the left that makes a short climb to a knoll. (If you reach the junction where the Coastal Trail and Matt Davis Trail split off, you've gone past it.) Take this spur trail, which in about 50 feet will lead you to the most awesome view of the day, taking in the entire Marin County coast. It's a good place to picnic or just sit and admire the world before heading back.

Options

You can continue on Coastal Trail past its junction with Matt Davis Trail for nearly three miles, until it intersects with West Ridgecrest Boulevard, adding up to six more miles to your out-and-back trip. Spring wildflowers are usually very good along this stretch.

Information and Contact

A $6 day-use fee is charged per vehicle. A trail map is available at Pantoll Ranger Station. For more information, contact Mount Tamalpais State Park, 801 Panoramic Highway, Mill Valley, CA 94941, 415/388-2070, website: www.parks.ca.gov.

Directions

From San Francisco, cross the Golden Gate Bridge and drive north on U.S. 101 for four miles. Take the Mill Valley/Stinson Beach/Highway 1 exit and continue straight for one mile to a stoplight at Shoreline Highway (Highway 1). Turn left on Shoreline Highway and drive 2.5 miles, then turn right on Panoramic Highway. Drive .9 mile until you reach an intersection where you can go left, straight, or right. Take the middle road (straight), continuing on Panoramic Highway for 4.3 more miles to the Pantoll Ranger Station and parking area. Turn left to park in the parking area, then walk across Panoramic Highway to the start of Pantoll Road. There is a small dirt parking area there, and across from it, on the southwest side of Pantoll Road, is the signed trailhead for the Coastal/Matt Davis Trail.

16 OCEAN VIEW, LOST TRAIL, & FERN CREEK LOOP

Muir Woods National Monument,
off Panoramic Highway near Mill Valley

Total distance: 3.4 miles round-trip

Hiking time: 1.5 hours

Type of trail: rolling terrain

Best season: year-round

The redwoods at Muir Woods National Monument are beauties. The foliage in the understory of the big redwoods—bays, sorrel, sword ferns, tanoak, and thimbleberry—is lush, green, and pretty year-round. Redwood Creek, which cuts through the center of the park, is a pristine, coursing stream.

Muir Woods is good—no doubt about it. The only problem with Muir Woods is its location: It's situated a bit too close to a major urban area. That means this little tiny national monument, not much larger than a few city blocks, gets visited by more than one million people each year.

How do you hike in the park and see its lovely redwoods without getting run over by the crowds? It's not easy. Summer is the busiest time, of course, so it's best to avoid May–September all together. Weekends tend to be more crowded than weekdays, but weekdays bring school groups. (Thirty sixth-graders on a field trip can be pretty boisterous.) The best choice? Try to show up early in the morning, as in 8 A.M. when the park gates open. (Phone the park for updated hours. In winter, the gates sometimes are not open until 9 A.M.) During the week, the first school buses and tour buses don't usually arrive until mid-morning. On the weekends, most visitors don't show up until late morning. An early start any day of the week should give you at least a two-hour window of peace among the redwoods. Winter and early spring are the least crowded and also the loveliest seasons, when Redwood Creek runs full and high.

And don't worry about visiting on a rainy day; just pack along your rain gear. A redwood forest is the best place to hike in the rain. You'll be partially protected by the big trees, and the drops of water on every fern, branch, and leaf only accentuate the beauty.

Start your trip from the entrance gate to Muir Woods, near the small visitors center. The only trail choice is the wide, paved path that runs along the bottom of the canyon, passing the most impressive redwoods.

forests of ferns at Muir Woods

You'll walk the entire length of this trail on your return; for now, bear right and in about 100 yards you'll reach a fork with Ocean View Trail. Ocean View Trail ascends up the hillside to the right. Take it and leave the pavement behind.

The path is completely forested, but the redwood trees are younger and smaller here, and interspersed with many Douglas firs. The climb is very moderately graded, and curves around the canyon until it reaches a junction with Lost Trail at 1.5 miles. Note this junction; then continue straight past it for another 200 yards until Ocean View Trail exits the forest just below Panoramic Highway, a busy road. A large boulder rests on the hillside between the trail and the road; this is the only spot along the trail where you can get a long-distance view. On a sunny day, it's a good resting place, looking down over the forests of Muir Woods below.

When you've had your fill of sunshine, return to the shady woods and the previously noted junction. Turn right on Lost Trail, now heading downhill. Lost Trail is very similar to Ocean View Trail in that it cuts through a young redwood, Douglas fir, and bay forest. Soon it descends more steeply on railroad-tie stairsteps, and in .7 mile it connects with Fern Creek Trail. Fern Creek is a narrower offshoot of Redwood Creek, the main stream that flows through Muir Woods' canyon. The path follows Fern Creek's delightful course for nearly a half mile, crossing it on two footbridges.

Near the end of the Fern Creek Trail you pass a sign marking the border of Muir Woods National Monument. In a few more steps, you're standing at the base of the Kent Memorial, a very large Douglas fir tree dedicated to the man who was responsible for the creation of Muir Woods National Monument. Congressman William Kent and his wife donated this land to the federal government; President Theodore Roosevelt declared it a national monument.

The loop trail ends with a .75-mile walk from the Kent Memorial back up the main trail to your starting point. Although this stretch of trail has the largest and most impressive redwoods, it also has the most people. Fortunately, most of the pavement has been removed in recent years. It has been replaced with a wooden boardwalk that allows the redwoods' roots to grow better. Admire the big trees and the clear stream of Redwood Creek, then head back to your car.

Options
A longer loop through Muir Woods is possible by following the Bootjack, Ben Johnson, and Hillside Trails. This 6.4-mile round-trip will lead you through some impressive woodland and definitely get you away from the crowds. Get a map at the Muir Woods entrance station before setting out.

Information and Contact

A $3 entrance fee is charged per adult; children 16 and under enter free. A free park map/brochure is available at the entrance station. For more information, contact Muir Woods National Monument, Mill Valley, CA 94941, 415/388-2595, website: www.nps.gov/muwo.

Directions

From San Francisco, cross the Golden Gate Bridge and drive north on U.S. 101 for four miles. Take the Mill Valley/Stinson Beach/Highway 1 exit and continue straight for one mile to a stoplight at Shoreline Highway (Highway 1). Turn left on Shoreline Highway and drive 2.5 miles, then turn right on Panoramic Highway. Drive .9 mile and turn left on Muir Woods Road. Drive 1.5 miles to the Muir Woods parking area.

17 LAGOON TRAIL

Golden Gate National Recreation Area,
off U.S. 101 near Sausalito

Total distance: 1.75 miles round-trip   **Hiking time:** 1 hour

Type of trail: mostly level terrain   **Best season:** year-round

You have to look long and hard to find a hiking trail in the Marin Headlands that is nearly level. Or you can head directly for the Lagoon Trail at Rodeo Lagoon and spare yourself a lot of searching. The trail begins conveniently at the Marin Headlands Visitor Center, where you can get a few natural and cultural history lessons before heading out on the scenic, easy path.

From the northwestern edge of the parking lot, start walking directly toward the ocean and Rodeo Beach. A trail veers off to the right, but continue straight ahead, marching toward the sea. Hiking on a wide gravel path, you can hear the rhythm of the ocean waves and watch the birds in Rodeo Lagoon. This natural lagoon is separated from the ocean by a narrow strip of beach. Winter storm waves occasionally wash over the beach, resulting in a mixed freshwater and saltwater environment that makes Rodeo Lagoon a happy home for brown pelicans, snowy egrets, diving wood ducks, and other water birds. Red-winged blackbirds and other songbirds like it too. Hope you brought your binoculars.

For a brief stretch, the foliage alongside the trail is very dense and high, and you can't see far in any direction. Walk past a feeder stream where horsetail ferns grow in thick clusters. The trail begins to climb, rising 100

footbridge across Rodeo Lagoon

feet above the lagoon and opening up your views. Across the water, you can see the buildings of the Headlands Institute and the Marine Mammal Center. The latter is a nonprofit organization that rescues and rehabilitates injured marine animals.

Where the trail drops back down again, nearly at the edge of Rodeo Beach, you are greeted by springtime poppies and deep blue lupine. The National Park Service is working diligently to remove invasive mats of nonnative ice plant from this area and give the native flowers a chance to flourish.

Follow the sandy trail straight out to the beach, or climb up on the bluffs on your left for a broad view of rocky sea stacks and the coast to the south. Most prominent is Bird Island, a giant sea stack that is only barely disconnected from the coast. Because of its separation, Bird Island is inaccessible to ground predators such as foxes, bobcats, raccoons, and people. It serves as a major rest stop for seabirds—as many as 1,200 brown pelicans have been counted on the island at one time. Bird Island is a small paradise for serious bird-watchers.

If you head straight for Rodeo Beach, you'll find it peopled by a mixed collection of fishing enthusiasts, dog walkers, bird-watchers, and beach-lovers. When it's sunny on Rodeo Beach, it's often windy. When it's foggy, it's generally still and peaceful. Look closely at the tiny, colorful pebbles on the beach. Some are semiprecious stones such as carnelians, jasper, and agates, but because this is a national park, collecting them is prohibited. Swimming at the beach is not recommended because of rip tides, although you will see hardy surfers riding the waves. The lagoon, also, is off-limits for swimming.

To finish out your trip, you can loop back by exiting the beach on a wooden footbridge, then walking along the north side of the lagoon, paralleling the road. I'd recommend a turnaround instead; just reverse your steps and enjoy this path all over again.

Options

Trails lead up the bluffs from both the north and south sides of Rodeo Beach, adding extensive out-and-back possibilities. Be sure to check posted signs for seasonal trail closures on these bluffs due to erosion problems.

Information and Contact

There is no fee. The Marin Headlands Visitor Center is open daily from 9:30 A.M.–4:30 P.M. A free map/brochure is available at the Marin Headlands Visitor Center, or by contacting the Golden Gate National Recreation Area, Building 1056, Fort Cronkhite, Sausalito, CA 94965, 415/331-1540, website: www.nps.gov/goga.

Directions

From San Francisco, cross the Golden Gate Bridge on U.S. 101 and take the first exit north of the bridge, Alexander Avenue. Turn left and loop back under the freeway, then turn right on Conzelman Road. (Coming southbound on U.S. 101, take the last Sausalito exit just before the Golden Gate Bridge.) Drive one mile on Conzelman Road, then turn right on McCullough Road and drive .9 mile. Turn left on Bunker Road and drive two miles. (Follow the signs for the Marin Headlands Visitor Center.) Park at the visitors center and locate the Lagoon Trail marker near the restrooms on the west side of the parking lot.

18 BAY VIEW LOOP

Point Pinole Regional Shoreline, off I-80 near Richmond

Total distance: 5.0 miles round-trip   **Hiking time:** 2.5 hours

Type of trail: mostly level terrain   **Best season:** year-round

Point Pinole Regional Shoreline is a little park with a big heart, a place of tranquility not far from the urban bustle of the East Bay. Few visitors other than avid fishing enthusiasts and dog walkers make the trip to the tip of

snowy egret at Point Pinole

Point Pinole, but those who do are surprised at how much their $4 park admission can buy. In addition to inspiring bay views, a fascinating history, and good pier fishing, the park offers volleyball courts, picnic areas, and more than 12 miles of winding dirt trails suitable for hiking or mountain biking.

Don't be put off by the drive in to the park. Point Pinole Regional Shoreline has some odd neighbors, including Chevron's oil refineries and a juvenile detention center. The Southern Pacific Railroad runs right alongside the park. But once you're inside the gates of Point Pinole, all is peaceful. On two weekend visits here, we found the place largely deserted except for a few hikers and bike riders. The ranger at the entrance kiosk told us that some people are discouraged by the park's Richmond address; others are put off by the $4 admission fee.

Start your hike on the main paved trail by the entrance kiosk. You'll notice a small mound planted with flowers and a plaque denoting the site of the Giant Powder Company from 1892 to 1960. When terrible explosions ruined its Berkeley and San Francisco factories, Giant Powder moved to remote Point Pinole to manufacture dynamite. Here they built a thriving company town and local railway.

Follow the paved road for 200 yards to a railroad bridge. Cross the bridge and take the signed trail on the left, Bay View Trail. The wide dirt trail skirts the edge of Point Pinole's peninsula and supplies continual views of San Pablo Bay. To the southwest, you see plumes of gas and steam rising from Chevron's oil refineries. To the west, Mount Tamalpais looms over Marin County. In the foreground are miles of open bay water, interrupted only by the San Rafael-Richmond Bridge and the East and West Brothers Islands. A few duck blinds dot the shoreline. Seabirds gather on the mudflats during low tide.

Due to a trail closure, the path moves away from the bay and into a eucalyptus grove for a brief stretch, then returns to the meeting of land and sea. Just under two miles from the trailhead, the path curves around the tip of Point Pinole's peninsula to reach its quarter-mile-long fishing pier. Walk out to the pier's end, then sit and sniff the salty air while you admire the views of Mount Diablo on your far right and Mount Tamalpais on your left. Look back toward shore and note the rugged coastal bluffs rising 100 feet above the bay. Point Pinole is the only place on this side of San Pablo Bay with shoreline cliffs; elsewhere the water is surrounded by flatlands.

The pier's Plexiglas shelters provide protection for fishing enthusiasts and hikers when the wind howls. If you're interested in fishing, note that you don't need a license to pier fish here. For those with luck, the catch may include sturgeon, striped bass, and kingfish.

From the pier, follow the paved road 100 yards south to a wooden bus shelter. (Shuttle buses ride this paved route from the parking lot to the pier every hour from 7:30 A.M.–2:30 P.M. For a buck, anglers who don't want to walk to the pier can catch a ride.) Beyond the bus shelter, take the signed Marsh Trail on the left. In just under a half mile you'll see a small pond on your right; turn left by the pond to stay on Marsh Trail.

Now facing eastward, your perspective on the bay is totally different. The Carquinez Bridge appears, as well as Vallejo and Napa. A large salt marsh lined with pickleweed borders the trail. The wide, gentle waters of San Pablo Bay remain constant.

Where Marsh Trail junctions with Cook's Point Trail, you'll see an odd structure sheltering a large hunk of metal. It's a black powder press remaining from the days of Giant Powder Company. Head past it on Marsh Trail to the edge of the bay; you can make a short loop to the right along the shoreline if you wish. Bird-watching is good near the salt marsh.

The return leg of the loop is Cook's Point Trail. This path will lead you all the way back to the park's picnic areas. From there, it's a short stroll over the railroad bridge and back to your car.

Information and Contact

A $4 day-use fee is charged per vehicle. Free trail maps are available at the parking area. For more information, contact the East Bay Regional Parks District, 2950 Peralta Oaks Court, P.O. Box 5381, Oakland, CA 94605-0381, 510/635-0135, website: www.ebparks.org.

Directions

From I-80 in Richmond, take the Hilltop Drive exit west. Turn right on San Pablo Avenue, then left on Richmond Parkway. Follow Richmond Parkway to the Giant Highway exit. Turn right and drive .75 mile to the park entrance on the left. Or, from U.S. 101 in Marin, take the San

Rafael-Richmond Bridge east (I-580), then take the first exit east of the bridge, signed for Castro Street and Richmond Parkway. Drive 4.3 miles on Richmond Parkway to the Giant Highway exit. Take the exit and drive .5 mile, then turn right on Giant Highway. Drive .75 mile to the park entrance on the left.

🔢19 OLD BRIONES ROAD & LAGOON TRAIL LOOP

Briones Regional Park, off I-680 near Pleasant Hill

Total distance: 5.0 miles round-trip   **Hiking time:** 2.5 hours

Type of trail: some steep terrain   **Best season:** November–April

For years I'd been hearing about how great the views were at Briones, but I never managed to make the trip. I had an attitude problem: Every time I looked at the Briones map, I envisioned a dry, hot desert, with giant dusty peaks to surmount, and maybe a few tumbleweeds blowing around. Hiking this far inland in the East Bay? Sorry, but I think I have some real important things I have to do.

Well, I finally made it to Briones, and I have a new attitude about the park. The secret is to go on a clear day in late fall, winter or spring (to get the best views and the coolest weather) and to start from the higher-elevation trailhead at Briones Road rather than the main trailhead at Alhambra Creek. This way your car does some of the climbing instead of your feet, and you get within easy hiking distance of some excellent vistas.

There are two prerequisites for enjoying this hike: 1) Don't go in the midday heat of summer; and 2) You must like bovines, or at least be amenable to them. Cows graze all over Briones.

The trail does have some fair ascents. Plus it's a long walk in wide open sunshine, so you need to come prepared with plenty of water and snacks, and don't forget to pick up your free trail map at the trailhead kiosk. Your trip begins with a climb on Old Briones Road, a fire road. Old Briones Road climbs gently for .75 mile and then levels out near—surprise—a small lagoon. On my first trip here, I had noticed "Maricich Lagoon" on the map, but I had imagined a crusty dust bowl with hawks circling overhead. Instead, the lagoon is a pretty little pond that is fenced in to keep the cows out. Ducks are often found floating peacefully on its surface.

At the lagoon, check the trail marker and make sure you continue right on Old Briones Road for another .25 mile. Then turn right on the Briones Crest Trail, heading for another set of ponds, Sindicich Lagoons. Now prepare to start getting those remarkable views.

Remarkable? How about Mount Diablo, San Pablo Bay, Point Pinole, Suisun Bay, and Honker Bay in the distance? Hey, what are all those ships lined up down there? That's the Mothball Fleet—old military ships that have been put out to pasture. You'll see the oil refineries along Contra Costa County's shoreline, often referred to as the Oil Coast. Not enough for you? Okay, let's toss in the Berkeley hills and the distinctive profile of Mount Tamalpais to the west. The whole of the Bay Area is brought into reach. And you're not even seeing it from the highest point in this park, which is Mott Peak to the south, named after William Penn Mott, champion of parks.

If you're feeling a bit tired from all the climbing you've done, now is the time to consider turning back instead of finishing out the loop. Because you've been going up for so long, you may think it's all downhill going back. Wrong. Shortly past the intersection with the Mott Peak Trail on the left, the Briones Crest Trail begins to descend. The only way to loop back to your car is to drop down below the trailhead and then circle around, which involves more ascent. The trail marker for the Mott Peak Trail, or somewhere close to it, is an excellent turnaround point for a four-mile round-trip hike.

Energetic types should continue farther on the Briones Crest Trail and

Briones Regional Park

bear right on the Lagoon Trail. Follow the Lagoon Trail for 1.25 miles and loop around to Toyon Canyon Trail. You'll head into a live oak forest, a nice change of pace from the sunshine and grasslands. Turn left on Toyon Canyon Trail and continue for one mile, then turn right for .25 mile on the Pine Tree Trail, nearing some estate homes. When you see the paved road you drove in on, either follow the road back to your car or the unsigned single-track trail that parallels the access road.

The trails at Briones have a lot of different users, besides hikers and all the bovines—dogs, bicyclists, horses and their riders—so keep your ears and eyes open for them. Always remember to give horses plenty of room. I saw every kind of trail user on my trip, and everyone was polite and friendly. Seems like at Briones, everyone, including me, gets their attitude adjusted.

Options
Make this an out-and-back hike instead of a loop. When you reach the trail sign for Mott Peak Trail, turn around and head back the way you came. If you continue on the loop, you'll have more mileage and more climbing.

Information and Contact
There is no fee. Free trail maps are available at the parking area. For more information, contact the East Bay Regional Parks District, 2950 Peralta Oaks Court, P.O. Box 5381, Oakland, CA 94605-0381, 510/635-0135, website: www.ebparks.org.

Directions
From I-680 north of Pleasant Hill, take Highway 4 west for three miles to the Alhambra Avenue exit. Turn south on Alhambra Avenue, drive .5 mile and bear right on Alhambra Valley Road. In about 50 yards, turn left on Briones Road and continue 1.5 miles to the trailhead.

20 MACDONALD TRAIL
Anthony Chabot Regional Park, off I-580 near Oakland

Total distance: 3.5 miles round-trip   **Hiking time:** 1.5 hours

Type of trail: rolling terrain   **Best season:** November–April

A little piece of paradise is available to hikers in the East Bay, and the big surprise is that it's only a 20-minute drive from the heart of downtown Oakland. Here's the scoop: Anthony Chabot Regional Park is nearly 5,000

Blue-eyed grass is a common springtime sight at Anthony Chabot Regional Park.

acres of grasslands and forest surrounding Lake Chabot, a bright-blue gem of a lake that provides quality fishing and boating as well as a reserve water supply for the city of Oakland. The East Bay Skyline National Recreation Trail, a 31-mile trail that traverses Contra Costa County between Berkeley and Walnut Creek, has an easement throughout the park. The Macdonald Trail follows a portion of it.

Pick up the Macdonald Trail at the Bort Meadow Staging Area. The path climbs gently right away and keeps climbing for the first mile. These open grassland hills give you plenty of reason to take your time and examine the abundant spring wildflowers. The Macdonald Trail is great for testing your knowledge of plants and grasses. Bring along a wildflower identification book and you can easily name more than 20 species. Most prevalent is blue-eyed grass, which, contrary to its name, is not blue but purple.

You'll pass through two cattle gates, one right at the beginning of the trail and one farther on. Close them behind you. In a few places, the main trail branches off to narrower trails, but stay on the wide main path. At 1.5 miles, you'll reach an intersection with the Parkridge Trail to your left, which connects to a bordering neighborhood. Stay on the Macdonald Trail as it starts to slope downward. Before it goes too far downhill—and this is that delicate point where you know you won't enjoy the return trip uphill— you should do an about-face and head back the way you came.

If you keep your eyes peeled, you will find my favorite destination and turnaround point. A quarter-mile past the Parkridge Trail junction, look for a tiny spur trail on the right that heads into dense foliage. This short spur leads you to a hidden wooden bench, which provides a place to rest and take in the view of the hills and grasslands to the east. It's a peaceful little spot overlooking a stunning vista. If you retrace your steps from here, you won't have to climb at all on your way back.

Pick a clear day in winter or spring, preferably one that combines blue skies with some big puffy clouds, or an early morning in summer before the temperatures heat up, and head to Chabot Park in the East Bay hills. You'll find that paradise is a lot closer than you thought.

Options
Just shorten or lengthen your route, and be sure to stop for a picnic somewhere along the trail or in Bort Meadow.

Information and Contact
There is no fee. Free trail maps are available at the parking area, or from any ranger kiosk in the park. For more information, contact the East Bay Regional Parks District, 2950 Peralta Oaks Court, P.O. Box 5381, Oakland, CA 94605-0381, 510/635-0135, website: www.ebparks.org.

Directions
From I-580 in Oakland, take the 35th Avenue exit and drive east (left). 35th Avenue becomes Redwood Road. Cross Skyline Boulevard and continue for 4.2 miles to the Bort Meadow Staging Area on the right. The trailhead is at the northwest end of the parking lot.

21 NORTH PEAK TRAIL TO PROSPECTORS GAP
Mount Diablo State Park, off I-680 near Danville

Total distance: 2.25 miles round-trip   **Hiking time:** 1 hour

Type of trail: some steep terrain   **Best season:** November–April

Most everybody thinks about making a trip to 3,849-foot Mt. Diablo from time to time. After all, you see it from just about everywhere in the Bay Area. It's not that it's the tallest mountain around San Francisco Bay (Mt.

Hamilton is taller); it just has a way of making its presence known, looming in the background of the lives of millions of East Bay residents.

When your time to visit Diablo arrives, the first thing you should do is drive up to the summit and see what it's like to look at the greater Bay Area from Mt. Diablo, rather than vice versa. Park as close to the summit building as possible, walk around the summit parking lot, and check out the view in all directions (on the clearest days, you can see all the way to the Sierra!) Then go inside the visitors center and take 10 minutes to learn about the landscape and geology of this big mountain called Diablo, which is Spanish for devil.

Despite its name, Diablo has a multitude of charms. Although its spectacular summit vista is the main attraction, easy hikers will be pleased to find a trail near the summit that makes a great winter or spring trip. To reach the trailhead, drive back down the summit road for about one mile to a gravel parking area signed as "Summit Trail." You'll find two trails here; don't take the upper Summit Trail, but rather the unsigned lower trail, which is the North Peak Trail. Start walking the path across the shoulder of the mountain at 3,800 feet in elevation, less than 100 feet below the summit.

Mt. Diablo has two summits, the main one with the paved road to the top and North Peak, which is 292 feet shorter at 3,557 feet. The North

© ANN MARIE BROWN

The cones of the gray pine can weigh up to four pounds.

Peak Trail takes you around the east side of the higher summit, then down to a saddle between the peaks called Prospectors Gap. The trail to Prospectors Gap weaves in and out of chaparral and grasslands, occasionally catching breezes from the north and west. The route is shaded by the summit in the afternoon, and the gap offers unimpeded views to the east and west.

The trail is not entirely easy, however. It drops 400 feet in elevation on the way to Prospectors Gap, then climbs back up on the return. The "up" is a bit of a challenge for your thighs, heart, and lungs, while the down gives your feet and knees a workout. I'd definitely advise wearing hiking boots on this trail, as there are some steep pitches with loose gravel and an uneven surface.

The flora on Mt. Diablo is quite unique. Even on this short walk on the North Peak Trail, you may see several spring wildflowers that are rarely seen in the rest of the Bay Area. Lucky hikers will spot Mount Diablo fairy lanterns, which grow nowhere else in the world. They have yellow, waxy-looking, nodding heads on stalks about five inches high. More prevalent are hooker's onions (foot-tall thin stalks with pink flower clusters at the top), purple fields of clarkia, red larkspur, dark blue lupine, orange California poppies, and tall mariposa lilies, with white tulip-shaped bowls and reddish-brown spots.

If you visit after the March-to-May wildflower season has passed, you'll still have California laurel, scrub oaks, and gray pines to keep you company along the trail. The scraggly-looking gray pines are similar to coulter pines, which also grow on Mt. Diablo, but they have forked trunks and a grayish color to their needles. Coulter pines grow straighter and taller. The gray pine is most remarkable for its big cones, which weigh between one and four pounds and are six to ten inches long. (The coulter pine's cones are even bigger.) As I walked, I heard a gray pinecone hit the ground with a resounding "bonk." Watch your head if you decide to sit under one of these trees.

You'll probably run across some wildlife on your trip to Diablo, too. I saw two deer on the summit road, a plethora of sagebrush lizards on the trail (they're the speediest lizards around), a big jackrabbit, and several varieties of butterflies flitting about the brush. At the summit, I was virtually surrounded by a swarm of ladybugs. There must have a ladybug convention, or perhaps they all took a tour bus to see the view.

There is only one important thing to remember about visiting Mt. Diablo: Never go in the blazing heat of summer; it just ruins all your fun. The best seasons to visit are winter, when you may even find snow on the summit; or spring, when the grasses are green and the wildflowers put on their show. Sunsets and sunrises are particularly spectacular, as is any day when the valley is fogged in. Diablo's summit usually sits above the fog, so you get the heavenly perspective of gazing down over a featherbed layer of puffy white clouds.

Options
From Prospectors Gap, North Peak Trail climbs on a fire road to the top of North Peak. This steep tromp has a 500-foot elevation gain in less than a mile, but if you're feeling energetic, the view is worth it.

Information and Contact

A $6 day-use fee is charged per vehicle. A map is available at the ranger kiosk or interpretive center. For more information, contact Mount Diablo State Park, 96 Mitchell Canyon Road, Clayton, CA 94517, 925/837-2525 or 925/837-0904, website: www.parks.ca.gov or www.mdia.org.

Directions

From I-680 at Danville, take the Diablo Road exit and head east. Follow Diablo Road for 2.9 miles (you must turn right at 0.7 miles to stay on Diablo Road). At a stop sign at Mount Diablo Scenic Boulevard, turn left. Drive 3.7 miles on Mount Diablo Scenic Boulevard (it becomes South Gate Road) to the park's southern entrance station. Continue to the junction with Summit Road, then turn right and drive to the summit (a total of 7.3 miles). After visiting the summit, drive back down Summit Road for one mile to the Summit Trail trailhead.

Alternatively, from I-680 in Walnut Creek, take the Treat Boulevard exit and go east for 1.2 miles. Turn right on Bancroft Road, which crosses Ygnacio Valley Road and becomes Walnut Avenue. Drive 1.6 miles on Walnut Avenue, then turn right on Oak Grove Road. Turn left immediately on North Gate Road and continue to the junction with Summit Road. Turn left and drive to the summit (a total of 12 miles).

22 BROOKS CREEK & MONTARA MOUNTAIN TRAILS

San Pedro Valley County Park, off Highway 1 near Pacifica

Total distance: 2.8 miles round-trip   **Hiking time:** 1.5 hours

Type of trail: some steep terrain   **Best season:** December–April

---

The first time you drive to San Pedro Valley County Park you may think you have the wrong directions. You head down Highway 1 into Pacifica, then turn off at a shopping center with a supermarket and a selection of fast-food chains. The place doesn't look much like a nature preserve.

But have patience, because you need only drive another couple miles before leaving the suburban entrapments behind. In a few minutes on the trail, you'll head up and away from the parking lots, noise, and traffic lights and enter a vastly different world.

If you're hiking in the rainy season, a surprise awaits. By hiking the

Brooks Creek Trail in winter or spring, you have a chance to see one of the Bay Area's prettiest waterfalls—Brooks Falls, a tall, narrow cascade of water that plunges 175 feet in three tiers. From a distance, it looks like one of the majestic tropical waterfalls of Hawaii.

Locate the trailhead for Montara Mountain Trail by the restrooms in San Pedro Valley County Park. A few feet beyond the trailhead, the trail splits: Montara Mountain Trail heads right and Old Trout Farm Trail heads left. Go left and gently uphill through a dense grove of eucalyptus. At trail junctions, small signs direct you "to Waterfall Viewing Area." Bear right at two forks, now following Brooks Creek Trail, and keep heading uphill. The well-graded path soon emerges from the trees to open views of the canyon amid coastal sage scrub, ceanothus, and monkeyflower.

Twenty minutes of well-graded climbing delivers your first glimpse of the waterfall, far off in the canyon on your left. Look for a narrow plume of water cascading down the mountainside. Unfortunately, no trails lead to the base of the waterfall; you can only view it from a distance. The best viewpoint is at a conveniently placed bench right along the trail. After a hard rain, you can hear and see the water crashing down the canyon slopes a quarter-mile away. If you want photographs, bring your telephoto lens.

From the manzanita-lined overlook, continue uphill on Brooks Creek Trail, gaining more views of Brooks Falls. The trail tops out on a ridge with an overlook of Pacifica and the ocean to the west and the Marin Headlands to the north. On the clearest days, even the Farallon Islands show up. Montara Mountain Trail takes off from here; to the left and two miles farther is the summit of Montara Mountain. For a 2.6-mile loop, turn right on Montara Mountain Trail and start to descend. You'll drop 500 feet in elevation through more stands of eucalyptus to reach the trailhead and parking area. If you happen to live in Pacifica, you might be able to pick out your house from the suburbs below as you descend.

Keep in mind that Brooks Falls is a seasonal waterfall. This loop trip makes a pleasant hike year-round, but you can view the falls only in the rainy season.

Options
You can shorten your hike considerably by just stopping at the viewing bench for Brooks Falls and then returning the way you came. This would make your walk about two miles round-trip, including a moderate 400-foot climb up to the falls' viewing spot.

Information and Contact
A $4 day-use fee is charged per vehicle. Free trail maps and park brochures are available at the trailhead. For more information, contact

San Pedro Valley County Park, 600 Oddstad Boulevard, Pacifica, CA
94044, 650/355-8289, website: www.eparks.net.

Directions
From San Francisco, take Highway 1 south into Pacifica. Turn east (left)
on Linda Mar Boulevard and follow it until it dead-ends at Oddstad Boulevard. Turn right and drive to the park entrance, located about 50 yards
ahead on the left. Park in the upper parking lot (to the right of the visitors
center as you drive in). Look for the trailhead signed "Montara Mountain
Trail" directly behind the public restrooms.

23 VALLEY VIEW TRAIL
San Pedro Valley County Park, off Highway 1 near Pacifica

Total distance: 2.0 miles round-trip   **Hiking time:** 1 hour

Type of trail: rolling terrain   **Best season:** year-round

Need a breather from the pressures of life in San Francisco or the Northern Peninsula? Want someplace to go where you can stretch your legs and
feel a whole lot better, but not use up the whole day? Head for San Pedro
Valley County Park in Pacifica. The Valley View Trail is a terrific one-hour
hike for anyone who wants a little bit of a workout and a big dose of sunshine and fresh air.

Children in particular will enjoy this trail, because they are virtually guaranteed of seeing wildlife. On my first hike here, within the first .25 mile I
saw three deer in a wide-open meadow, despite the fact that it was the middle of the day. As I continued, I spotted more than a dozen lizards (always
popular with the under-12 crowd), several species of songbirds and hawks,
and a rabbit. You may even see a bobcat or coyote on rare occasions.

An interesting feature of this trail is that it's rated for use by disabled
persons with "mountain wheelchairs" and a buddy. The hard-packed dirt
trail has a 400-foot elevation gain, and parts of it become quite narrow
and uneven, so some wheelchair users may choose to travel only a portion
of the trail. Weiler Ranch Road, which is the return leg of this loop hike,
is even more wheelchair-friendly. It's also popular with people pushing
baby strollers.

It takes about 30 minutes to gently ascend the Valley View Trail. You'll
have to work just hard enough to say hello to your cardiovascular system.
As you climb, you'll be rewarded with lovely meadow, canyon, hillside,

and finally ocean views. When you reach the top of the ridge, you'll be surprised at how high you've climbed, because the trail has an easy grade that makes the ascent smooth. In springtime, you'll find several huge patches of purple Douglas irises on the ridge top—as many as 100 showy flowers in each patch. From this high point, you have 20 minutes of easy walking down to Weiler Ranch Road, where you turn right and head back to your starting point.

Showy Douglas irises are easily spotted on the Valley View Trail.

Options

To explore more of the park, try a 4.6-mile loop on Hazelnut Trail and Weiler Ranch Road, starting from behind the visitors center. From the group picnic area, take wide and level Weiler Ranch Road up the valley for 1.2 miles, then turn right on Hazelnut Trail. You'll gain 400 feet as you switchback up a ridge through a mixed bouquet of tall chaparral plants—everything from common coyote brush to uncommon chinquapin. From the loop's highest points, you gain surprising views of the Pacific Ocean (even the Farallon Islands on the clearest days) and San Pedro Creek Canyon. The downhill side of the loop is routed through a veritable forest of hazelnut, the trail's namesake.

Information and Contact

A $4 day-use fee is charged per vehicle. Free trail maps and park brochures are available at the trailhead. For more information, contact San Pedro Valley County Park, 600 Oddstad Boulevard, Pacifica, CA 94044, 650/355-8289, website: www.eparks.net.

Directions

From San Francisco, take Highway 1 south into Pacifica. Turn east (left) on Linda Mar Boulevard and follow it until it dead-ends at Oddstad Boulevard. Turn right and drive to the park entrance, located about 50 yards ahead on the left. Park in the lower parking lot (to the left of the visitors center as you drive in). Look for the sign at the northeast end of the parking lot pointing toward the group picnic area. Follow the paved path over a bridge, through the group picnic area, and then straight ahead for the trailheads for Weiler Ranch Road and the Valley View Trail.

24 WHITTEMORE GULCH TRAIL
Purisima Creek Redwoods Open Space Preserve,
off Highway 35 on the San Francisco Peninsula

Total distance: 2.2 miles round-trip   **Hiking time:** 1 hour

Type of trail: some steep terrain   **Best season:** year-round

Purisima Creek Redwoods Open Space Preserve is a hiker's heaven. With breathtaking ocean views, towering redwood and fir trees, a year-round creek, and plentiful wildlife and wildflowers, the preserve shows off some of the best features of the Santa Cruz Mountains. Purisima delivers on its Spanish name—it's pristine.

You can access the 3,200-acre preserve from two trailheads on Skyline Boulevard or one on Higgins Purisima Road in Half Moon Bay. Purisima's trails traverse the slopes between Skyline Ridge and the coast, a 1,600-foot elevation change. Choose any path and you'll have to go up and then down, or down and then up.

This easy hike begins at the preserve's northern entrance on Skyline Boulevard, a mere half-hour drive from San Francisco. This is an "upside down" hike, in which you'll go downhill first, then uphill on your return. Even though it's a relatively mellow ascent, bring plenty of water and snacks to sustain you on the return trip.

From the Skyline trailhead, follow the single-track, hikers-only trail to the right of the wide fire road. Switchback your way down the trail, enjoying the shade of Douglas firs, tanoaks, and madrones. From February–June, the woodland understory is littered with dense clusters of light blue forget-me-nots. Look down at your feet; it appears as if you are walking amid blue-and-white clouds.

The narrow trail ends a half-mile out. Turn right on North Ridge Trail, a fir tree-lined fire road, and follow it for .5 mile. A left turn on Whittemore Gulch Trail puts you back on single-track. You'll pass through a seasonal gate used for blocking the trail to equestrians and mountain bikers during the wet season, then begin a series of long switchbacks downhill. The path opens out to chaparral-covered slopes with views of Half Moon

Bay and the San Mateo coast. A short spur trail leads to an overlook with a railing to lean on; the coast vista is widest from here.

This overlook makes a fine turnaround spot for a 2.2-mile round-trip. You may be tempted to continue farther, but just be aware that if you do, you'll have a substantial climb on the way back out. The trail continues from this overlook railing for another two miles to a dense redwood and Douglas fir forest along Purisima Creek. If you have the time and energy, it is worth seeing. If you don't, it's time to wave good-bye to the coast and head back uphill.

Options

Two miles south on Skyline Boulevard is another trailhead for Purisima Creek Redwoods Open Space Preserve. From here, the .6-mile Redwood Trail, a wheelchair- and stroller-accessible path, winds through towering redwoods. You can connect to Purisima Creek Trail for a longer out-and-back hike.

Information and Contact

There is no fee. Free trail maps are available at the trailhead. For more information, contact the Midpeninsula Regional Open Space District, 330 Distel Circle, Los Altos, CA 94022, 650/691-1200, website: www.openspace.org.

Directions

From San Francisco, drive south on I-280 for 19 miles to the Highway 92 cutoff. Head west on Highway 92 toward Half Moon Bay for 2.7 miles, then turn south (left) on Highway 35 (Skyline Boulevard) and drive 4.2 miles to the Purisima Creek Redwoods Open Space Preserve parking area on the right. The Whittemore Gulch Trailhead is at the southwest end of the parking lot.

25 TAFONI TRAIL

El Corte de Madera Open Space Preserve,
off Highway 35 on the San Francisco Peninsula

Total distance: 2.6 miles round-trip   **Hiking time:** 1.5 hours

Type of trail: rolling terrain   **Best season:** year-round

Although mountain bikers come to El Corte de Madera Open Space Preserve for different reasons, the main attraction for hikers at this wooded, 2,800-acre preserve is the monolithic sandstone formations at the end of

looking up at the sandstone monoliths

the Tafoni Trail. The formations stand completely alone in the forest; they're unlike anything else you see along the trail. The rest of the preserve is primarily trees and more trees, including some magnificent old Douglas firs and younger redwoods. You hike through acres of forest, then suddenly they appear— huge sandstone beasts looming 50 feet high. Just as suddenly, there are no more of them, just dense trees again. It's as if Mother Nature told the delivery company to drop the sandstone off at the wrong location.

Many trails run through the preserve, but for the majority of this trip you stay on the wide main fire road known as Tafoni Trail. You'll hike on a gentle uphill grade for the first 1.2 miles, then reach a major four-way junction. Turn sharply right to head to the sandstone formations. In just a few hundred yards, you'll reach a sign announcing the "tafoni" ahead. Turn right on a single-track path (this is the only trail in the preserve that is reserved for hikers only) and descend to the 50-foot-high outcrops. From a newly constructed observation deck, built in 2002, you have a good vantage point for gazing in awe at the tafoni.

Although it sounds like an Italian dessert, tafoni is a type of sandstone that is formed by years of weathering. (It was named for an Italian geologist.) A unique combination of coastal fog, tectonic upthrust, and sandstone cliffs provide the right ingredients for tafoni. The "glue" that holds the sandstone's individual sand grains together eventually erodes away, leaving honeycomb patterned, lace-like crevices and holes in the smooth rock.

When you've finished admiring these geological oddities, retrace your steps to the previous junction and head right on the 100-yard-long spur trail signed for Vista Point. This spot offers a view of the coast and a level, open area for picnicking.

Information and Contact

There is no fee. Free trail maps are available at the trailhead. For more information, contact the Midpeninsula Regional Open Space District, 330 Distel Circle, Los Altos, CA 94022, 650/691-1200, website: www.openspace.org.

Directions

From San Francisco, drive south on I-280 for 19 miles to the Highway 92 cutoff. Head west on Highway 92 toward Half Moon Bay for 2.7 miles, then turn south (left) on Highway 35/Skyline Boulevard and drive 8.5 miles to the Skeggs Vista Point parking area on your left. (It is 1.6 miles south of the intersection with Kings Mountain Road, and 3.8 miles north of Skylonda.) You can't turn left into the parking area; you must drive farther south and find a safe place to make a U-turn. After parking, walk 50 yards north on Skyline and cross the road to access Tafoni Trail.

26 PALO ALTO BAYLANDS NATURE TRAIL
Palo Alto Baylands Preserve, off U.S. 101 in Palo Alto

Total distance: 1.25 miles round-trip

Hiking time: 30 minutes

Type of trail: mostly level terrain

Best season: year-round

You might feel a little skeptical about a hike that parallels the Palo Alto Municipal Airport runway. Is it possible to have a nature experience in the midst of suburban sprawl? It doesn't seem likely. But you can at the Palo Alto Baylands Preserve and its accompanying Baylands Interpretive Center and trails.

The Interpretive Center is a picturesque wooden structure resting on stilts high above the mudflats and pickleweed of South San Francisco Bay. And the hike, which follows the airport runway for some distance, has many pleasant and surprising features. For starters, the area is teeming with bird life. On my trip, one particular species caught my eye because of its unique markings—black stripes on its wings and a pale orange head. It was an American avocet, easily identified by the side-to-side motion it makes with its head as it feeds in shallow water. Orioles zoomed back and forth across the trail, ambitiously building their nests underneath the pilings of the interpretive center. Also present were the usual wetlands birds: coots, ducks, egrets, herons, pelicans, and an abundance of western sandpipers (more than 100,000 of them show up here at one time). The sandpipers fly in precise patterns right along the water's edge, as if the entire flock was radio-controlled.

All these birds can't be wrong. The Palo Alto Baylands is a sanctuary amid the chaos of the Silicon Valley, with more than 2,000 acres of preserved marshland. The birds don't seem to mind the neighboring airport, nor the power lines and electrical towers that line the bay.

The walk is as level as can be, but never dull. You start walking on the trail in front of the interpretive center, head out for .5 mile until you reach a bench at the end of the trail, then head back. When you're not watching the wildlife, it's interesting to watch the small planes take off at the airport. You're far enough away so that their noise is not bothersome, but close enough to make out the details of the planes.

Don't miss a visit to the interpretive center, if it's open, and a stroll on the wooden boardwalk that extends from its back side for 800 yards across the tidal marshlands. This allows you a remarkable perspective on the Bay—you are in the middle of it, instead of watching from its edges. At the boardwalk's end is an observation deck, situated at the exact boundary where marshland meets open water. It's the kind of place you can sit for a long time, gazing at the always-in-motion bay flow.

The Palo Alto Baylands Preserve was created in the 1960s by some smart folks in Palo Alto. More acreage was added later to include a huge salt marsh, a duck pond, and a seasonal freshwater marsh that is fed by millions of gallons of treated wastewater from the nearby Palo Alto sewage treatment plant. The preserve is a fine example of the right way to protect precious wetlands.

One more surprise is in store for bird-watchers: The Palo Alto Baylands is home to a healthy population of colorful ring-necked pheasants, exotic birds imported from Asia that were introduced in the United States in the 1800s as a game bird. For many years, a pheasant farm was located just north of what is now the interpretive center. After the farm's demise in the 1960s, the birds continued to thrive in the wild. If you're lucky, you may hear a pheasant making its clamorous call, or catch sight of its bright gold and forest-green colors as you hike.

Information and Contact

There is no fee. For more information, contact Palo Alto Baylands Interpretive Center, 1451 Middlefield Road, Palo Alto, CA 94301, 650/329-2506, website: www.ci.palo-alto.ca.us.

Directions

From U.S. 101 in Palo Alto, take the Embarcadero exit east. Drive about a half mile, passing the golf course, airport and yacht harbor, until you reach a sharp right turn. Park in the lot on the right. The interpretive center is across the road; the trailhead is directly in front of it.

27 RUSSIAN RIDGE LOOP
Russian Ridge Open Space Preserve,
off Highway 35 on the San Francisco Peninsula

Total distance: 4.4 miles round-trip **Hiking time:** 2 hours

Type of trail: rolling terrain **Best season:** year-round

Russian Ridge Open Space Preserve is more than 1,500 acres of windswept ridge-top paradise. We're talking location, location, location, as in directly off Skyline Boulevard (Highway 35), near the well-to-do town of Portola Valley. The weather may be foggy along the coast, but the sun is usually shining brightly on Skyline. From the preserve's 2,300-foot elevation, you can look out and above the layer of fog blanketing the ocean. What pleasure to appreciate its cotton candy appearance without being stuck in the thick of it.

In spring, Russian Ridge will charm you with colorful wildflowers and verdant grasslands. In summer and fall, the hillsides turn to gold and the grasses sway in unison to the ridge-top winds. On the rare days of winter when snow dusts this ridge, you can pull out your cross-country skis and glide along the slopes! On a clear day in any season, you'll be wowed by the vistas from 2,572-foot Borel Hill, the highest named point in San Mateo County.

mule's ears in Russian Ridge Open Space Preserve

Although many people visit this preserve for the views, Russian Ridge doles out much more. Its acreage combines several plant environments, including lush grasslands, creeks, springs, and oak-shaded canyons. It is home to substantial wildlife, including a variety of raptors, coyotes, and mountain lions. Most impressive are the spring wildflowers. Every April and May, the grasslands explode in a fireworks display of colorful mule's ears, poppies, lupine, goldfields, Johnny jump-ups, and blue-eyed grass. Russian Ridge is considered to be one of the best places in the Bay Area to see wildflowers.

This 4.4-mile loop circles the preserve. Take the Bay Area Ridge Trail uphill from the parking lot, heading for the top of grassy Borel Hill in less than a mile. (Stay right at two junctions.) The 2,572-foot summit of Borel Hill is just high enough to serve up a 360-degree view of the South Bay, Skyline Ridge, and all the way west to the Pacific Ocean. Mount Diablo looms in the eastern horizon and Mount Tamalpais guards the north. This has to be one of the most inspiring lookouts on the Peninsula.

From the summit, descend gently for .5 mile to a major junction of trails near Skyline Boulevard. Bear left on Mindego Trail, then shortly turn right on Bay Area Ridge Trail. Ridge Trail narrows, curving around grassy knolls and producing more views of the coast and the bay. To the southwest you can see Mindego Hill, an ancient volcanic formation that may be the source of this ridge's scattered rock outcrops.

At a junction with Hawk Trail, turn left to head southeast and start your loop back. Descend to the junction of Mindego Trail and Ancient Oaks Trail, then follow Ancient Oaks Trail. This short trail leads you through a remarkable forest of gnarled, moss-covered oak trees interspersed with equally gnarled Douglas firs, plus some madrones and ferns. You may want to linger a while in this strange, enchanted woodland, at least long enough to climb a few trees. Then turn left at the next junction and cruise back out into the sunlight to rejoin Bay Area Ridge Trail. Watch for a wooden bench along this open stretch that is nearly overwhelmed by bright-orange California poppies in spring. A plaque on its side reads: "There is great peace in this natural beauty. We must all help to preserve it."

Options

The Caltrans Vista Point on Skyline Boulevard, 1.1 mile north of the main Russian Ridge entrance at Alpine Road, is the trailhead for the easy 2.5-mile Clouds Rest and Meadow Loop in Coal Creek Open Space Preserve. The trail's highlight is a walk around flower-dotted Coal Creek Meadow, which provides memorable views of the Peninsula and South Bay. From the Vista Point parking area, walk 50 yards north on Skyline to Clouds Rest Road. Turn right and walk .3 mile to the trailhead. Where the path splits, take the right fork to head straight for the scenic meadow.

Information and Contact

There is no fee. Free trail maps are available at the trailhead. For more information, contact the Midpeninsula Regional Open Space District, 330 Distel Circle, Los Altos, CA 94022, 650/691-1200, website: www.openspace.org.

Directions

From I-280 in Palo Alto, take the Page Mill Road exit west. Drive 8.9 winding miles to Skyline Boulevard (Highway 35). Cross Skyline Boulevard to Alpine Road. Drive 200 feet on Alpine Road and turn right into the Russian Ridge entrance.

Or, from the junction of Highways 35 and 9 at Saratoga Gap, drive seven miles north on Highway 35 (Skyline Boulevard). Turn left on Alpine Road and then right into the preserve entrance.

28 HORSESHOE LAKE LOOP

Skyline Ridge Open Space Preserve,
off Highway 35 in the Los Altos hills

Total distance: 1.5 miles round-trip

Type of trail: rolling terrain

Hiking time: 45 minutes

Best season: year-round

Skyline Ridge Open Space Preserve is the most developed of all the Midpeninsula Regional Open Space preserves. It has a big entrance sign on Skyline Boulevard and three large-sized parking lots instead of meager dirt pullouts along the road. If your reason for hiking is to get away from it all, you might want to head somewhere else. But Skyline Ridge's Horseshoe Lake Trail is such a special little walk, you should come here anyway and check it out.

The preserve is easy to spot—it's located right next to a huge Christmas tree farm, where all the conifers are exactly the same size and grow in neat rows like good soldiers. From the parking lot, you head out on the trail by the map and signboard, walking through fields of wildflowers to little Horseshoe Lake. Along the way, you'll cross a parking lot reserved for wheelchair-users so they can take a wheelchair-accessible trail to the lake.

The walk to the lake's western edge is only .3 mile in length. Once there, you can stay for a while and then head back for a short leg stretcher, or make a loop around the lake for a longer, 1.5-mile walk. Lots of people do the former—you'll see plenty of picnickers, families, and older folks who just show up for a brief stroll to the lake. Benches are provided so you can

Horseshoe Lake, Skyline Ridge Open Space Preserve

sit and enjoy the scene. True to its name, the lake is horseshoe-shaped. It is nicely protected from the wind by ridges on the north and south side.

If you hike the loop, you'll connect to a trail that's open to bikers and equestrians for .25 mile, then climb above the lake and wind up at yet another parking lot—this one for cars with horse trailers. From there, you have a hillside meadow walk (open to hikers only), which brings you back to the north side of the lake and then to the wheelchair-user parking lot. Simply retrace your steps back to your car.

Horseshoe Lake is particularly popular with families and children, because parents with baby strollers can maneuver the route and older children enjoy exploring the lake's shoreline and watching for wildlife. Numerous picnic tables are situated near the water. Because the trail is so short, you can leave the Power Bars at home and pack a real picnic.

The trail is also a good place to teach children about wildflowers. Skyline Ridge has basically the same variety of plant life as nearby Russian Ridge and Long Ridge, but you can see more flowers in a shorter walk. Purple, vine-like spring vetch, orange California poppies, and dark-blue lupine are most prevalent.

Options

From the same trailhead parking lot, you can hike the Ridge Trail to Alpine Pond, where the Daniels Nature Center is open on weekend afternoons. This 3.2-mile round-trip features lovely open grasslands, views, and spring wildflowers.

Information and Contact

There is no fee. Free trail maps are available at the trailhead. For more information, contact Midpeninsula Regional Open Space District, 330 Distel Circle, Los Altos, CA 94022, 650/691-1200, website: www.openspace.org.

Directions

From I-280 or U.S. 101 on the San Francisco Peninsula, take Highway 84 west to Skyline Boulevard (Highway 35). Turn left on Highway 35 and drive 7.8 miles south to the Skyline Ridge parking area on the right. (From the South Bay, take Highway 9 west to the junction with Highway 35. Turn north on Highway 35 and drive 5.4 miles to the Skyline Ridge parking area on the left.) Park in the lot farthest to the right. Wheelchair users can follow the signs and park in the lot closer to the lake and the wheelchair-accessible trail.

29 PETER'S CREEK TRAIL & LONG RIDGE ROAD

Long Ridge Open Space Preserve, off Highway 35 in the Los Altos hills

Total distance: 4.6 miles round-trip

Hiking time: 2.5 hours

Type of trail: rolling terrain

Best season: year-round

Long Ridge Open Space is a peaceful 2,000-acre preserve along Skyline Boulevard near Saratoga Gap. Its hiking, biking, and equestrian trails are perfect in all seasons—warm and windy in summer, crisp and golden in autumn, fern-laden and mossy in winter, and gilded with wildflowers in spring.

From the Grizzly Flat trailhead, only one pathway enters Long Ridge. It's the start of Peter's Creek Trail, which soon junctions with the Bay Area Ridge Trail. The latter makes a tight switchback and heads north; you'll continue straight on Peter's Creek Trail. Once you get moving, the sight and sound of Skyline Boulevard quickly disappear as the trail drops below the road and into a pristine canyon of grasslands and forest. Fields of wildflowers and rolling grasses in the foreground are framed by a forest of Douglas firs and oaks ahead. Some people walk only as far as this first, open meadow, spread out a picnic, then head home.

At a junction with Long Ridge Trail, turn left to stay on Peter's Creek Trail and begin a gentle ascent through oaks, firs, and bay laurel. Babbling Peter's Creek, a major tributary of Pescadero Creek, meanders along at your side. Ferns and moss-covered boulders line the stream. Woodland wildflowers include tiny two-eyed violets (heart-shaped leaves with white-and-purple flowers) and purple shooting stars.

The trail wanders in and out of meadows and forest, passing an old apple orchard and ranch site. The trees still bear delicious apples in autumn; in winter, their bare branches are lined with a shaggy, gray-green lichen. At 1.6 miles, you'll reach a small pond with huge reeds and a sea of horsetails growing around its edges. Watch for pond turtles sunning themselves. On the far side of the pond is private property belonging to the Jikoji Buddhist retreat center.

The spring flower show continues as you hike. Look for *brodiaea,* columbine, wild roses, blue-eyed grass, white irises, poppies, lupine, and huge ceanothus bushes with sprays of blue flowers. The variety of species is remarkable.

A few switchbacks lead you to the top of the ridge, where you meet up with Long Ridge Road. At this 2,500-foot elevation, expansive views are yours for the taking. Turn right on Long Ridge Road and traipse along, "oohing" and "aahing" at the panorama of neighboring Butano Ridge and the forests of the Pescadero Creek watershed. Be sure to pause at the

Long Ridge's sunny, exposed ridgeline

bench commemorating Pulitzer prize-winning author Wallace Stegner, who lived in this area and aided in the conservation of Long Ridge.

After this sunny, view-filled stint, take Long Ridge Trail back into the forest to finish out the loop. The path makes a wide circle around to the north and then east through a dense forest of leafy oaks, then reconnects with the start of Peter's Creek Trail.

Long Ridge's trails are multiuse; you may share your trip with mountain bikers or equestrians. If that concerns you, wait until the rainy season to visit, when the Open Space District closes the trails to everyone but hikers. The preserve is at its best then anyway; the ideal time to visit is on a clear winter day soon after a rainstorm.

Information and Contact

There is no fee. Free trail maps are available at the trailhead. For more information, contact Midpeninsula Regional Open Space District, 330 Distel Circle, Los Altos, CA 94022, 650/691-1200, website: www.openspace.org.

Directions

From I-280 or U.S. 101 on the San Francisco Peninsula, take Highway 84 west to Skyline Boulevard (Highway 35). Turn left on Highway 35 and drive 10 miles south to the Long Ridge/Upper Stevens Creek County Park/Grizzly Flat parking area. (From the South Bay, take Highway 9 west to the junction with Highway 35. Turn north on Highway 35 and drive 3.2 miles to the Long Ridge/Upper Stevens Creek County Park/Grizzly Flat parking area.) The trail is on the west side of the road.

30 SKYLINE TRAIL TO SUMMIT ROCK
Sanborn-Skyline County Park,
off Highway 35 near Saratoga Gap

Total distance: 0.8 mile round-trip   **Hiking time:** 30 minutes

Type of trail: mostly level terrain   **Best season:** year-round

Although there is another, more prominent entrance to Sanborn-Skyline County Park, the Summit Rock trailhead offers the shortest walk to Summit Rock, the best lookout around for viewing the South Bay. Why is it the best? Because Summit Rock is perched at 3,000 feet in elevation, high enough to get an occasional dusting of snow in winter, in a dramatic contrast to the flat—oh so flat—peninsula bay lands below. From Summit

enjoying the view from Summit Rock

Rock, you can see the Santa Clara Valley spread out below you in all its suburban splendor.

In addition to the far-away views, you'll have a chance to see lots of action close up at Summit Rock. Local rock climbers use the steep east side of the rocky outcrop to practice their stuff. Anyone can hike up the western, back side of the rock—that's where this trail takes you—but the steep front side is reserved for those with ropes and harnesses. It's fascinating to sit on top of the rock and watch the climbers inch their way up.

The Skyline Trail to Summit Rock leads through a pretty hardwood forest, filled with Douglas firs, oaks, California laurels, and madrones. As you walk on a dirt path lined with fir needles, you may find yourself having thoughts (or at least olfactory memories) of Christmas. To reach your destination, simply head out on the Skyline Trail, which is clearly signed to Summit Rock. When you come to a four-way intersection, turn left toward the valley of the South Bay, and walk out of the forest and into an open area. A short climb up a steep dirt hill will put you right at the base of Summit Rock. From there you can clamber around to find the best view.

Options

After visiting Summit Rock, return to the four-way junction and walk south (left), following Skyline Trail for as long as you like. The trail continues for several more miles.

Information and Contact

There is no fee. For more information and a free map, contact Sanborn-Skyline County Park, 16055 Sanborn Road, Saratoga, CA 95070, 408/867-9959 or 408/355-2200, website: www.parkhere.org.

Directions

From I-280 or U.S. 101 on the San Francisco Peninsula, take Highway 84 west to Skyline Boulevard (Highway 35). Turn left on Highway 35 and drive 14.6 miles south, past Highway 9, to the Summit Rock parking area on the left. (From the South Bay, take Highway 9 west to the junction with Highway 35. Turn south on Highway 35 and drive 1.4 miles to the Summit Rock parking area on the left.) The trailhead starts on the south side of the parking lot.

31 SARATOGA GAP & RIDGE TRAIL LOOP

Castle Rock State Park, off Highway 35 near Saratoga Gap

Total distance: 5.2 miles round-trip

Hiking time: 2.5 hours

Type of trail: some steep terrain

Best season: year-round

Hello, hikers, and welcome to Swiss Cheese State Park. Oops, that's Castle Rock State Park, of course, but all those holey sandstone rocks look more like *fromage* than *châteaux*. Call it what you like, Castle Rock is one of the most surprising parks in the entire Bay Area. In five miles of hiking, you can visit a 50-foot waterfall in winter and spring, gaze at miles of Santa Cruz Mountains wildlands, and explore several large sandstone formations, including the local rock climbers' favorite, Goat Rock.

In recent years, Castle Rock has also become one of the most popular parks in the Bay Area. Because the park is used by rock climbers as well as hikers, weekends can be very crowded. For the best experience, plan your trip for a weekday, or get an early morning start on the weekends.

Take Saratoga Gap Trail from the far side of Castle Rock's parking lot, heading right. (The trail is signed "to campground.") The pleasure begins immediately as you travel downhill, walking along rocky, fern-lined Kings Creek through a mixed forest of Douglas firs, black oaks, and madrones. The seasonal stream begins as a trickle at the parking lot, then picks up flow and intensity as it heads downhill alongside the trail.

It's a mere .8 mile to Castle Rock Falls, which flows with vigor in the wet season. After 15 minutes on the trail, you find yourself standing on a large wooden viewing deck, perched on top of the waterfall. Because you're at its brink, the fall is a bit difficult to see. You'll be torn between searching for the best view of its 50-foot drop and admiring the miles of uninhabited Santa Cruz Mountains' wildlands. It's hard to say whether this deck was built for viewing the waterfall or the canyon vista. Both are incredible. From the viewing deck, continue on Saratoga Gap Trail for another 1.8 miles. The terrain changes quickly from a shady, mixed woodland to a sunny, exposed slope with views all the way out to Monterey Bay and the Pacific Ocean. Spring and summer bring forth colorful blooms on bush monkeyflower and other sun-loving chaparral plants. As you progress along the trail, you'll notice an ever-increasing number of sandstone outcrops that have been hollowed and sculpted by wind erosion. In some places, the sandstone becomes the trail surface. You'll have to scramble over a few small boulders to continue on your way.

Castle Rock State Park's holey sandstone

At 2.5 miles from its start, Saratoga Gap Trail junctions with Ridge Trail and the spur to Castle Rock Trail Camp. Pay a visit to the pleasant, forested campsites if you wish (water and picnic tables are available), or just turn sharply right on Ridge Trail, beginning the return of your loop. After a half-mile uphill hike through a dense madrone forest, you emerge on an open ridge. (Ridge Trail roughly parallels Saratoga Gap Trail, but at a higher elevation.)

Another half mile of gentle ascent takes you past a connector trail to Saratoga Gap Trail. Just beyond is a short spur to the Emily Smith Bird Observation Point. This forested knoll is a good spot to look for raptors, although views are severely limited by the leafy black oaks.

Nearly four miles into the loop you reach the spur trail for Goat Rock. Turn right and follow it for .25 mile. (The left fork leads to a fascinating interpretive exhibit on the park's geology; you can also loop around to Goat Rock from there.)

You're likely to see rock climbers strutting their stuff on the steep south side of Goat Rock, but the north side is easily accessible on two feet. Signs along the path encourage hikers to visit a neighboring overlook area instead of climbing on the 100-foot-high rock, due to its steep and potentially dangerous drop-offs. Take your pick. The overlook features a great view of the Santa Cruz Mountains parading down to the Pacific Ocean, and often more solitude than Goat Rock. If you're sure-footed and cautious, the smooth back side of Goat Rock is a great place to climb up and examine the sandstone closely, as well as enjoy more high views.

Beyond Goat Rock, Ridge Trail continues eastward until it reconnects with Saratoga Gap Trail just above Castle Rock Falls. Turn left and make a short, half-mile climb back up the creek canyon to the trailhead.

Options
Don't leave the park without walking the .7-mile loop trail to Castle Rock, the park's namesake rock formation. A spur trail on the right, just before you return to the parking lot on the hike outlined above, will take you there. And in spring, the park's Summit Meadows Trail should not be missed. The trailhead is at Sempervirens Point, a drive-up overlook on the south side of Highway 9, 1.9 miles west of Skyline Boulevard. If the view of the Santa Cruz Mountains from the overlook inspires you, take this two-mile flower-filled walk from the point's north end through Summit Meadows.

Information and Contact
A $3 day-use fee is charged per vehicle. A trail map/brochure is available at the entrance kiosk. For more information, contact Castle Rock State Park, 15000 Skyline Boulevard, Los Gatos, CA 95020, 408/867-2952, website: www.parks.ca.gov.

Directions
From I-280 or U.S. 101 on the San Francisco Peninsula, take Highway 84 west to Skyline Boulevard (Highway 35). Turn left on Highway 35 and drive 15.7 miles south, past Highway 9, to the Castle Rock State Park parking area on your right. (From the South Bay, take Highway 9 west to the junction with Highway 35. Turn south on Highway 35 and drive 2.5 miles to the Castle Rock State Park parking area.) The trailhead is on the west side of the parking lot, opposite the entrance.

32 SEQUOIA AUDUBON TRAIL

Pescadero Marsh Natural Preserve,
off Highway 1 near Pescadero State Beach

Total distance: 2.4 miles round-trip

Type of trail: mostly level terrain

Hiking time: 1 hour

Best season: year-round

Pescadero Marsh Natural Preserve is a 500-acre coastal marsh that backs the scenic San Mateo Coast along Highway 1. Considered to be one of the largest and most important freshwater and brackish marshes in California, Pescadero Marsh serves the important function of water filtration, water storage, and groundwater recharge for Pescadero and Butano creeks. In addition, the marsh is critical habitat for a diverse assemblage of wildlife, including thousands of migratory birds traveling on the Pacific Flyway.

There's one other thing about Pescadero Marsh: it's beautiful. Despite being bordered by Highway 1 to the west, the preserve is a peaceful oasis that is marked by the deep, rich blues and greens of plentiful water and foliage. *Plein-air* painters often drive up alongside the preserve, pull out their brushes and canvases, and try to capture the marsh's voluptuous hues.

The preserve has three trails, which unfortunately are not contiguous. The southern trail along Butano Creek is accessed from a trailhead on Pescadero Road, just 75 yards from its junction with Highway 1. The preserve's North Pond Trail is accessed by parking at the northernmost Pescadero State Beach parking lot. (Walk across the highway, then follow the trail as it curves around the east side of Pescadero Marsh's freshwater pond.) Sequoia Audubon Trail is the longest of the

great egret fishing at Pescadero Marsh
Natural Preserve

© ANN MARIE BROWN

three trails, and it is accessed by parking in the state beach lot just south of the highway bridge over Pescadero Creek.

Because of its length and diversity, Sequoia Audubon Trail is the preference of most hikers. The trail travels alongside Pescadero Creek for 1.2 miles, providing prime opportunities for wildlife-watching. It begins on the beach on soft sand. Walk underneath the highway bridge and head inland, soon gaining hard earth beneath your shoes. You'll notice that the ground heats up as you get away from the coastal winds and move into thick vegetation. Spring and summer wildflowers bloom along the trail, including coastal paintbrush, monkeyflower, yellow bush lupine, and nonnative purple and yellow ice plant. A couple of gnarled, low-lying eucalyptus trees grow along the path.

A veritable jungle of wetlands and coastal foliage, the marsh attracts more than 200 species of birds (more than 60 species nest here), as well as numerous mammals and amphibians. Almost everyone who comes to Pescadero Marsh gets rewarded with wildlife sightings. On one trip, we saw two deer wading up to their knees through the marsh waters, half a dozen bullfrogs under a footbridge by the creek, one large turtle, scads of minnows and water bugs, and birds galore—ducks, egrets, godwits, great egrets, redwing blackbirds, swallows, and four great blue herons doing a little fishing. The herons nest in the eucalyptus trees above the marsh.

In late winter, you might get the chance to see steelhead trout swimming up Pescadero Creek to spawn. Or watch for the endangered San Francisco garter snake slithering along the trail.

The far end of Sequoia Audubon Trail climbs above the marsh to a viewing area, where a bench affords a vista of the entire wetlands and the ocean beyond. An interpretive sign identifies different birds of prey you may see soaring above you. Hawks, kites, and owls are most common.

If bird-watching is your thing, the best birding times at Pescadero Marsh are late fall and early spring. But there's one prerequisite for a spring hike in the marsh—make sure you wear long pants and long sleeves. Pescadero Marsh happens to be the tick capital of the world, and it may be one of California's greatest natural greenhouses for poison oak. If the trail hasn't been cleared recently, you may think they grow the stuff commercially here.

Options

A side trip that's a must is a coastal walk along Pescadero's rocky beaches, starting from the lot where you parked your car. The coastline features long sandy stretches, interesting rock formations, tidepools, and plentiful harbor seals lounging around on the rocks. Also, check with rangers about occasional guided hikes into Pescadero Marsh. Phone 650/879-2170 for a current schedule.

Information and Contact

There is no fee. For more information, contact California State Parks, Bay Area District, 250 Executive Park Boulevard, Suite 4900, San Francisco, CA 94134, 415/330-6300, website: www.parks.ca.gov.

Directions

From Highway 1 in Half Moon Bay, drive south for 17 miles to just north of Pescadero Road, near Pescadero State Beach. Park in the state beach parking lot south of the highway bridge over Pescadero Creek, on the west side of the highway. Walk to the north side of the bridge (use the pedestrian walkway on the west side), take the stairs to the sand, then follow the trail underneath the bridge and up the canyon.

33 SEQUOIA TRAIL

Big Basin Redwoods State Park, off Highway 9 near Felton

Total distance: 3.6 miles round-trip

Type of trail: rolling terrain

Hiking time: 1.5 hours

Best season: year-round

Sure, everybody knows that Berry Creek Falls is the prime destination of hikers in Big Basin Redwoods State Park. The catch is that it takes four to six hours to make the round-trip hike, covering about nine miles with a lot of up-and-down in between. But what everybody doesn't know is that there's another pretty waterfall in Big Basin, and you can get to it in less than two miles of nearly level hiking from park headquarters.

Sempervirens Falls is a waterfall that anyone can hike to, even small children with their parents. The Sequoia Trail takes you there in 1.8 miles. After you see it, you can just turn around and hike back (for a round-trip of 3.6 miles) or make a longer loop trip out of it by returning on the Shadowbrook Trail (for a round-trip of five miles).

The best time to visit is after winter or early spring rains. The wet season turns Sempervirens Falls into a gushing 25-foot-tall cascade of water, about four feet wide at the top, with two miniature cascades flowing into it from above. The waterfall is perfectly framed by fallen redwood trees on either side and a large clear pool at its base.

Even if the waterfall is not flowing hard when you visit, the trail that leads to it is still a delightful journey into a redwood world. The big trees, which reach more than 300 feet tall in Big Basin, never fail to take your breath away, no matter how many times you've seen them. Mixed in with

© ANN MARIE BROWN

Sempervirens Falls, Big Basin Redwoods State Park

the redwoods are Douglas fir, tan oak, and California laurel, as well as thousands upon thousands of ferns lining the forest floor. Springtime brings wild ginger, trillium, and azalea blooms.

To get started, follow the Sequoia Trail from park headquarters. You don't even need to remember the trail's name, because all the trail markers read "Sempervirens Falls" on your way out and "Park Headquarters" on your way back. What could be easier than that?

Portions of the Sequoia Trail are routed near a park road, but it gets little traffic and shouldn't disturb your hike. Most of the time, you won't even notice it's there, and no wonder—the forest surrounding you is certain to keep your attention.

A nice feature of this hike is its convenient location to park campgrounds. If you are staying at Sky Meadow Group Camp, Wastahi Campground, or Huckleberry Campground, you can access the falls directly from your campground by either the Sequoia or Shadowbrook trails, rather than driving and parking at park headquarters.

Options
After visiting the falls, loop back on Shadowbrook Trail instead of retracing your steps. This will make a five-mile round-trip.

Information and Contact
A $6 day-use fee is charged per vehicle. A trail map is available at park headquarters or the entrance station. For more information, contact Big Basin Redwoods State Park, 21600 Big Basin Way, Boulder Creek, CA 95006, 831/338-8860, website: www.bigbasin.org.

Directions

From Santa Cruz, take Highway 9 north and drive approximately 12 miles to Boulder Creek. At Boulder Creek, turn left on Highway 236. Follow it for about 10 miles to Big Basin Redwoods State Park Headquarters. Park in the lot across from park headquarters, then walk back toward the headquarters building. The trailhead is located to the right of the building near the 15-minute parking spots.

34 WATERFALL LOOP TRAIL

Uvas Canyon County Park, off U.S. 101 near Morgan Hill

Total distance: 3.5 miles round-trip   **Hiking time:** 2 hours

Type of trail: mostly level terrain   **Best season:** December–April

---

Uvas Canyon County Park is a little slice of waterfall heaven on the east side of the Santa Cruz Mountains. Although the drive to reach it is a long journey from the freeway through grasslands and oaks, it delivers you to a surprising redwood forest at the park entrance. Suddenly, you've entered another world.

Uvas Canyon is a small park with camping and picnicking facilities and a short stretch of hiking trails in its 1,200 acres, but it's living proof that good things come in small packages. If you're short on time, you can walk the one-mile Waterfall Loop Trail and see Black Rock Falls and several smaller cascades on Swanson Creek. If you're in the mood to stretch your legs, you can make a 3.5-mile loop out to Alec Canyon, then take the uphill trail .5 mile to Triple Falls on Alec Creek.

The park has enough waterfalls to make any waterfall-lover happy. Just make sure you show up in the rainy season, because that's when Uvas Canyon is at its best. Water seems to pour from every crack in the hillsides. By mid-summer, the falls run dry. The canyon is filled with oaks, laurels, big-leaf maples, and Douglas firs, all thriving in the moist environment around Swanson Creek.

Start your trip at the Black Oak Group Picnic Area by the gated dirt road. Head straight (not uphill on the road) to connect to the short loop trail through the canyon. Cross Swanson Creek on a footbridge, then bear right at the fork and head directly for Black Rock Falls, .25 mile away. You'll find the waterfall on your right, pouring 30 feet down a side canyon over—you guessed it—black rock. Take a few pictures, then continue on the trail, heading for Basin Falls. This waterfall is 20 feet high and surrounded

Uvas Falls in Uvas Canyon County Park

by moss-covered rocks. It makes a shapely S-curve at it carves its way down canyon. Next you'll reach Upper Falls, a little shorter in height than the other falls, but just as enchanting.

At Upper Falls, it's decision time: Either head back and take the other side of the Waterfall Loop Trail for a short and level one-mile hike, or continue up Swanson Creek and follow the winding Contour Trail to Alec Canyon and Triple Falls. For the longer trip, follow Contour Trail through a dense oak and Douglas fir forest, crossing a few small ravines. Where the trail junctions with Alec Canyon Trail, turn right and hike .5 mile to Manzanita Point. Here, at an opening in the abundant manzanita bushes, you gain wide views of the South Bay and Diablo Range on clear days.

A short distance farther in the chaparral and soon you enter Alec Canyon's second-growth redwood forest. In the late 1800s, the virgin redwoods in this canyon were cut for lumber to build the nearby mining town of New Almaden. The trail you're following is an old logging road.

Turn right on the short spur trail to Triple Falls. True to its name, Triple Falls is a series of three cascades, totaling 40 feet in height. If you wish, you can find a seat right alongside the cascading fall. Or backtrack to Alec Canyon Trail, turn right, and head for a picnic table right alongside the creek. To finish the loop, follow the road back to Black Oak Picnic Area, a steep .75 mile descent.

So which waterfall at Uvas Park is the best? Uvas rangers say that if you're only going to see one cataract in the park, see Upper Falls. My favorites are Basin Falls and Triple Falls. Your favorite? Better go see them all and decide.

Options

If you didn't time your Uvas Park visit for the winter waterfall season, head for a trail with a radically different demeanor that isn't dependent on the weather: The Nibbs Knob Trail. This 3.6-mile out-and-back trip involves a 1,600-foot climb on a rather steep and exposed fire road. It leads to 2,694-foot Nibbs Knob, a forested summit with peek-a-boo views of the high peaks of the Santa Cruz Mountains, Skyline Ridge, and the mountains and foothills of the Diablo Range. On very rare clear days, the Sierra Nevada can be spotted from here. The trail begins at the Upper Bench Youth Camp. Hike 1.5 miles and then turn right on the .25-mile spur trail to Nibbs Knob. A picnic table is located at the top.

Information and Contact

A $4 day-use fee is charged per vehicle. Free maps are available at the park visitors center. For more information, contact Uvas Canyon County Park, 8515 Croy Road, Morgan Hill, CA 95037, 408/779-9232, website: www.parkhere.org.

Directions

From U.S. 101, heading south in Morgan Hill, take the Bernal Road exit. At the stoplight, turn right, then right again, to access Monterey Highway. Turn left (south) on Monterey Highway. Turn right on Bailey Avenue and drive 2.8 miles to McKean Road. Turn left on McKean Road and drive six miles (McKean Road becomes Uvas Road). Turn right on Croy Road and drive 4.5 miles to the park (continue past Sveadal, a private camp/resort). Park near park headquarters or in one of the picnic area parking lots. The trail is the gated dirt road at Black Oak Picnic Area.

Chapter 7

© ANN MARIE BROWN

Santa Cruz and Big Sur

Santa Cruz and Big Sur

I t wouldn't be easy to choose the most spectacular stretch of California coastline, but if pressed, most beach connoisseurs would agree there is no place as visually stunning as the 130 miles of cliffs, rocks, and waves that run from Davenport to San Simeon.

There's nothing not to like here, from the mild climate to the wild landscape. Much of this area is isolated, undeveloped, and difficult to access, with high cliffs and few roads. Hiking in this land means wandering along gravel beaches, pausing to watch sunsets over glimmering seas, and walking in the shadows of giant redwoods.

Whereas towns are few and traffic is light on shore, a different story unfolds out at sea. Every winter and spring, like clockwork, thousands of gray whales pass by on their long migrations. Traveling from their summer home in Alaska's Bering Sea to their winter breeding grounds in Baja, then back again a few months later, the whales display occasional flashes of fins or tails and leave hundreds of frothy spouts as their calling cards. Whale-watching is at its best from December to May, on days when the sea is flat and deep blue, with no wind or whitecaps. Hikers have a chance to witness this great natural spectacle from coast-side trails at several Santa Cruz and Big Sur parks, and also while driving scenic Highway 1.

The Santa Cruz and Big Sur region also contains one of California's most unusual national parks, Pinnacles National Monument. Its jagged cliffs, crags, and peaks are not part of any nearby mountain range; instead they are the remains of an ancient volcano that erupted 200 miles to the southeast. Although rock climbers flock to the vertical surfaces of the high crags, easy hikers can follow well-built trails that tunnel through caves and ascend over and around the pinnacles. Springtime brings a spectacular display of wildflowers in the park's grasslands. The strange landscape of Pinnacles is just another reason that this region is a winning destination for lovers of the outdoors.

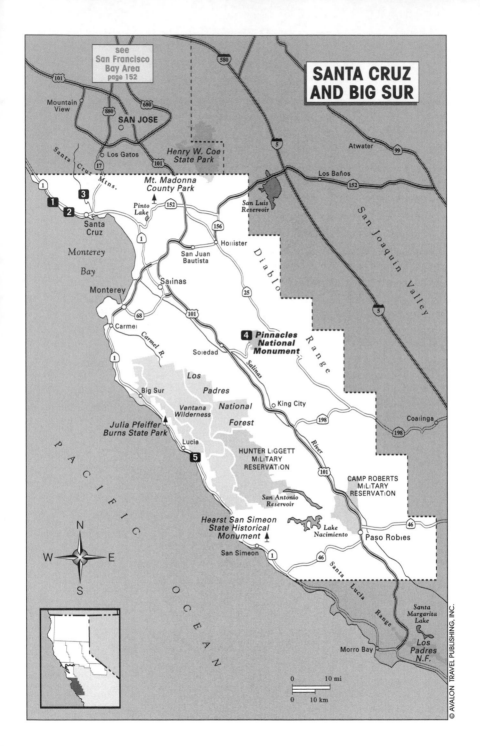

Contents

1. Davenport Beach Walk 236
2. Old Landing Cove Trail 238
3. Loch Trail 240
4. Bear Gulch Caves & Overlook 242
5. Limekiln Trail 244

1 DAVENPORT BEACH WALK

City of Davenport, off Highway 1 in Davenport

Total distance: 2.0 miles round-trip

Type of trail: mostly level terrain

Hiking time: 1 hour

Best season: year-round

Many beaches in Northern California are spectacular, but some beaches are a cut above. Davenport Beach is one of them. The beach is usually sunny, not foggy, it is typically uncrowded, and it graciously provides its admirers with a fine hike along coastal bluffs and then down a rocky staircase to the sand. From the water's edge, you can walk to the north to visit sea caves at low tide, or south to an ocean-bound stream that carves a sculpted canyon through the bluffs.

Start the hike from the parking area across from the Davenport Post Office. Cross the railroad tracks, then look to your left to pick up the trail again (about 15 feet away). From here you simply follow the edge of the oceanside bluff, paralleling the beach.

The bluffs here are a classic example of a wave-cut terrace. They are formed as this part of the coast rises and is jolted upward from geological activity that takes place over the course of thousands of years. The story of a wave-cut terrace goes something like this: Eons ago, as a warming climate melted glaciers, the sea rose and cut into the landmass. This created beach-

Davenport Beach

es and bluffs that grew larger as sand and gravel were washed down them. Subsequent geologic activity moved the earth's plates, lifting the beaches to form seaside terraces. The nonstop action of waves and wind sculpts and erodes the terraces. Even now, new terraces are being formed under water. As the coastline continues to rise, the bluffs will continue to change.

Besides being ancient geological wonders, the grass-topped bluffs provide exposed, windblown habitat for coastal wildflowers, including Indian paintbrush, wild strawberry, coast lupine, and monkeyflower. Even if the flowers aren't blooming, there is plenty to admire from this perch above the sea. The carved-out rocks along the shore and the continual crashing of the waves will compete for your attention.

Head south along the bluffs for .3 mile until you reach the chalky sandstone cliffs that have eroded into a wide natural staircase to the beach. Descend to the sand and walk to the south side of the cove, where you can hike up and around a high-walled streambed that carries runoff from the hills to the sea, or examine the eroding cliffs that drop right to the water's edge.

If the tide is low, walk to the north end of the beach, where you'll find sea caves carved deep into the wave-cut terraces. Some extend back into the land mass farther than your eyes can see in the darkness. The sandstone and mudstone of the terraces erodes in little carved pockets, which create a rippled effect on the rock. It's like a miniaturized surface of the moon.

The wind is almost always blowing on the Davenport coast, so come prepared for it. In summer, this is often a great beach for sunbathing and swimming, but you're likely to need warmer clothes for hiking on the windswept bluffs.

Information and Contact
There is no fee or managing agency for this beach. For food and lodging in Davenport, contact the Davenport Cash Store/Bed and Breakfast Inn, 31 Davenport Avenue, Davenport, CA 95017, 831/426-4122, website: www.davenportinn.com.

Directions
From Santa Cruz, drive north on Highway 1 for 11 miles to the yellow flashing light in Davenport. Turn left at the light into the dirt parking area (across from the post office and Ocean Street). The trail starts at the north end of the parking lot.

2 OLD LANDING COVE TRAIL

Wilder Ranch State Park, off Highway 1 near Santa Cruz

Total distance: 2.5 miles round-trip

Hiking time: 1.5 hours

Type of trail: mostly level terrain

Best season: year-round

Wilder Ranch State Park is a favorite park of mountain bikers, and often what bikers find appealing, hikers don't. Bikers like long fire roads that go forever so they can pedal to their heart's content; hikers like narrow paths that lead to a stellar destination in not too many miles. Bikers like the wide-open road; hikers like the meandering trail.

The good news is that Wilder Ranch has trails that are good for both parties. The park is large enough to have a variety of paths, plus plenty of room for everybody. Most riders stick to the inland side of the park, across Highway 1, where the fire roads crisscross the grassy hillsides. If hikers stay on the ocean side of the park, they don't have to fear being mowed down by speeding mountain bikers. And luckily, on the ocean side of the park lies the Old Landing Cove Trail, a gem of a coastal walk that offers several great surprises, including a seal rookery, some spectacular beaches, and a hidden fern cave.

seal rookery at Wilder Ranch State Park

The Old Landing Cove Trail starts from the parking lot, at a sign that simply reads "Nature Trail." Begin walking on a level dirt road through the park's agricultural preserve of brussels sprouts fields. Yes, it's true, Wilder Ranch's biggest claim to fame is not its historic ranch buildings, nor its excellent trail system, nor its spectacular beaches and coastal vistas. It's the fact that 12 percent of our national brussels-sprouts production happens right here within the park's boundaries. One question: Who's eating all of them, anyway?

Follow the trail toward the coast, then turn right and head out along the sandstone and mudstone bluffs. The first beach you'll reach, Wilder Beach, is a critical habitat area for the endangered snowy plover and is fenced off and protected as a natural preserve.

No matter; there are plenty of other beaches to explore. In another .125 mile you'll come to the trail's namesake, the old landing cove. The cove is a remarkably narrow inlet where small schooners pulled in to anchor and load lumber in the late 1800s. Sizing up the limited cove, you gotta think: Those guys sure must have known how to steer.

Just off Old Landing Cove is a huge flat rock where harbor seals hang out, lying around in the sun all day to keep their flippers warm. You can't get a good look at the seals on the rock until you walk past the Old Landing Cove and turn around, which means your best view of the seals comes on your return trip.

For now, keep walking along the blufftops. The highlight of this hike is the descent to the beach to see Wilder Ranch's fern cave, the oceanside home of a collection of bracken and sword ferns. They hang from the small cave's ceiling just low enough to tickle the top of your head. The fern cave is hidden in the back of a U-shaped cove, but the trick is that it's almost impossible to know which cove is the right one. (The spur trail to the beach can be difficult to spot.) Here's the key to finding the fern cave: The Old Landing Cove Trail is a numbered interpretive trail, so keep your eyes peeled for post number 8. A few yards beyond it is the cove with the fern cave; a narrow spur trail leads down to it. (Another way to know you're in the right spot is to look back toward the park entrance; you should be directly across from the California and United States flags that fly over the entrance kiosk.)

Because it's located in the back of the cove, the fern cave is partially protected from the salty ocean air. An underground spring gives the ferns life and keeps them moist and cool. The floor of the cave is covered in driftwood that has been collected from the sea by the constant motion of the tide.

After exploring and admiring the sea cave, return to the top of the bluffs and the Old Landing Cove Trail. Walk .25 mile farther north, heading to the next beach cove, known as Sand Plant Beach. This cove has a wider and more visible trail leading down to it, and it features a perfect crescent-shaped strip of sand—the ideal place to have a picnic lunch or sit and watch the waves come in.

Options
Where the Old Landing Cove Trail ends at the crescent-shaped beach, you can walk to the beach's far side and pick up another blufftop trail, the Ohlone Bluff Trail. The path continues northward, heading to Strawberry Beach in .6 mile and Three Mile Beach in another .7 mile.

Information and Contact
A $6 day-use fee is charged per vehicle. A park map is available at the entrance kiosk. For more information, contact Wilder Ranch State Park, 1401 Old Coast Road, Santa Cruz, CA 95060, 831/423-9703, website: www.parks.ca.gov.

Directions
From Santa Cruz, drive north on Highway 1 for four miles. Turn left into the entrance to Wilder Ranch State Park, then follow the park road to its end and park in the main parking area. Take the trail marked "Nature Trail" from the southwest side of the parking lot.

❸ LOCH TRAIL
Loch Lomond Recreation Area, off Highway 9 near Felton

Total distance: 2.0–5.0 miles round-trip   **Hiking time:** 1–2 hours

Type of trail: rolling terrain   **Best season:** March–September

---

Every summer, when I was a kid, my parents took my sisters and me hiking and fishing at a big lake surrounded by a beautiful forest. We'd explore around the lake, learn about the trees and plants that grew there, watch for wildlife, and go trolling in our little motorboat. Mostly we'd cruise near the shoreline in the hopes of catching some fish. We'd always take a break at midday, pull up our boat on an island on the lake, sit on a rock, and eat some sandwiches. Then we'd hike in the woods some more, or just sit on the shoreline and admire the scenery.

As an adult, I never thought I'd find any place in urban California to match that lake of my memories. I thought that in order to take a hike near a peaceful, pretty lake, I'd have to travel far from the hustle and bustle of

Northern California's cities. But then I went to Loch Lomond Reservoir, just 10 miles north of Santa Cruz, and found out what I'd been missing.

The Loch Trail at Loch Lomond Recreation Area follows the shoreline of a large, deep blue reservoir through a Douglas fir and redwood forest. After a pleasant mile along the water's edge, the trail connects with a fire road (Highland Trail) that climbs up and around the hillside above the lake. More ambitious hikers will want to follow the latter and make a loop out of the hike. Less ambitious hikers will think the first mile is just fine. It's a level, easy, out-and-back hike from the boat launch ramp and park store.

The distance you hike is up to you; just follow the trail as far as you wish along the lake. You might stop to drop a line in the water or picnic at one of the many shaded tables near the shoreline, or you might just meander along, admiring the pretty lake as you walk. If you turn around before the trail starts to head seriously uphill, you'll have a two-mile round-trip. Go as far as Fir Cove, a little sandy inlet where a stream pours down from the hills into the lake. If you're in the mood for a longer trip, you can follow the trail until it connects with Highland Trail, then take Highland Trail uphill to a great view of the lake. You can make a five-mile loop by hiking back downhill on either the trail or the paved park road.

If the good hiking isn't enough to motivate you, here's the final selling point for Loch Lomond Reservoir: When you visit, not only do you get to take a peaceful lakeside stroll, but you can even rent a little motorboat, do some fishing for trout, bass, or bluegill, and then pull up your boat on the lake's island and have a picnic.

Pack up the peanut butter and jelly and the Audubon field guides—suddenly I feel like I'm 12 years old again.

Options
Follow Loch Trail for 1.5 miles to its junction with Highland Trail. Take Highland Trail uphill, then loop back downhill on the park road for a five-mile round-trip.

Information and Contact
A $4 day-use fee is charged per vehicle. Check your calendar before you go: Loch Lomond Recreation Area is open only from March 1–September 15. A free trail map/park brochure is available at the entrance station. For more information, contact Loch Lomond Recreation Area, 100 Loch Lomond Way, Felton, CA 95018, 831/335-7424, website: www.ci.santa-cruz.ca.us.

Directions
From Santa Cruz, take Highway 9 north and drive approximately seven miles to Felton. At Felton, turn right on Graham Hill Road and drive .5

mile, then turn left on Zayante Road and drive 2.5 miles to Lompico Road. Turn left again and drive 1.5 miles to West Drive. Turn left one more time and drive to Sequoia Road, then enter the park. (The route is well signed for Loch Lomond Recreation Area.) Follow the park road all the way to the lake and park as close as possible to the boat ramp and park store. The trailhead for the Loch Trail begins by the boat ramp, right at the water's edge.

4 BEAR GULCH CAVES & OVERLOOK

Pinnacles National Monument, off Highway 25 near King City

Total distance: 3.0 miles round-trip   **Hiking time:** 1.5 hours

Type of trail: mostly level terrain   **Best season:** November–May

---

Bear Gulch Caves are a crowd pleaser at Pinnacles National Monument. Sure, the park has terrific hiking trails, hundreds of first-class rock climbing sites, abundant spring wildflowers, and fascinating geological features. But what many Pinnacles visitors want to do is explore Bear Gulch Caves.

That's partly because they have waited so long to do so. From 1997 until 2003, the Bear Gulch Caves were closed continually, sometimes due to flooding, but mostly in order to protect the endangered bats that nested inside. But a new policy went into effect in 2004 in which the Park Service uses a system of gates to keep at least some portion of the caves open to visitors most of the year. As park biologists studied the cave-dwelling bats, they realized that the bats don't use the entire cave system year-round—only certain regions in certain seasons. With a system of lockable gates in place, rangers will be able to close off the portion of the caves the bats are using, and allow visitors to explore the rest of the caves.

Your hike through the caves begins just beyond the Bear Gulch Visitor Center on the Moses Spring Trail, also signed for Bear Gulch Caves. Pick up an interpretive brochure at the visitors center or the trailhead and you'll learn to identify the flora of the Pinnacles. The first .25 mile is nothing out of the ordinary, just a pleasant walk through oaks, gray pines, and buckeye trees. In spring, the buckeye flowers smell so sweet, they can make you giddy.

Shortly you'll enter and exit a rock tunnel that was built by an ambitious trail crew in the 1930s. Just beyond it, at a fork, take leave of the Moses Spring Trail, which goes up and over the Bear Gulch Caves instead of through them. Bear left for Bear Gulch Caves and turn on your flashlights. Now the fun begins: You'll squeeze through clefts in the rock, duck your head under ledges, and climb down rocky staircases. You'll walk into water-sculpted volcanic caverns where only occasional beams of sunlight flash through the ceiling. You'll twist and turn through narrow passageways in which the only sound is the dripping of water on the walls. If you don't have a good light with you, you may bump into a few boulders or tree roots, or get lost momentarily. But no worries—small painted arrows on the cave walls keep you going in the right direction. Every moment of this

tunnel near the entrance to Bear Gulch Caves

spelunking expedition feels like an adventure, even though it's easy enough for a six-year-old to accomplish. Adults love it as much as kids; these caves are just plain fun. If you were a bat, you might want to live here too.

If you're wondering what made these intriguing caves and the surrounding rocky spires and crags of Pinnacles National Monument, they are the result of an ancient volcano that erupted some 200 miles to the southeast, in the northern San Fernando Valley. Movement along the San Andreas Fault carried these rock formations many miles from the rest of the volcano's remains and deposited them in the smooth, grassy hills of this inland valley. Water erosion over many thousands of years did a final job on the Pinnacles's mighty rock formations, creating deep, tunnel-like canyons covered by and partially filled with huge boulders. These tunnels form the Bear Gulch Caves, and also the Balconies Caves on the park's west side.

After exiting Bear Gulch Caves, head back to the visitors center on the Moses Spring Trail. At the visitors center, pick up the trail across the road, signed as Condor Gulch Trail to the High Peaks Trail and Overlook. It's a solid 30-minute uphill climb to the overlook on a comfortably graded trail. In spring, a cascading stream parallels the path. The scent of wild sage and rosemary is enticingly aromatic, and your eyes will be drawn to the fascinating colorful lichen growing on the equally colorful rocks. That is, until you start getting views of the high pinnacles, which will surely divert your attention. The overlook, a giant volcanic boulder with a metal railing, is a great place to stand and admire the high peaks of the Pinnacles and look down on the rocky valley below.

Options
Hike beyond the overlook on the Condor Gulch Trail. In .7 mile you'll reach the High Peaks Trail, where you can turn left and access one of the most exciting trail stretches in the park. High Peaks Trail leads through a maze of cliffs and spires by utilizing handholds and footholds in the rock, stairsteps blasted out of the rock, and metal railings to hold you on the rock. It's great fun.

Information and Contact
There is a $5 entrance fee at Pinnacles National Monument, good for seven days. Park maps are available at the entrance station. For more information, contact Pinnacles National Monument, 5000 Hwy. 146, Paicines, CA 95043, 831/389-4485, website: www.nps.gov/pinn.

Directions
From King City on U.S. 101, take the First Street exit and head east. First Street turns into Highway G13/Bitterwater Road. Follow it for 15 miles to Highway 25, where you turn left (north). Follow Highway 25 for 14 miles to Highway 146. Go left on Highway 146 and drive 4.8 miles to the park visitors center, then continue beyond it to the parking lot at the end of the road. If this lot is full, park by the visitors center and walk down the road to the trailhead.

5 LIMEKILN TRAIL
Limekiln State Park, off Highway 1 near Lucia

Total distance: 2.5 miles round-trip   **Hiking time:** 1.5 hours

Type of trail: mostly level terrain   **Best season:** year-round

Compared to its larger neighbors to the north in Big Sur, Limekiln State Park is a small park, with a relatively quiet campground and only one main hiking trail. Developed facilities are few, but you will find a lovely redwood forest, a perennial creek and waterfall, and an easy hiking trail that leads to a set of 1800s limekilns that were used to make bricks and cement.

old limekiln at Limekiln Creek State Park

Start hiking from the far end of the campground on the signed path through the forest. The route parallels pretty Limekiln Creek, a watercourse that's surrounded by big redwoods, ferns, rocks, and sorrel. Cross a bridge immediately past the campground, and then in another .2 mile, cross a second bridge.

Immediately past the second bridge you'll see a side trail on the right, across the stream. Make note of it for your return trip, then keep heading into the canyon toward the limekilns. You'll cross one more footbridge, then come to the four big kilns, which look like giant smokestacks with mossy, brick bottoms. In 1880, the Rockland Cement Company fired limestone in these metal kilns, using this canyon's redwoods for firewood. Cargo ships carried the limestone bricks and cement, as well as redwood lumber, to build the prospering new city of San Francisco. As a result of all this activity, the redwoods you see today in Limekiln Canyon are mostly second growth. Still, they are large and beautiful.

Beyond the kilns, a sign marks the end of the trail. Turn around here and head back to the trail junction by the second footbridge. If the stream level is low enough, you can rock-hop across the stream (or if you're lucky, a seasonal bridge will be in place), then head up the spur trail toward Limekiln State Park's waterfall. You'll need to cross and recross the creek several times, and in winter and spring, you might get your hiking boots wet.

Your scramble ends at the base of the waterfall, where Limekiln Falls pours 100 feet down a nearly vertical sheet of limestone. On one May visit, the waterfall's flow fanned out to 25 feet wide at the base. In contrast to the dark and shady redwood forest you've been hiking in, the light is surprisingly bright by the waterfall. The waterfall's limestone cliff prevents any trees from growing nearby and blocking out the light.

Information and Contact
A $6 day-use fee is charged per vehicle. A trail map is available at the entrance kiosk. For more information, contact Limekiln State Park, c/o Big Sur Station, Hwy. 1, Big Sur, CA 93920, 831/667-2403 or 831/667-2315, website: www.parks.ca.gov.

Directions
From Big Sur, drive south on Highway 1 for 26 miles to Limekiln Creek State Park on the east side of the highway. (It's 2.5 miles south of Lucia.) The trailhead is at the far side of the campground.

Chapter 8

© ANN MARIE BROWN

Yosemite and Mammoth Lakes

Yosemite and Mammoth Lakes

Plunging waterfalls, stark granite, alpine lakes, pristine meadows, giant Sequoias, and raging rivers—you'll find them all in the Yosemite and Mammoth Lakes region, which encompasses not only world-famous Yosemite National Park but also the popular recreation areas of Mammoth Lakes and the Eastern Sierra.

The centerpiece of this region, of course, is Yosemite National Park, a must-see on every hiker's itinerary. From Yosemite Valley's famous waterfalls—three of which are among the tallest in the world—to the towering granite domes and glistening meadows of Tioga Pass, Yosemite is a place that can only be described in superlatives.

As scenic as the national park itself are the resort areas just to the east, particularly Mammoth Lakes and June Lake on the U.S. 395 corridor, as well as the surrounding wilderness areas—Hoover, Ansel Adams, and John Muir. The alpine lakes of this region are a major draw for day hikers, but equally as compelling are the Eastern Sierra's alpine meadows, fir and pine forests, and sagebrush-covered plains. This is a region known for its unusual diversity, including volcanic craters, hot springs, lava flows, and the strange beauty of Mono Lake, an ancient and majestic body of water covering 60 square miles.

More uncommon geologic features are found nearby at Devils Postpile National Monument. This 800-acre national park preserves the Devils Postpile—a "pile" of 60-foot-high basalt columns that are remnants of an ancient lava flow—plus breathtaking 101-foot Rainbow Falls.

Key to enjoying your experience in the Yosemite and Mammoth Lakes region is planning your visit for the least crowded months of the year. Summer weekends are the busiest time and best avoided, especially in the national park. After school starts in September, the crowds lessen substantially. Likewise, if there is a perfect time to visit the Eastern Sierra, it's in the transition between summer and winter. Autumn transforms the scenic canyons and pristine lakeshores into a wave of blazing color. Aspens, willows, and cottonwoods turn showy hues of orange, yellow, and red. The trees generally begin their color change early in September; peak viewing time is usually late September and early October.

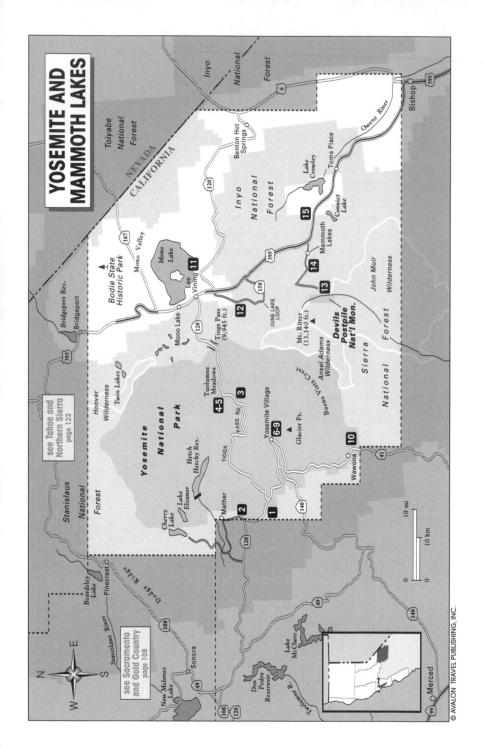

Contents

1. Merced Grove 252

2. Lukens Lake Trail 254

3. Tenaya Lake Trail 256

4. Dog Lake Trail 258

5. Lembert Dome Trail 260

6. McGurk Meadow Trail 262

7. Sentinel Dome Trail 264

8. Taft Point Trail 266

9. Panorama Trail 268

10. Mariposa Grove of Big Trees 270

11. Mark Twain Scenic Tufa Trail 272

12. Parker Lake Trail 275

13. Devils Postpile & Rainbow Falls 277

14. Emerald Lake & Sky Meadows 279

15. Hot Creek Geothermal Area Trail 281

#

Yosemite National Park, off Highway 120 in Yosemite

Total distance: 3.0 miles round-trip

Hiking time: 1.5 hours

Type of trail: rolling terrain

Best season: May–October

There are three giant sequoia groves in Yosemite National Park—Merced, Tuolumne, and Mariposa. Because the Merced Grove is tucked into a western corner of the park and is the smallest of the groves, it is the least visited and most peaceful. Generally, the Merced Grove only gets traffic from people who enter Yosemite at the Big Oak Flat entrance station, then drive by it on their way to Yosemite Valley. It's a fine place to go for an easy walk through a lovely mixed forest, and of course, to be awed by the big sequoias. Think of this as a simple, beautiful nature walk, perfect on any day, in any season.

The hiking trail is a closed-off dirt road that was Yosemite's first carriage road. It is level for the first .5 mile until it reaches a junction. Take the left fork and head downhill through a mixed forest of white firs, incense cedars, ponderosa pines, and sugar pines. Azaleas bloom in early summer beneath the conifers' branches.

You reach the first trees of the small sequoia grove at 1.5 miles. First

old cabin at the Merced Grove

you see a group of six sequoias along the trail to your right. They are not of record-breaking size, but they're certainly impressive. Walk a few more feet down the trail and you spot two more big trees on the left and one on the right—they're getting bigger as you go. A total of only 20 sequoias are found in this grove, but because they grow quite close together, they make a stately impression.

The sequoias in the Merced Grove were "discovered" in 1833 by the Walker party, a group of explorers headed by Joseph Walker who were looking for the best route through the Sierra Nevada. Most likely local Native American tribes had long known about the location of the big trees.

The largest, granddaddy sequoias of the grove are found directly across the road from a handsome old log cabin. The cabin was originally built as a retreat for the park superintendent, but it is no longer used. Have a seat near the largest trees, pull a sandwich from your pack, and stay a while. For your return, simply retrace your steps from the cabin, hiking back uphill.

Options

You can hike farther, beyond the cabin, but the trail becomes more overgrown and obstacle-ridden with fallen trees. In the winter, the Merced Grove is one of Yosemite's best snowshoeing destinations, even for beginners. It's harder work to snowshoe this trail than to hike it, but seeing the sequoias in snow makes it all worthwhile.

Information and Contact

There is a $20 entrance fee at Yosemite National Park (good for seven days). Park maps are available for free at the entrance kiosk. For more information, contact Yosemite National Park Public Information Office, P.O. Box 577, Yosemite National Park, CA 95389, 209/372-0200, website: www.nps.gov/yose.

Directions

From the Arch Rock entrance station at Yosemite National Park, drive east into the park for 4.5 miles to the turnoff for Tioga Road/Highway 120, which is Big Oak Flat Road. Turn left and drive 13.5 miles (past the Tioga Road/Highway 120 turnoff) to the Merced Grove parking area on the left.

Or, from the Big Oak Flat entrance station on Highway 120, drive south into the park for 4.3 miles to the Merced Grove trailhead on your right.

2 LUKENS LAKE TRAIL

Yosemite National Park, off Highway 120 in Yosemite

Total distance: 1.5 miles round-trip

Type of trail: rolling terrain

Hiking time: 1 hour

Best season: June–October

The Lukens Lake Trail is the perfect introductory lake hike for families in Yosemite National Park. It has all the best features of a long, backpacking trip to a remote alpine area, without the long miles, steep hills, and heavy weight to carry. Anyone can do it, and everyone will have a good time.

As you head out of the Yosemite Valley floor and up Tioga Pass Road, the trailhead parking area for Lukens Lake is one of the first you'll reach. If you've been cruising around the Valley, your body has become accustomed to a 4,000-foot elevation, but Lukens Lake is set at more than 8,000 feet. This can take some getting used to—don't be surprised if you're huffing and puffing a little more than you'd expect as you hike uphill. Fortunately, the trail to the lake is only .75 mile long and gains only 200 feet in elevation, so your body gets a chance to adapt to its new heights without much of a strain on your cardiovascular system.

After parking at the Lukens Lake pullout, cross the road to reach the trailhead. The wide trail climbs gently through a red fir forest for .5 mile until it reaches a saddle, where it descends to the lake in another .25 mile.

A flower-filled meadow lines the shores of Lukens Lake.

If this is your first hike on Tioga Road, you'll notice many differences in this forest environment from others at lower elevations. The red firs, with their red-brown, deeply engrained bark, look a little like ponderosa pines but are redder in color and have distinctive needles and cones. Whereas ponderosa pines grow at about 4,000 feet in elevation, red firs prefer areas of heavy winter snowfall, between 7,000 and 8,000 feet in elevation, where the soil is well drained. They grow to be very large (more than 150 feet tall) and cluster in thick stands, making it nearly impossible for other plants to grow near or around them.

Lukens Lake is surrounded by a large and beautiful meadow, filled with mountain wildflowers such as shooting stars and bluebells. At this high elevation, you may find patches of snow along the trail and in the shady forest until late in July. Soon after snowmelt, you'll find huge emerald-green corn lilies growing in standing water. The meadow can be totally flooded until midsummer, its shallow waters shimmering in the afternoon sun. If it is dry, you can cross the meadow and continue on the trail to the far side of the lake, where there are good picnic spots on its north side. In late summer, most hikers choose to swim. Because Lukens Lake is quite shallow, the water is surprisingly warm for this high elevation. Don't expect the smooth granite bottom that you find at many lakes in the high country—Lukens Lake is grassy and muddy underneath its blue waters.

Options
The trail continues from the back side of Lukens Lake to White Wolf Campground and then all the way to Ten Lakes and the Grand Canyon of the Tuolumne River. Hike as far as you please.

Information and Contact
There is a $20 entrance fee at Yosemite National Park (good for seven days). Park maps are available for free at the entrance kiosk. For more information, contact Yosemite National Park Public Information Office, P.O. Box 577, Yosemite National Park, CA 95389, 209/372-0200, website: www.nps.gov/yose.

Directions
From Merced, drive 70 miles northeast on Highway 140 to Yosemite National Park. Enter Yosemite at the Arch Rock entrance station, then drive 4.5 miles and turn west (left) on Big Oak Flat Road (signed for Highway 120). Drive 9.3 miles, then turn right on Tioga Road/Highway 120. Drive 16.3 miles on Tioga Road, past the entrance to White Wolf Campground, to the trailhead for Lukens Lake. Park in the turnout on the right side of the road, then cross the road to reach the trailhead.

3 TENAYA LAKE TRAIL

Yosemite National Park, off Highway 120 in Yosemite

Total distance: 2.0 miles round-trip

Hiking time: 1 hour

Type of trail: mostly level terrain

Best season: June–October

Lots of people drive east down Tioga Road in a big rush to get to Tuolumne Meadows, but when they see giant Tenaya Lake right along the road, it stops them in their tire tracks. Luckily, the 150-acre, sapphire-blue lake has a parking lot and picnic area at its east end, where you can leave your car and take a stroll down to the lake's edge.

Whereas most people stop at the white-sand beach and picnic tables to swim, sunbathe, or watch the rock climbers on nearby Polly Dome (across the highway), it's better to leave the crowds behind and take a hike around the lake. From the parking lot, follow the trail west to the lake, then turn left and walk to the south side of the beach. Pick up the trail there that leads along the lakes' forested south side, far from the road on the north side. You'll have to rock-hop across a small, shallow stream to access the trail, which comes in from the east (it travels all the way to Tuolumne Meadows).

The mostly level path meanders alongside the lake, then continues beyond it to Olmsted Point. You can hike as far as you like and then turn around. The best parts of the trail are in the first mile from the beach, before you connect with the busier trails on the southwest side of the lake. The lakeside forest is very lush in summer, with plenty of wildflowers growing in the understory of Douglas firs, spruce, hemlocks, and pines. The trees make the trail remarkably private, despite the proximity of Tioga Road and Tenaya Lake's beach and picnic area. Swimming is best on the lake's southwest side; although there is no sandy beach like on the east side, the shoreline is protected from the wind and fairly private.

For all its beauty, the lake has a grim history. In 1852, the United States government sent soldiers to round up the Yosemite American Indians and "resettle" them on reservations. Members of the Ahwahneeche tribe, who were native to Yosemite Valley, fled to this remote lake to escape the roundup. The Ahwahneeches and their chief, Teneiya, were captured and resettled on the Fresno River. Even there, angry whites continued to persecute them, seeking vigilante justice for alleged crimes. Chief Teneiya died in 1853, and Lake Tenaya was named for him, with a slight change in spelling.

The Ahwahneeches had their own name for Lake Tenaya—"Pywiack," or Lake of Shining Rocks. It's a name well earned by the wall of polished granite framing the water.

Tenaya Lake

Options
Continue hiking beyond the lake's western edge, following the trail as far as you wish. If you walk all the way to Olmsted Point and back, it will be a five-mile round-trip.

Information and Contact
There is a $20 entrance fee at Yosemite National Park (good for seven days). Park maps are available for free at the entrance kiosk. For more information, contact Yosemite National Park Public Information Office, P.O. Box 577, Yosemite National Park, CA 95389, 209/372-0200, website: www.nps.gov/yose.

Directions
From Merced, drive 70 miles northeast on Highway 140 to Yosemite National Park. Enter Yosemite at the Arch Rock entrance station, then drive 4.5 miles and turn west (left) on Big Oak Flat Road (signed for Highway 120). Drive 9.3 miles, then turn right on Tioga Road/Highway 120. Drive 16.3 miles on Tioga Road, to the farthest (eastern) edge of Tenaya Lake. Park in the picnic area; the trailhead is located by the parking lot. (There is another Tenaya Lake picnic area .5 mile west of this one; make sure you drive all the way to the picnic area on the far east side of the lake.)

4 DOG LAKE TRAIL

Yosemite National Park,
off Highway 120 near Tuolumne Meadows

Total distance: 3.0 miles round-trip   **Hiking time:** 2 hours

Type of trail: some steep terrain   **Best season:** June–October

Dog Lake is an easy-to-reach destination from Tuolumne Meadows, and a perfect place for families to spend an afternoon picnicking or swimming at a charming alpine lake. Keep in mind that although this is a relatively easy hike, the air is very thin at this elevation and even a moderate climb can feel difficult, especially if you're not acclimated.

The trail begins by the restrooms at the Lembert Dome parking lot. Initially, you'll walk through a pretty meadow, with views of snowy Cathedral Peak and Unicorn Peak in the distance. (Guess which is which—their names tell you all you need to know.) Notice how the trail is dug a few inches into the ground to keep hikers on a single, definitive route and protect the fragile meadow. In spring, colorful wildflowers add contrast to the emerald-green grasses.

Immediately after you cross the meadow, you reach a huge horizontal slab of granite, marked by rock trail cairns to show you the way. Next

© ANN MARIE BROWN

Mount Dana and Mount Gibbs rise above Dog Lake.

comes a trail split—Dog Lake to the left and Lembert Dome to the right; you head left.

Now your climb begins in earnest, as you ascend a sandy, rocky trail to the top of a ridge behind Lembert Dome. The dome is behind your right shoulder as you mount the ridge; you have plenty of opportunity during the 500-foot climb to stop and admire it as you catch your breath. The forest surrounding you is primarily lodgepole pines and firs. If you hike this trail early in summer, a stream accompanies you on your left for much of the climb. By late summer, it goes dry.

After a half mile of huffing and puffing, you'll cross the streambed and top the ridge. The trail flattens out, but you're not done climbing yet. A more moderate grade takes you to a junction with the Young Lakes Trail to your left. Bear right here and you'll reach Dog Lake in less than .25 mile.

After the hefty climb, Dog Lake is a joy to see. Set at 9,240 feet in elevation, the lake is wide, shallow, and deeply blue. The colorful red peaks to the east are Mount Dana and Mount Gibbs. Although the lake's edges are grassy and partially forested, you can still hike around its perimeter. If you head to your right from the main trail, you'll reach a pretty meadow and sandy swimming area on the lake's far side. Getting there requires a stream crossing, but it's very shallow and narrow by summer.

Some people toss a line in the water. We've witnessed plenty of fishing taking place at Dog Lake, but not much catching. Nobody seems to mind. One important caveat for this trip, however: If you are visiting in July, don't forget the mosquito repellant. During the hatch season, the insects are vicious.

Note that a separate hiking trail leads to Dog Lake from near Tuolumne Lodge. This trail is about the same length and grade as the trail from the Lembert Dome parking lot, but it begins on the south side of Tioga Road. The trail crosses the highway and then proceeds up the eastern flank of Lembert Dome to the lake. This trail is not quite as scenic, although it is usually less crowded.

Options

Add on a one-mile side trip to Lembert Dome on your return from Dog Lake. Leaving the lake, you'll pass the junction with the Young Lakes Trail. Stay left and continue downhill a third of a mile farther, to where a trail sign for Lembert Dome and Tuolumne Lodge points left. Take it; you'll pass a small pond on your left, then see an unmarked spur trail on your right that leads to the base of the dome. Pick any route up the granite slabs to the summit. (See the following trail description on Lembert Dome.) For your return trip from either Dog Lake or Lembert Dome, make sure you follow the trail signs for "Lembert Dome Parking." Otherwise, you could wind up back at the horse stables or Tuolumne Lodge instead of at your car; several other trails connect with this trail.

Information and Contact
There is a $20 entrance fee at Yosemite National Park (good for seven days). Park maps are available for free at the entrance kiosk. For more information, contact Yosemite National Park Public Information Office, P.O. Box 577, Yosemite National Park, CA 95389, 209/372-0200, website: www.nps.gov/yose.

Directions
From Merced, drive 70 miles northeast on Highway 140 to Yosemite National Park. Enter Yosemite at the Arch Rock entrance station, then drive 4.5 miles and turn west (left) on Big Oak Flat Road (signed for Highway 120). Drive 9.3 miles, then turn right on Tioga Road/Highway 120. Drive 39 miles on Tioga Road, past Tenaya Lake, to the east side of Tuolumne Meadows and the parking lot for Lembert Dome picnic area on the left (north) side of the road (the road sign also notes the trailheads for Soda Springs, Dog Lake, and Glen Aulin). Park in the parking lot and locate the trailhead next to the restrooms, on the west (left) side of Lembert Dome.

5 LEMBERT DOME TRAIL
Yosemite National Park,
off Highway 120 near Tuolumne Meadows

Total distance: 2.5 miles round-trip   **Hiking time:** 1.25 hours

Type of trail: some steep terrain   **Best season:** June–October

When you see 800-foot-high Lembert Dome from the trailhead and parking area, you'll never think you can make it to the top. It just seems too big and imposing to be scaled without ropes and carabiners. But the secret of Lembert Dome is that although the west side is an intimidating sheer face—the playground of technical climbers—the northeast side is nicely sloped.

Granite domes, a common geological feature in the Sierra, are essentially large rounded rocks, formed by the creation of slowly expanding granite. As the granite expands, cracks form, creating individual layers of rock near the surface. Over time, a process called exfoliation occurs, in which these outer layers of rock break apart and fall off, removing all sharp corners and angles from the rock and leaving a smooth round dome. Lembert Dome is a special kind of granite dome called a roche moutonnée. This is a French geologic term that designates a dome with one sheer side and one sloping side. It roughly means "rock sheep."

To hike to Lembert Dome, take the trail by the restrooms that is signed for both Dog Lake and Lembert Dome. In less than .25 mile, the trail splits off from the path to Dog Lake. You'll take the right fork for Lembert Dome and begin to climb more steeply through a lodgepole pine forest. The sandy, rocky, well-worn trail can make somewhat tricky footing, which is even trickier on the way back down. As you pass underneath Lembert Dome's west side, you'll see rock climbers dangling from the granite high above you, and hear their commanding shouts to their companions.

The trail curves around the back (north) side of the dome and becomes rather faint, then disappears completely once you're on hard granite. Pick your own route to Lembert Dome's exposed summit. You'll see other hikers going every which way—some make a beeline for the top, others switchback and lateral their way over to it.

Any way you get there, the effort is completely worthwhile. The views from the top of Lembert Dome (elevation 9,450 feet) are outstanding, taking in all of Tuolumne Meadows and its surrounding peaks. The steepness of the dome combined with its high vista can be downright dizzying, so if you're afraid of heights, hold on to your hiking partner. The wind often howls on top, adding to the excitement.

For your return from Lembert Dome, make sure you follow the trail signs for "Lembert Dome Parking." Otherwise, you could wind up back at the horse stables or Tuolumne Lodge instead of at your car; several other trails connect with the Lembert Dome Trail.

Options
Add on a side trip to Dog Lake; see the previous trail description.

Information and Contact
There is a $20 entrance fee at Yosemite National Park (good for seven days). Park maps are available for free at the entrance kiosk. For more information, contact Yosemite National Park Public Information Office, P.O. Box 577, Yosemite National Park, CA 95389, 209/372-0200, website: www.nps.gov/yose.

Directions
From Merced, drive 70 miles northeast on Highway 140 to Yosemite National Park. Enter Yosemite at the Arch Rock entrance station, then drive 4.5 miles and turn west (left) on Big Oak Flat Road (signed for Highway

120). Drive 9.3 miles, then turn right on Tioga Road/Highway 120. Drive 39 miles on Tioga Road, past Tenaya Lake, to the east side of Tuolumne Meadows and the parking lot for Lembert Dome picnic area on the left (north) side of the road (the road sign also notes the trailheads for Soda Springs, Dog Lake, and Glen Aulin). Park in the parking lot and locate the trailhead next to the restrooms, on the west (left) side of Lembert Dome.

6 McGURK MEADOW TRAIL
Yosemite National Park, off Glacier Point Road in Yosemite

Total distance: 2.0 miles round-trip

Hiking time: 1 hour

Type of trail: rolling terrain

Best season: June–October

The McGurk Meadow Trail is an often-overlooked path that leads through a fir and pine forest to a pristine, mile-long meadow with a stream meandering through its center. It's easily as beautiful (although not nearly as large) as Tuolumne Meadows, but without all the people. The trail also travels right past an old pioneer cabin still standing in half-decent repair, a remnant of bygone days when sheep and cattle ranchers grazed their stock in Yosemite.

After parking at the pullout, walk west along the road for about 70 yards to the McGurk Meadow trailhead sign. Fifteen minutes of downhill hiking on a forested trail will bring you to the pioneer cabin, only .8 mile from the trailhead. Built with logs and nails, the cabin must have been used only in the summer, as its front door is so low that it would be covered by snow in the winter.

After you pass the old cabin, a few more footsteps

corn lilies at McGurk Meadow

take you to the edge of McGurk Meadow, where a trail sign points you to Dewey Point in three miles and Glacier Point in seven. No need to hike that far, though, since this meadow is a perfect destination in and of itself. A footbridge carries you over a small stream, which cuts long, narrow "S" marks end over end through the tall grass.

For a too-brief period, usually in July and August, McGurk Meadow abounds with wildflowers. If you time your trip carefully, you can see a stunning display of purple, alpine shooting stars with tiny rings of white and yellow, their stigma tips pointing to the ground like bowed heads. Hundreds of corn lilies may also be in flower, along with patches of penstemon, Indian paintbrush, gentian, lupine, and yampah.

My July walk revealed other signs of spring in the meadow, including several flitting butterflies and a centipede who was slowly making her way across the footbridge. Because the growing season is so short at this 7,000-foot elevation, plants and animals don't waste any time on warm days. They focus their efforts on growing, reproducing, and storing food for the long winter to come.

Cross the footbridge and walk to McGurk Meadow's far side, where the trail turns right and skirts the meadow's edge as it abuts with the forest. You'll add another .25 mile to your trip by walking the path along the length of the pristine meadow. When the trail heads away from the meadow and deeper into the forest, turn around and retrace your steps.

Options
You can continue for another three miles to Dewey Point, a breathtaking overlook on the south wall of Yosemite Valley. This will make an eight-mile round-trip from where you left your car.

Information and Contact
There is a $20 entrance fee at Yosemite National Park (good for seven days). Park maps are available for free at the entrance kiosk. For more information, contact Yosemite National Park Public Information Office, P.O. Box 577, Yosemite National Park, CA 95389, 209/372-0200, website: www.nps.gov/yose.

Directions
From Merced, drive 70 miles northeast on Highway 140 to Yosemite National Park. Enter Yosemite at Arch Rock, then drive 6.3 miles into the valley and turn right at the fork for Highway 41/Wawona/Fresno. Drive 9.2 miles on the Wawona Road/Highway 41 and turn left on Glacier Point Road. Drive 7.5 miles to the trailhead for McGurk Meadow. The trailhead is on the left side of the road. A parking pullout is found about 70 yards farther, also on the left.

7 SENTINEL DOME TRAIL

Yosemite National Park, near Glacier Point in Yosemite

Total distance: 2.2 miles round-trip

Type of trail: rolling terrain

Hiking time: 1 hour

Best season: June–October

It's hard to believe you can get so much for so little, but on the Sentinel Dome Trail, you can. The granite dome is located about a mile west of Glacier Point, and its elevation is 1,000 feet higher than the point's. That means stellar views are yours for the asking. The Sentinel Dome Trail gives you a complete understanding of the word "panorama." You'd expect a view like this to come with a price, but since the trailhead is conveniently located at 7,700 feet in elevation, reaching the top of Sentinel Dome at 8,122 feet requires only a brief ascent. Even very small children can make it to the top. Make sure you bring your camera for this trip, because few places in the park offer such panoramic views. In all of Yosemite Valley, only Half Dome is a higher summit, and reaching it is a heck of a lot more work.

A nearly level one-mile walk leads you to the base of Sentinel Dome. From the Taft Point/Sentinel Dome trailhead, take the path to the right. Hike very gently uphill on the easy-to-follow trail. The terrain is mostly exposed granite except for some Jeffrey pines and white firs. In summer, tiny purple-and-white mountain wildflowers bring a splash of color to the ground.

You'll enter a grove of old-growth fir trees and then approach Sentinel Dome from the southeast side. Your trail meets up with an old, once-paved road, which leads around the right side of the dome to its northern flank. (Stay left at two junctions.)

the stark granite of Sentinel Dome

© ANN MARIE BROWN

You're deposited right at the base of Sentinel Dome. Leave the trail to climb up the granite slope. The route is obvious, and you'll probably see others ahead of you. In a matter of a few minutes, you're on top.

The view is breathtaking. You can see both Lower and Upper Yosemite Fall and the Middle Cascades—this is one of the few places in the park where you can see all three sections that make up the complete Yosemite Falls. Half Dome is easy to spot, and just to the left of it are two twin domes, Basket Dome and North Dome. Behind Half Dome is Quarter Dome, which is situated at the head of deep, forested Tenaya Canyon; behind Quarter Dome you can see Pywiack Cascade streaming down the mountainside. In front of Half Dome is Liberty Cap and Nevada Falls, and farther to the right is Bunnell Cascade, which slides straight down to Bunnell Point. In case you weren't counting, that's five waterfalls in one peek (and on one peak). Of course, if you visit much later than July, not all of these falls will be flowing. Early in the summer is the best time to take in the view.

Expect the wind to be fierce on top of Sentinel Dome. Although there's almost no soil structure at all, a few plants manage to dig their roots into the hard granite and survive. Among them are tiny wildflowers tucked into creases in the rock. Sentinel Dome used to have a very large and frequently photographed Jeffrey pine at its summit, but it finally gave way to the forces of nature.

Options

To make a longer day out of your trip to Sentinel Dome, you can easily combine this hike with the following trail to Taft Point. That trail begins at the same trailhead but heads in the opposite direction. It is also possible to make a loop hike from Sentinel Dome to Taft Point, by connecting with the Pohono Trail (north of the dome) and following it to the west for 1.5 miles until it junctions with the Taft Point Trail.

Information and Contact

There is a $20 entrance fee at Yosemite National Park (good for seven days). Park maps are available for free at the entrance kiosk. For more information, contact Yosemite National Park Public Information Office, P.O. Box 577, Yosemite National Park, CA 95389, 209/372-0200, website: www.nps.gov/yose.

Directions

From Merced, drive 70 miles northeast on Highway 140 to Yosemite National Park. Enter Yosemite at Arch Rock, then drive 6.3 miles into the valley and turn right at the fork for Highway 41/Wawona/Fresno. Drive 9.2 miles on the Wawona Road/Highway 41 and turn left on Glacier Point

Road. Drive 13.2 miles to the trailhead for Sentinel Dome and Taft Point (two miles before the end of the road at Glacier Point). The trailhead is on the left side of the road.

⑧ TAFT POINT TRAIL
Yosemite National Park, near Glacier Point in Yosemite

Total distance: 2.2 miles round-trip   **Hiking time:** 1 hour

Type of trail: rolling terrain   **Best season:** June–October

---

It's not so much the sweeping vista from Taft Point that you remember, although certainly the point's views of Yosemite Valley and its north rim are stunning. Instead, what sticks in your mind is the incredible sense of awe that you felt, one perhaps mixed with a little fear and a lot of respect, as you peeked over the edge of Taft Point's 3,000-foot cliff, or looked down into The Fissures in Taft Point's granite—huge cracks in the rock that plunge hundreds of feet down toward the valley.

The Taft Point Trail starts off innocently enough from the same trailhead as the Sentinel Dome Trail (see the previous trail description). Take the path to the left through a dense forest of Jeffrey pine, lodgepole pine, and white fir. In the first .25 mile, you pass by a large pile of white quartz on your right, its orange and gray veins visible upon closer inspection.

Continue through the forest and cross a couple of small creeks, including one that is surrounded by dense corn lilies and grasses. At nearly one mile out, the trees disappear and you begin to descend along a rocky slope. The trail more or less vanishes on the granite; just head toward Yosemite Valley. In a few hundred feet, you reach the edge of the cliff you're standing on. You expect to be able to see some distance down, but nothing can prepare you for how far down it is.

If you can stop your knees from knocking, walk a few hundred feet farther, contouring along the edge of the cliff. Head for the metal railing you see at the high point on top of Profile Cliff. On the way, you'll pass a few of The Fissures, remarkably skinny clefts in the cliff that drop straight down to the valley below. One of The Fissures has a couple of large granite boulders captured in its jaws; they're stuck there waiting for the next big earthquake or Ice Age to set them free. Then they'll make a half-mile, one-way journey to the valley floor.

The high overlook on Profile Cliff caps off the trip. Its railing, a meager piece of metal, performs an important psychological job. Although it's only a

the dramatic dropoff from Taft Point

hand rail, it takes away some of the fear of peering 3,500 feet straight down, because you can clutch it tightly while you gawk at the view. If you have kids with you, be sure to keep a firm handhold on them.

At 7,503 feet in elevation, Profile Cliff is approximately the same height as 7,569-foot El Capitan, which means you get the same kind of unnerving view as those daring rock climbers on El Cap. Squint carefully, or pull out your binoculars, and you can see those El Capitan climbers almost directly across from you.

Also in view are Upper Yosemite Fall across the valley, the Merced River cutting down in front of El Capitan, and tiny cars parked near the meadow by its side. From this height you can't see Lower Yosemite Fall, which is obscured in the canyon, but you get a rare look at the stream that feeds the upper falls.

Walk another hundred yards to the west to reach Taft Point proper, which has even better views of El Capitan. There is no railing here, but the clifftop is broad enough so that you can locate a safe, and view-filled, picnic spot.

Options

To make a longer day out of your trip to Taft Point, you can easily combine this hike with the previous trail to Sentinel Dome. The best option is to hike back on the Taft Point Trail for .5 mile, then bear left at a trail junction. Follow the Pohono Trail for 1.5 miles to the Sentinel Dome cutoff, then turn right and follow the trail uphill to the dome. To finish out your loop, you can circle back to the parking lot on the Sentinel Dome Trail.

Information and Contact

There is a $20 entrance fee at Yosemite National Park (good for seven days). Park maps are available for free at the entrance kiosk. For more information, contact Yosemite National Park Public Information Office, P.O. Box 577, Yosemite National Park, CA 95389, 209/372-0200, website: www.nps.gov/yose.

Directions

From Merced, drive 70 miles northeast on Highway 140 to Yosemite National Park. Enter Yosemite at Arch Rock, then drive 6.3 miles into the valley and turn right at the fork for Highway 41/Wawona/Fresno. Drive 9.2 miles on the Wawona Road/Highway 41 and turn left on Glacier Point Road. Drive 13.2 miles to the trailhead for Sentinel Dome and Taft Point (two miles before the end of the road at Glacier Point). The trailhead is on the left side of the road.

9 PANORAMA TRAIL

Yosemite National Park, near Glacier Point in Yosemite

Total distance: 4.0 miles round-trip

Type of trail: some steep terrain

Hiking time: 2 hours

Best season: June–October

A trip to Yosemite always takes your breath away. It's one world-class natural wonder after another—Bridalveil Falls, Cathedral Rock, Half Dome, Yosemite Falls, El Capitan, Vernal and Nevada Falls . . . Every one of these features is worthy of its very own park.

Tons of people drive their cars through the valley floor to visit these famous landmarks. Many of them also make the trip to Glacier Point to line

view of Half Dome, Vernal Falls, and Nevada Falls from the Panorama Trail

© ANN MARIE BROWN

up at the railing and see the splendor from up high. But of all the ways to see Yosemite's sights, a short walk on Glacier Point's Panorama Trail is one of the best.

The Panorama Trail starts at 7,230 feet in elevation, just to the right of the viewing area and picnic tables at Glacier Point. Several trails start from this trailhead, but you'll take the Panorama Trail, heading toward Illilouette Falls, a rushing cascade on Illilouette Creek. That's ill-ill-ew-et, with the accent on the second "ill."

Head off downhill on the trail, switchbacking through a fire-scarred pine forest. You'll notice how the fire meandered on its route, burning some areas and sparing others. The sparse remaining forest provides an open view, which includes spectacular Vernal and Nevada Falls. These two famous waterfalls, written about by John Muir and photographed by Ansel Adams, can't be seen simultaneously from the canyon bottom because one is lower and set back farther than the other. But here on the Panorama Trail, you can see them both from above. Vernal Falls (the lower one), is a wide, block-shaped waterfall that drops more than 300 feet into a gorge. Nevada Falls, narrower and taller at 594 feet, is shaped like an inverted V.

No steps are taken on the Panorama Trail without a glimpse of something dramatic. You'll have continual chances to admire the gleaming granite of Half Dome, Quarter Dome, and Liberty Cap, plus the glistening cascades of Vernal, Nevada, and Illilouette falls. You'll have a bird's-eye view—3,000 feet down—of the entire east side of Yosemite Valley.

Keep an eye on your energy for this hike; since it is all downhill for two miles to Illilouette Falls, you need to save your strength for the return trip uphill. If you're feeling tired, there's no need to go all the way to the falls, as there are plenty of visual rewards along the way.

After a series of switchbacks, the Panorama Trail junctions with a trail leading to Mono Meadow, but continue left for Illilouette Fall. In a few minutes more you reach an overlook directly across from the waterfall. You may be surprised to find that you've approached the fall sideways, rather than from behind or in front. That's because Illilouette doesn't pour from the back of a canyon; it rushes over its side cliff, where the creek drops 370 feet over a granite lip. The canyon is pencil-thin with vertical rock walls, so the only vantage point is from the side. It's a memorable sight. "Illilouette" sounds like a French name, but it's not; it's actually an awkward English translation of a Yosemite word, which was originally something like "Tooloolaweack." To the American Indians, the word was the name for the place where they gathered to hunt for deer.

After you've admired the waterfall, follow the trail as it descends and then crosses a bridge over Illilouette Creek, just above the falls. Posted signs warn hikers not to swim here, because the bridge is only about 50 yards above the drop. Enjoy the granite and white-water scenery by the bridge and rest up: You have a 1,200-foot climb back to Glacier Point.

Options
Ambitious hikers can follow the Panorama Trail all the way downhill to Yosemite Valley, but even though the trip is mostly downhill, it's still a strenuous 8.5 miles with 3,200 feet of elevation loss, and a workout for your knees. At Yosemite Valley, you will need to have a car shuttle arranged to take you back to Glacier Point. Or you can arrange to take the Hiker's Bus from Yosemite Lodge to Glacier Point in the morning, and then hike back down to your car in the Valley in the afternoon. Phone 209/372-1240 for bus fees and pickup times.

Information and Contact
There is a $20 entrance fee at Yosemite National Park (good for seven days). Park maps are available for free at the entrance kiosk. For more information, contact Yosemite National Park Public Information Office, P.O. Box 577, Yosemite National Park, CA 95389, 209/372-0200, website: www.nps.gov/yose.

Directions
From Merced, drive 70 miles northeast on Highway 140 to Yosemite National Park. Enter Yosemite at Arch Rock, then drive 6.3 miles into the valley and turn right at the fork for Highway 41/Wawona/Fresno. Drive 9.2 miles on the Wawona Road/Highway 41 and turn left on Glacier Point Road. Drive 15.7 miles to Glacier Point (at the end of the road). Park in any of the parking lots, then walk to the viewing area, across from the café and gift shop. Look for the Panorama Trail sign about 150 feet southeast of the café building, on your right.

10 MARIPOSA GROVE OF BIG TREES
Yosemite National Park, off Highway 41 in southern Yosemite

Total distance: 2.0 miles round-trip   **Hiking time:** 1 hour

Type of trail: rolling terrain   **Best season:** May–October

Giant sequoias are the largest living things on earth in terms of volume. That, quite simply, is the single most important reason that hundreds of people each day tour the Mariposa Grove in Yosemite National Park.

Sure, the trees are also old—as much as 3,000 years—but they're not the oldest living things on earth. They're the biggest.

The Mariposa Grove is the largest of Yosemite's three sequoia groves, with more than 250 trees, and also the most developed, with a big parking lot, restrooms, and a museum. Motorized trams run through the grove, so visitors can alternate riding and walking without getting too tired to see the forest for the trees, or the trees for the forest. But why ride the trams when you can walk this easy, two-mile loop?

Begin your hike at the trailhead by the parking lot, and head immediately for the Fallen Monarch, a big sequoia that fell more than 300 years ago. It was made famous by an 1899 photograph of the U.S. Cavalry and their horses standing on top of it. Even though it has been on the ground all these centuries, its root ball and trunk are still huge and intact, a testament to how long it takes for sequoias to decay. That's because of a surfeit of tannic acid in the sequoia's wood.

Continue to hike gently uphill on the obvious trail through the forest. The sequoias are mixed in with lots of other trees, especially white firs, sugar pines, and incense cedars; the giants appear sporadically, like treasures in a treasure hunt. Your next "find" is the Bachelor and Three Graces (an odd reference to one big tree with three smaller trees at its side). Then turn right and start a steeper uphill climb to the Grizzly Giant. This is the largest tree in the Mariposa Grove, with a circumference of more than 100 feet. The tree has one particularly impressive branch that is almost seven feet in diameter. It's also one of the oldest giant sequoias in this grove, at approximately 2,700 years old. Thinking about this gives you a little perspective on your short time on Earth.

Now start to descend to the California Tunnel Tree, which was tunneled in 1895 so stagecoaches could drive through it. Just beyond the California Tree, you'll see a trail marker that points you to the Upper Grove and Museum. This marker is the turnaround point for the short tour of the grove, so turn left to circle back to the parking area. For your return, you can take the fork that leads past the Bachelor and Three Graces and the Fallen Monarch again, or you can stay straight at the next junction and make a slightly wider loop back to the parking lot.

Note that to get the most out of your trip, you must visit the Mariposa Grove either very early in the morning or late in the day, when the crowds have lessened and the forest is quiet. The best time to visit the big trees is in the early and late hours, when you have the chance to see more playful ground squirrels than tourists with video cameras. And also know that in the summer months, the grove is so popular that parking at the trailhead is just about impossible. Make your trip more pleasant by parking at the Wawona Store, then riding the free shuttle bus into the grove.

Options

A longer, 6.5-mile loop is also possible in the Mariposa Grove. Just beyond the California Tree, follow the trail sign for the Upper Grove and Museum. There are many more wonderful tree specimens to be admired, a small sequoia museum that is open in the summer months, and almost always less people than on the lower loop.

Information and Contact

There is a $20 entrance fee at Yosemite National Park (good for seven days). Park maps are available for free at the entrance kiosk. A guide and map to the Mariposa Grove is available at the trailhead. For more information, contact Yosemite National Park Public Information Office, P.O. Box 577, Yosemite National Park, CA 95389, 209/372-0200, website: www.nps.gov/yose.

Directions

From Merced, drive 70 miles northeast on Highway 140 to Yosemite National Park. Enter Yosemite at Arch Rock, then drive 6.3 miles and turn right at the fork for Highway 41/Wawona. Drive 32 miles to the Mariposa Grove access road, then turn east and drive two miles to the grove parking lot. (If you enter Yosemite on Highway 41 at its southern entrance, the grove access road is on the right, just after you pass the southern entrance kiosk.) Note that during the summer months, the Mariposa Grove parking lot fills up and driving into the grove can be difficult. During the busy season, leave your car at the Wawona Store in Wawona and ride the free shuttle bus to the grove.

11 MARK TWAIN SCENIC TUFA TRAIL
Mono Lake Tufa State Reserve, off U.S. 395 near Lee Vining

Total distance: 1.0 mile round-trip   **Hiking time:** 30 minutes

Type of trail: level terrain   **Best season:** June–October

You'll never fully understand all the fuss about Mono Lake until you finally make the trip and see how strange and beautiful the place really is. When you arrive, the first thing you notice is that the lake is immense in size. Gazing at it from the highway, you might feel as if you've been turned around and have driven west instead of east, because here is this glorious, wide-open body of water that looks remarkably like the ocean.

But Mono Lake is three times as salty as the ocean and 80 times as alkaline. Not only that, the lake is remarkably old. Its age is estimated at 700,000 years, one of the oldest lakes in North America. And its geographical setting is spectacular, located just east of the Sierra crest and west of the Nevada State border. That means Mono Lake is framed by snow-capped mountains on one side and sagebrush plains on the other—a strange melding of extreme landscapes. Luckily for easy hikers, Mono Lake can be seen via a terrific walk on the Mark Twain Scenic Tufa Trail in Mono Lake Tufa State Reserve.

Mark Twain visited Mono Lake in 1863 and wrote about it extensively in his book *Roughing It*. He was fascinated by the tufa structures found near the edges of the lake—off-white, coral-like formations that are formed when underwater springs containing calcium are released from the lake bottom and combine with the lake's water. This forms calcium carbonate, the chemical expression for tufa. The tufa formations grow upright, swelling into odd vertical shapes as much as six feet high as spring water pushes upward inside them. The tufas only stop growing when exposed to air, which in effect ruins the chemistry experiment.

The Mark Twain Scenic Tufa Trail takes you on a perfectly level, one-mile walk around the tufa formations and the southern edge of Mono Lake. You'll pass some high-and-dry inland tufas on your way to the lakeshore, where you'll see miniature tufa islands in the water. You can touch the tufa, which feels surprisingly hard, almost like concrete, although it appears brittle to the eye. Some hikers wade in to the lake or take a swim; others enjoy bird-watching along the shore. Most people just walk around feeling a bit dazed, amazed at this strange place they've just discovered.

© ANN MARIE BROWN

tufa spires on the edge of Mono Lake

In addition to the tufa chemistry lesson, there's also a wildlife lesson to be learned on this trail. Mono Lake's islands are important nesting grounds for California gulls; in fact, 85 percent of the gulls that live on the California coast were born here. The lake's population of tiny brine shrimp feeds the gulls and the loons, grebes, pintails, and huge number of migratory birds that visit. From April–November, you can see brine shrimp clustered in thick masses near the lake surface.

The main controversy surrounding Mono Lake regards the regulation of its water level. In 1941, four streams that fed Mono Lake were diverted into the California Aqueduct to provide water for Los Angeles. The lake started to shrink rapidly, losing an average of 18 inches per year. As the water level dropped, a land bridge to the islands was formed. Coyotes and other predators could now access the gulls' nesting area, which was bad news for the birds. Elevation markers along the trail show what the lake level was in different years. In 1941, the lake's elevation was 6,417 feet. In 1993, it was down to 6,376 feet. Today, it's the job of the Water Resources Board to regulate the level of Mono Lake so that its resources remain protected. The lake level has been kept stable since the 1990s, although it is not as high as it once was.

Mono Lake is unlike anything else you'll find in California. A hike along the shoreline of the huge turquoise lake with its bald islands and strange tufa structures leaves you with a great appreciation for what Mark Twain called "one of the strangest freaks of nature to be found in any land."

Options
You can add on a three-mile, round-trip hike to Panum Crater, a volcanic crater in the state reserve, by driving your car back (west) along Highway 120 for two miles to the turnoff for the Panum Crater trailhead.

Information and Contact
There is no fee. For more information, contact Mono Lake Tufa State Reserve, P.O. Box 99, Lee Vining, CA 93541, 760/647-6331, website: www.parks.ca.gov.

Directions
From the town of Mammoth Lakes, drive three miles east on Highway 203 to its junction with U.S. 395. Take U.S. 395 north for 20 miles to the Mono Lake South Tufa exit, which is also Highway 120 east. (If you're traveling south on U.S. 395, the Mono Lake South Tufa exit is five miles south of Lee Vining.) Turn east and drive 4.6 miles until you reach a dirt road on your left that is signed for South Tufa Area parking. Turn left and drive one mile to the parking area and trailhead.

12 PARKER LAKE TRAIL

Inyo National Forest/Ansel Adams Wilderness,
off U.S. 395 near Grant Lake

Total distance: 3.6 miles round-trip

Type of trail: rolling terrain

Hiking time: 2 hours

Best season: June–October

The Parker Lake Trail in the Ansel Adams Wilderness is a quintessential study in contrasts. The first part of the trip takes place in open sagebrush plains, the second part in a shady aspen forest along a stream, and the third part at a glacial lake where the mountain wind ricochets off the lake surface. You get a little bit of everything on this trail.

The trail to Parker Lake has a 400-foot elevation gain, but unfortunately most of it occurs right at the beginning, giving you no opportunity for a warm-up. You'll climb hard at the start for 15–20 minutes, but the rest of the hike is on a gently rolling trail. If you can manage the first half mile, you can do the whole trip. As you ascend, be sure to stop, turn around,

and catch your breath while you gaze at the far-off views of Mono Lake. If you just trudge up the hill without pausing, you'll miss out on the vistas.

In the first stretch of trail, the air is pungent with the smell of sage, which seems to grow everywhere. In spring and summer, the sage is joined by profusely flowering, yellow mule's ears. As you walk, you may get buzzed by a cicada, a large insect that makes its home in the sagebrush.

As you ascend, you'll be joined by Parker Creek on your right, which can run quite forcefully after snowmelt. But soon the trail levels out and things begin

Parker Lake

© ANN MARIE BROWN

to change. You come closer to the stream, then enter a grove of quaking aspens, bearing white bark and small, round leaves that quake in the wind. The aspens are a refreshing sight on the trail, signifying shade and nearby water.

Wildflowers are more varied and profuse in this wetter area—blue and purple forget-me-nots, yellow alpine butterweed, light lavender hooker's onion, dark blue irises, pale-orange paintbrush, and dark-blue brewer's lupine with its silver-tipped leaves. Even mariposa lilies, with their tulip shape and yellow-and-red spots, make an appearance.

As you keep walking, the surrounding forest changes again. You'll enter a grove of immense Jeffrey pines, mixed in with tall and narrow lodgepole pines. You may hear the sound of busy woodpeckers at work in the pines.

Pass by a trail spur on your left that leads to Silver Lake, then head into a peaceful, shady dell close to Parker Creek. The raging stream you saw at the beginning of your hike is now tamed and quieted; you're closer to its headwaters. Aspens, pines, and wildflowers abound. Now the trail levels out completely for the last .25 mile to Parker Lake.

Prepare for another abrupt scenery change as you arrive. The lake is picturesque glacial water set in a basin below Mt. Lewis at 12,300 feet, Parker Peak at 12,861 feet, and Mt. Wood at 12,900 feet. When I visited, two ducks were floating peacefully across the water, despite the nearly gale-force winds that whipped down the snow-capped mountains and across the lake's surface. With an aspen grove at the far end of the lake completing the picture, the scene is like a postcard, too beautiful to be believed.

If the wind is too strong for a picnic at Parker Lake, head back down the trail for .25 mile to the protected and peaceful aspen grove you passed on the way in.

Information and Contact
There is no fee. For more information, contact Inyo National Forest, Mono Basin Scenic Area Visitor Center, P.O. Box 429, Lee Vining, CA 93541, 760/647-3044, website: www.fs.fed.us/r5/inyo.

Directions
From Lee Vining, drive five miles south on U.S. 395 to the Highway 158 turnoff for the June Lake Loop (make sure you take the northern end of the loop; not the southern end that is five miles farther south at June Lake Junction). Turn right and drive 1.3 miles on Highway 158, then turn right on a dirt road signed for Parker and Walker Lakes. Drive 2.4 miles to the Parker Lake trailhead at the end of the road (stay straight at all junctions).

13 DEVILS POSTPILE & RAINBOW FALLS

Devils Postpile National Monument,
off U.S. 395 near Mammoth Lakes

Total distance: 5.0 miles round-trip

Hiking time: 2.5 hours

Type of trail: rolling terrain

Best season: June–October

What the heck is the Devils Postpile? People ask themselves this question time and time again as they read the road signs while driving up U.S. 395 on their way to Mammoth Lakes for skiing or fishing vacations. Getting the answer requires only a short walk in Devils Postpile National Monument—.75 mile round-trip—but if you add in a few more miles, you'll see spectacular Rainbow Falls as well.

There's one catch, though. The road into the park is narrow, steep, and winding, and because of that, you can't just drive in any time you want. During daylight hours, visitors must purchase an access pass and ride a shuttle bus (see Directions, below). And one more catch: solitude lovers should seriously consider making a weekday visit. The trail to Devils Postpile and Rainbow Falls is incredibly popular; summer weekends bring a continual parade of hikers.

You'll start hiking at the trail by the ranger station. The footpath begins in a pretty meadow alongside the headwaters of the San Joaquin River. If you time

the Devils Postpile

your trip right, you will be wowed by the meadow wildflowers, especially the masses of shooting stars and Indian paintbrush. In a mere .4 mile on a level, easy trail, your curiosity will be sated as you reach the base of the Devils Postpile. What is it? It's a pile of volcanic rock posts or columns made from lava that was forced up from the earth's core. At the base of the standing columns is a huge pile of rubble—the crumbled remains of columns that collapsed. Notice the shapes of the various lava columns; some are almost perfectly straight, while others curve like tall candles that have been left out in the sun.

The Mammoth Lakes area is volcano country. Less than 100,000 years ago, lava filled this river valley more than 400 feet deep. As the lava began to cool from the air flow on top, it simultaneously cooled from the hard granite bedrock below. This caused the lava to harden and crack into tall, narrow pieces, forming nearly perfect columns or posts. The Devils Postpile is considered to be the finest example of lava columns in the world.

After examining the base of the Postpile, take the trail on either side of it up to its top. You can stand on the columns and marvel at the fact that they are all nearly the same height. Under your feet, the tops of the columns look like honeycomb, or tiles that have been laid side by side. A bonus is that the view of the San Joaquin River from the top of the Postpile is quite lovely.

When you're ready, return to the base of the Postpile and continue past it on the well-marked trail to Rainbow Falls. You'll skirt in and out of the monument boundary and Inyo National Forest as the trail descends gently through lodgepole pines. The forest fire damage you'll notice was caused by a wildfire in 1992. The sound of the San Joaquin River is always apparent, although you won't see the stream again until you get close to the waterfall.

At a trail junction directing you straight to Rainbow Falls or left to Reds Meadows, continue straight. After a stream crossing on a two-log bridge, the path begins its final descent to Rainbow Falls. The anticipation mounts as you walk closer to a big channel in the river gorge. The gorge is cut very steeply, with almost no foliage on its walls—just stark, vertical rock. The roar of Rainbow Falls can be heard before you see it; the trail brings you in above the falls. If you're hiking in the late morning, you'll see Rainbow Fall's namesake—two big, beautiful rainbows arcing over the waterfall's mist. The angle of the midday sun on the water droplets creates the perfect recipe for a rainbow.

Keep walking past the lip of the falls. You'll see that Rainbow Falls's drop makes a grand statement, plunging 101 feet over hard rock. The trail has two viewing areas for the falls, about 30 yards apart. A path from the second viewpoint descends steep granite steps to the base of the falls. Ferns and moss grow on the rock at the cliff bottom; they benefit from the waterfall's constant mist.

Options

Just hike to Devils Postpile and back for a less than one mile round-trip. Or to see Rainbow Falls via a shorter, two-mile round-trip, start your hike farther down the road at Reds Meadows Resort. The trailhead is at a signed parking area just before you reach the resort.

Information and Contact

Between the hours of 7 A.M.–7 P.M. you must park your car and take the shuttle bus into the monument. The bus ride is free, but each visitor must purchase an access pass at the cost of $7 per adult; $4 per child. If you are planning to camp in the monument, you may drive your own car instead of riding the bus, but still you must purchase an access pass. For more information, contact Devils Postpile National Monument, P.O. Box 501, Mammoth Lakes, CA 93546, 760/934-2289, website: www.nps.gov/depo. Or contact Inyo National Forest, Mammoth Ranger Station and Visitor Center, P.O. Box 148, Mammoth Lakes, CA 93546, 760/924-5500, website: www.fs.fed.us/r5/inyo.

Directions

From the town of Mammoth Lakes near U.S. 395, take Highway 203 west for four miles, then turn right on Minaret Road (which is still Highway 203) and drive 4.5 miles to the Devils Postpile entrance kiosk, .25 mile beyond Mammoth Mountain Ski Area. Buy an access pass and board the bus here; disembark at the Devils Postpile Ranger Station.

14 EMERALD LAKE & SKY MEADOWS
Inyo National Forest, off U.S. 395 near Mammoth Lakes

Total distance: 4.0 miles round-trip   **Hiking time:** 1 hour

Type of trail: rolling terrain   **Best season:** June–October

There are so many day-hiking trails to choose from in the Mammoth Lakes Basin, you could easily visit for two weeks, hike a different trail every day, and not even scratch the surface. With Sierra scenery this lovely and accessible, it's difficult to decide even where to start.

You might as well start from the door of your tent, which means from the popular Cold Water Campground across the road from Lake Mary. One of the least busy trails in this beautiful region is the Emerald Lake Trail, which leads to a destination that is no longer much of a lake—every summer it slowly dries up, so that by August the lake is really just a pond. The lake itself isn't the reason for taking this trip, it's the myriad flowers that line the path and the banks of Cold Water Creek. Among the wide variety of flower species to be seen and admired, one standout is the tall, orange leopard lilies, a flower that is showy enough to be in a florist's shop. For flower lovers, a hike on this trail in July can be like a trip to heaven. Even after the blooming season has passed, the lodgepole pine forest and expansive meadows this trail visits are well worth the trip.

You climb from 8,900 feet at the trailhead to 9,300 feet at the lake, and then a few hundred feet more to the meadows beyond. In early summer, when the lake still has a fair share of water, it lives up to its name; it is a pretty emerald color. But its best feature is a gorgeous backdrop of craggy granite peaks rising straight up to the sky, framing the blue water. The lake (or pond, to be more precise) is small and C-shaped, and surrounded by big boulders—perfect spots for sunbathing or reading a book.

After you've caught your breath at Emerald Lake, continue on the trail that follows along its inlet stream. As you hike through the forest, you have a good chance of seeing belding ground squirrels—light brown squirrels that are often mistaken for chipmunks. They have a shrill whistle and are usually spotted running along the ground or sitting upright on their back haunches.

Three brief climbs lead you past small Gentian Meadow to the southeast edge of huge Sky Meadows, which is filled with wildflowers throughout the summer. Beyond the meadows, permanent snowfields decorate the granite cliffs of Mammoth Crest. The meadows are usually very wet, even in late summer, but try to find a dry spot where you can sit down and just breathe in the scenery.

Options
Several other trails lead from Cold Water Campground. Another easy trail that is about one mile in length is the trail to Heart Lake, which begins by the Mammoth Consolidated Mine Exhibit at the edge of the campground. Heart Lake is more of a lake than Emerald Lake, described above, and its trail also shows off myriad wildflowers.

Information and Contact
There is no fee. For more information, contact Inyo National Forest, Mammoth Ranger Station and Visitor Center, P.O. Box 148, Mammoth Lakes, CA 93546, 760/924-5500, website: www.fs.fed.us/r5/inyo.

Directions
From U.S. 395 in Lee Vining, drive 5 miles south to the Mammoth Lakes/Highway 203 cutoff. Take Highway 203 west for four miles, through

the town of Mammoth Lakes, to the intersection of Highway 203/Minaret Road and Lake Mary Road. Continue straight on Lake Mary Road and drive 3.8 miles to a fork just before Lake Mary; bear left and drive .6 mile to the Cold Water Campground turnoff on the left. Turn left and drive through the camp to the trailhead parking lot.

15 HOT CREEK GEOTHERMAL AREA TRAIL
Inyo National Forest, off U.S. 395 near Mammoth Lakes

Total distance: 2.0 miles round-trip   **Hiking time:** 1 hour

Type of trail: rolling terrain   **Best season:** June–October

The only problem with relaxing in a hot tub is that after a while, you always get too hot. But that rule doesn't apply at Hot Creek, where you soak in a natural hot spring while cold, river water flows past you and regulates your temperature. Sounds good, yes? But before you jump into the soothing waters, you should take a walk on one of the most unusual streamside trails in Northern California.

Your adventure starts with a three-mile drive on a dirt and gravel road to the Hot Creek Geothermal Area parking lot. There, you'll find changing rooms and restrooms for bathers, and interpretive signs explaining what makes this area bubble and boil. Looking down at Hot Creek from the parking area above, you glimpse the strange landscape of your upcoming hike: Clear and narrow Hot Creek curves gracefully through a canyon of sagebrush and volcanic rocks. Near its edges, two bright aqua pools are isolated

Hot Creek

from the stream's flow. Their full-boil status can be seen even from 100 feet above. The pools' steam rises ominously upward, warning visitors of their ferocious heat. Without Hot Creek flowing through these hot springs to cool their boil, the pools are liquid fire, unfit for humans or animals.

Hot Creek Geothermal Area is what remains from a 700,000-year-old volcanic eruption. The creek canyon is part of a 10- by 18-mile depression called a caldera, which was formed when eruptions blasted molted rock from beneath the earth's surface and caused the ground to sink hundreds of feet. The hot springs are the result of mountain runoff filtering down through the earth's crust and being heated by molten rock or magma, then being pushed back up to the surface in the caldera.

Posted signs and fences indicate where you can and can't roam, due to the unstable nature and unpredictable temperatures of this geologic area. Your dog may accompany you on your walk, but keep him leashed and under control to keep him safe. Children, too, should be watched very carefully, as their natural curiosity could lead them into dangerously hot water.

The hiking trail along Hot Creek is completely level, but to access it you must descend about 100 yards on a short paved trail from the parking lot. When you reach the canyon bottom, the first thing you'll notice is the pervasive smell of sulfur. Look around at the hot pools and vents, then cross the footbridge to the north side of the stream and walk to your left (west) on the dirt trail. A parallel trail is located on the south side of the stream, but it's usually occupied by fly-fishing enthusiasts. (If you walk the north side of the creek, you'll have less chance of disturbing anybody's casting. Fishing Hot Creek is hard enough as is.)

Although the hot springs area is quite popular with bathers, the crowds fade away as you walk westward along Hot Creek. You wander along a clear and shallow stream that is neatly bordered by fascinating volcanic formations, sagebrush, and thick reeds at the stream's edge. Ground squirrels and lizards scurry among the rocks, startled by your footsteps. Hot Creek's canyon is very narrow, and as you round each curve you gain spectacular views of the snowy Sierra Nevada straight ahead.

Walk as far as you like and then retrace your steps back to the hot springs area. If you've brought your bathing suit, you can finish up your walk with a dip in the warm waters in the middle of the river.

Options
You can extend your walk much farther along Hot Creek, as this trail leads almost three miles one-way toward the Hot Creek Fish Hatchery.

Information and Contact
There is no fee. For more information, contact Inyo National Forest,

Mammoth Ranger Station and Visitor Center, P.O. Box 148, Mammoth Lakes, CA 93546, 760/924-5500, website: www.fs.fed.us/r5/inyo.

Directions

From U.S. 395 in Lee Vining, drive 28 miles south, 2.8 miles past the Mammoth Lakes/Highway 203 cutoff, to the Hot Creek Fish Hatchery exit, where you turn left (northeast). Drive three miles on Hot Creek Hatchery Road, past the Fish Hatchery, to the Hot Creek Geothermal Area. Turn left into the parking lot. The trailhead is located by the restrooms.

© ANN MARIE BROWN

Index

*Page numbers in **bold** are references to maps.*

A

Abbotts Lagoon: 157
Alamere Falls: 164
Alec Canyon Trail: 227, 228
Alice Kent Trail: 166–169
Alpine Lake: 171
Alpine Pond: 215
Ancient Oaks Trail: 213
Angora Lakes Trail: 145–146
Ansel Adams Wilderness: **234,** 275
Anthony Chabot Regional Park: 198
Arroyo Hondo Creek: 165
Arroyo Trail: 166
Audubon Canyon Ranch/Bolinas Lagoon: 166

B

Balconies Caves: 243
Bale Grist Mill State Historic Park: 99, 100–101
Barnabe Peak: 170
Barth's Creek: 185
Basin Falls: 227–228
Bass Lake: 164
Bay Area Ridge Trail: 213
Bay View Loop: 193–196
Baylands Interpretive Center: 210
beach trails: author's top five 10–11; Bluff Trail 93–95; Coastal Trail 22–23, 28–30; Davenport Beach Walk 236–237; Ecological Staircase Nature Trail 84–86; Enderts Beach Trail 20–21; Fern Canyon Trail 24–26; Fort Ross Cove Trail 96–97; Headlands Trail 80–81; Indian Nature Trail 162–164; Johnstone Trail 162–164; Kehoe Beach Trail 156–158; La Laguna Trail 78–80; Lagoon Trail 191–193; Marshall Beach Trail 160–162; Old Landing Cove Trail 238–240; Rim Trail 34–35; Sequoia Audubon Trail 223–225; Shoreline Trail 178–181; Skunk Cabbage Trail 28–30; Yurok Loop 22–23
Bear Gulch Caves & Overlook: 242–244
Ben Johnson Trail: 190
Benstein Trail: 184–186
Big Basin Redwoods State Park: **152,** 225
Big Hendy Grove: 90–91
Big Sur area: 231–246, **234**
Big Tree Area: 38–39
Bill's Trail: 170
Bird Island: 192
Bird Rock: 155
Black Rock Falls: 227
BLM Folsom Resource Area: 114
Bluff Trail: 93–95
Bodega Bay: 155
Boiling Springs Lake: 69
Bolinas Lagoon Preserve: 166–167
Bon Tempe Lake Loop: 171–173
Bootjack Trail: 190
Borel Hill: 213
Bothe-Napa Valley State Park: **76,** Coyote Peak Trail 97–99; History Trail 100–101; Ritchey Canyon Trail 97–99
Briones Crest Trail: 197–198
Briones Regional Park: 196
Brokeoff Mountain: 70
Brooks Creek Trail: 203–205
Brooks Falls: 204
Brown Creek Trail: 26–28
Bull Creek Flats Trail: 38–39
Bumpass Hell Trail: 69–71
Burney Falls: 56
Butano Creek Trail: 223

C

Caltrans Vista Point: 213
Cantara Loop Trail: 46–47
Canyon Trail: 101–103
Carson Falls Trail: 176–178
Cascade Falls Trail (Lake Tahoe Basin Management Unit): 143–145
Cascade Falls Trail (Marin County Open Space District): 174–175
Cascade Lake: 143
Cascades, The: 66
Castle Dome: 54
Castle Lake Trail: 48–49
Castle Rock: 222
Castle Rock State Park: 220

Cataract Loop Trail: 184–186
Cathedral Trees Trail: 27
Chamberlain Creek Falls: 82–83
Chaos Crags: 63–65
Chaos Jumbles: 64
children, hiking with: 7–8; *see also* family trails
China Camp State Park: 178
Chinese Gulch Trail: 91–93
Clear Creek Vista Trail: 63
Cliff Lake: 67–69
clothing: 3–5
Clouds Rest: 213
Coal Creek Open Space Preserve: 213
Coastal Trail (Mount Tamalpais State Park): 186–188
Coastal Trail (Redwood National Park): 21, 22–23, 28–30
Cold Boiling Lake: 71
Cold Water Creek: 280
Condor Gulch Trail: 243, 244
Contour Trail: 228
Cook's Point Trail: 195
Coyote Peak Trail: 97–99
Crags Lake: 63–65
Crags Trail: 55
Crescent Beach Overlook: 20

D

D. L. Bliss State Park: 141
Daniels Nature Center: 215
Davenport Beach Walk: 236–237
Devil's Gulch Creek: 169–170

Devil's Punchbowl Trail: 86–87
Devils Postpile: 277–279
Devils Postpile National Monument: **234,** 277
Dewey Point: 263
Diamond Peak: 70
Discovery Trail: 90
Dog Lake Trail: 258–260
dogs, trails permitting: Angora Lakes Trail 145–146; Bay View Loop 193–196; Benstein Trail 184–186; Bon Tempe Lake Loop 171–173; Cantara Loop Trail 46–47; Carson Falls Trail 176–178; Cascade Falls Trail (Lake Tahoe Basin Management Unit) 143–145; Cascade Falls Trail (Marin County Open Space District) 174–175; Castle Lake Trail 48–49; Cataract Loop Trail 184–186; Chamberlain Creek Falls 82–83; Davenport Beach Walk 236–237; Dry Creek Falls 111–113; Emerald Lake Trail 279–281; Enderts Beach Trail 20–21; Fern Falls Trail 131–132; Frazier Falls Trail 132–134; Fuller Lake Trail 139–140; Halsey Falls Trail 127–129; Hat Creek Trail 58–60; Hedge Creek Falls Trail 52–53; Horsetail Falls Trail 147–148; Hot Creek Geothermal Area Trail 281–283; Kehoe Beach Trail

156–158; Lagoon Trail 191–193; Lagoon Trail Loop 196–198; Lake Shasta Overlook Trail 60–61; Lily Lake Trail 131–132; Loch Trail 240–242; Macdonald Trail 198–200; McCloud Falls Trail 50–52; Mickey O'Brien Trail 184–186; Old Briones Road 196–198; Palo Alto Baylands Nature Trail 210–211; Parker Lake Trail 275–276; Phyllis Ellman Trail 181–183; Pine Mountain Trail 176–178; Sardine Lakes Trail 136–137; Sky Meadows 279–281; Smith Lake Trail 129–131; Stevens Creek Trail 114–115; Waterfall Loop Trail 227–229; Wild Plum Loop Trail 138–139
Dry Creek Falls: 111–113

E

East Bay Skyline National Recreation Trail: 199
Ecological Staircase Nature Trail: 84–86
El Capitan: 267
El Corte de Madera Open Space Preserve: 208
El Dorado Mine: 62
Eldorado National Forest: **122,** 147
Emerald Lake Trail: 279–281
emergencies: 4
Emily Smith Bird Observation Point: 221
Enderts Beach Trail: 20–21

F

Fairy Falls: 111
Fairy Falls Trail: 113
Fallen Leaf Lake: 145
Falls Loop Trail: 88–89
Falls Trail: 56
False Klamath Cove: 22
False Klamath Rock: 23
family trails: Angora Lakes Trail 145–146; author's top five 9; Bear Gulch Caves & Overlook 242–244; Bumpass Hell Trail 69–71; Canyon Trail 101–103; Cascade Falls Trail 143–145; Enderts Beach Trail 20–21; Frazier Falls Trail 132–134; Fuller Lake Trail 139–140; Grass Lake Trail 124–125; Halsey Falls Trail 127–129; Hat Creek Trail 58–60; Headlands Trail 80–81; Hedge Creek Falls Trail 52–53; Horseshoe Lake Loop 214–216; Kehoe Beach Trail 156–158; Lukens Lake Trail 254–255; Madora Lake Trail 126–127; Sentinel Dome Trail 264–266; Sequoia Trail 225–227
Fern Canyon Nature Trail: 164–166
Fern Canyon Trail (Prairie Creek Redwoods State Park): 24–26
Fern Canyon Trail (Russian Gulch State Park): 88–89
Fern Creek Loop: 188–191
Fern Falls Trail: 131–132
first-aid: 4

Fisk Mill Cove: 93, 94
flashlights: 4
Flume Trail: 55
food: 3
Foothill Trail: 27
forest trails: Benstein Trail 184–186; Big Hendy Grove 90–91; Bon Tempe Lake Loop 171–173; Brown Creek Trail 26–28; Bull Creek Flats Trail 38–39; Canyon Trail 101–103; Cataract Loop Trail 184–186; Chamberlain Creek Falls 82–83; Coastal Trail 28–30; Coyote Peak Trail 97–99; Enderts Beach Trail 20–21; Falls Loop Trail 88–89; Fern Canyon Nature Trail 164–166; Fern Canyon Trail 88–89; Fern Creek Loop 188–191; Fuller Lake Trail 139–140; Griffin Trail 166–169; Hermit Hut Trail 90–91; History Trail 100–101; Indian Nature Trail 162–164; Johnstone Trail 162–164; Kent Trail 166–169; Lady Bird Johnson Grove 30–31; Limekiln Trail 244–246; Long Ridge Road & Trail 216–218; Lost Trail 188–191; Lukens Lake Trail 254–255; Mariposa Grove 270–272; Merced Grove 252–253; Mickey O'Brien Trail 184–186; Mill Creek Trail 61–63; North Loop Trail 166–169; Ocean View Trail

188–191; Peter's Creek Trail 216–218; Peterson Trail 18–19; Rhododendron Trail 26–28; Ritchey Canyon Trail 97–99; Root Creek Trail 54–56; Russian Ridge Loop 212–214; Sand Pond Interpretive Trail 134–136; Sequoia Trail 225–227; Simpson-Reed Trail 18–19; Skunk Cabbage Trail 28–30; Smith Lake Trail 129–131; South Fork Loop Trail 26–28; Stairstep Falls Trail 169–171; Tafoni Trail 208–210; Tall Trees Grove 31–33; Whittemore Gulch Trail 207–208
Fort Ross Cove Trail: 96–97
Fort Ross State Historic Park: 96
Frazier Creek: 133
Frazier Falls Trail: 132–134
Fuller Lake Trail: 139–140

G

geological interest, hikes with: author's top five 12; Bear Gulch Caves & Overlook 242–244; Bumpass Hell Trail 69–71; Chaos Crags 63–65; Davenport Beach Walk 236–237; Devil's Punchbowl Trail 86–87; Devils Postpile 277–279; Headlands Trail 86–87; Hot Creek Geothermal Area Trail 281–283; Lembert Dome Trail 260–262;

Mark Twain Scenic Tufa Trail 272–274; Rainbow Falls 277–279; Rim Trail 34–35; Root Creek Trail 54–56; Tafoni Trail 208–210

Glacier Point: **234,** 268–270

Goat Rock: 221–222

Gold Bluffs Beach: 25, 28

Gold County: 105–117, **108**

Golden Gate National Recreation Area: 191

Grass Lake Trail: 124–125

Grassy Lake: 128

Gray Eagle Creek: 128

Grey Rocks: 54

Griffin Trail: 166–169

H

Halsey Falls Trail: 127–129, 132

Hat Creek Trail: 58–60

Hatton Trail: 19

Hawk Trail: 213

Haypress Creek: 138

Hazelnut Trail: 206

Headlands Trail (MacKerricher State Park): 80–81

Headlands Trail (Russian Gulch State Park): 86–87

Headwaters Trail: 56–58

Heart Lake: 280

Heart's Desire Beach: 163

Hedge Creek Falls Trail: 52–53

Henderson Overlook: 167

Hendy Woods State Park: 90

Hermit Hut Trail: 90–91

High Peaks Trail and Overlook: 243–244

Highland Trail: 241

hiking tips: 3–8

Hillside Trail: 190

historic sites, trails with: Coastal Trail 22–23; Fern Canyon Nature Trail 164–166; Fort Ross Cove Trail 96–97; Headlands Trail 80–81; History Trail 100–101; Limekiln Trail 244–246; McGurk Meadow Trail 262–263; Mill Creek Trail 61–63; Phyllis Ellman Trail 181–183; Shoreline Trail 178–181; Tomales Bay Trail 158–160; Tomales Point Trail 154–156; Yurok Loop 22–23

History Trail: 100–101

Hog Island: 155

Home Creek: 25

Hookton Slough Trail: 36–37

Horseshoe Lake Loop: 214–216

Horsetail Falls Trail: 147–148

Hot Creek Geothermal Area Trail: 281–283

Humboldt Bay National Wildlife Refuge: 36

Humboldt Redwoods State Park: **16,** 38

IJK

Illilouette Fall & Creek: 269

Indian Beach: 163

Indian Creek Trail: 55

Indian Nature Trail: 162–164

Inyo National Forest: **234;** Emerald Lake Trail 279–281; Parker Lake Trail 275–276; Sky Meadows 279–281

Jackson Demonstration State Forest: **76,** 82

James Irvine Trail: 25

Jamison Falls/Jamison Lake: 125

Jedediah Smith Redwoods State Park: **16,** 18

Jepson Trail: 163–164

Johnstone Trail: 162–164

Jug Handle State Reserve: 84

Kehoe Beach Trail: 156–158

Kent Lake: 172

Kent Memorial: 190

Kent Trail: 166–169

kids, hiking with: 7–8; *see also* family trails

Kings Creek Falls: 65–67

Klamath Overlook: 23

Kruse Rhododendron State Reserve: 91

L

La Laguna Trail: 78–80

Lady Bird Johnson Grove: 30–31

Lagoon Creek: 23

Lagoon Trail: 191–193

Lagoon Trail Loop: 196–198

Laguna Point Seal Watching Station: 80

Lagunitas Lake: 172

Lake Britton: 56, 57

Lake Chabot: 199

Lake Cleone: 78–79

Lake Lagunitas: 173

Lake Shasta: 60–61

Lake Shasta Overlook Trail: 60–61

Lake Tahoe: **122** 141, 143

Lake Tahoe Basin Management Unit: Angora Lakes Trail 145–146; Cascade Falls Trail 143–144

lake trails: Angora Lakes Trail 145–146; author's

top five 11; Bon Tempe Lake Loop 171–173; Castle Lake Trail 48–49; Chaos Crags 63–65; Cliff Lake 67–69; Crags Lake 63–65; Dog Lake Trail 258–260; Emerald Lake Trail 279–281; Fern Falls Trail 131–132; Fuller Lake Trail 139–140; Grass Lake Trail 124–125; Horseshoe Lake Loop 214–216; La Laguna Trail 78–80; Lake Shasta Overlook Trail 60–61; Lily Lake Trail 131–132; Loch Trail 240–242; Lukens Lake Trail 254–255; Madora Lake Trail 126–127; Mark Twain Scenic Tufa Trail 272–274; Parker Lake Trail 275–276; Rubicon Trail 141–143; Sardine Lakes Trail 136–137; Shadow Lake 67–69; Sky Meadows 279–281; Smith Lake Trail 129–131; Tenaya Lake Trail 256–257; Terrace Lake 67–69

Lakes Basin: 127–128, 131, 132, 136

Lassen Geothermal System: 69

Lassen Volcanic National Park: **44,** Bumpass Hell Trail 69–71; Chaos Crags 63–65; Cliff Lakes 67–69; Crags Lake 63–65; Kings Creek Falls 65–67; Shadow Lake 67–69; Terrace Lake 67–69

Lembert Dome Trail: 260–262

Lighthouse Trail: 142

Lily Lake Trail: 131–132

Limekiln Creek/Limekiln Falls: 245

Limekiln State Park: 244

Limekiln Trail: 244–246

Little Castle Lake: 49

Little Hendy Grove: 91

Little Hot Springs Valley: 69

Little Jamison Creek: 125

Loch Lomond Recreation Area: 240

Loch Trail: 240–242

Long Lake: 128

Long Ridge Open Space Preserve: 216

Long Ridge Road/Long Ridge Trail: 216–218

Lost Trail: 188–191

Lukens Lake Trail: 254–255

M

Macdonald Trail: 198–200

MacKerricher State Park: **76,** Headlands Trail 80–81; La Laguna Trail 78–80

Madora Lake Trail: 126–127

Mammoth Lakes: 247–283, **250**

Manzanita Lake: 63

maps: **16, 44, 76, 108, 122, 152, 234, 250**

Maricich Lagoon: 196

Marin County Open Space District: 174

Marin Islands: 182

Marin Municipal Water District: Benstein Trail 184–186; Bon Tempe Lake Loop 171–173; Carson Falls Trail 176–178; Cataract Loop Trail 184–186; Mickey

O'Brien Trail 184–186; Pine Mountain Trail 176–178

Mariposa Grove of Big Trees: 270–272

Mark Twain Scenic Tufa Trail: 272–274

Marsh Trail: 195

Marshall Beach Trail: 160–162

Matt Davis Trail: 186–188

McArthur-Burney Falls Memorial State Park: 56

McCloud Falls Trail: 50–52

McCloud River: 50

McCloud River Preserve: 51

McClures Beach: 156

McGurk Meadow Trail: 262–263

Meadow Loop: 213

Mendocino area: 73–103, **76**

Merced Grove: 252–253

Mickey O'Brien Trail: 184–186

Mill Creek: 62–63, 100

Mill Creek Trail: 61–63

Mindego Trail: 213

Mono Lake Tufa State Reserve: 272

Montara Mountain Trail: 203–205

Morgan Springs: 69

Moses Spring Trail: 242

Mott Peak Trail: 197

Mount Conard: 70

Mount Diablo: 200–202

Mount Diablo State Park: **152,** 200

Mount Diller: 70

Mount Shasta: **44,** 51

Mount Tamalpais: 171

Mount Tamalpais State Park: 186

Mount Tehama: 70
Muir Woods National
 Monument: 188

NO

Navarro River: **76,** 90
Nibbs Knob Trail: 229
Nickel Creek Nature
 Trail: 20–21
Northern Sierra: 119–148,
 122
North Loop Trail:
 166–169
North Peak Trail: 200–203
North Pond Trail: 223
North Ridge Trail: 207
North Trail: 89
Ocean View Trail:
 188–191
Ohlone Bluff Trail: 240
Old Briones Road:
 196–198
Old Landing Cove Trail:
 238–240
Old Spenceville Road
 Trail: 113
Old Trout Farm Trail: 204
Olmsted Point: 256

P

Pacific Crest Trail: 55,
 56–58, 139
Palo Alto Baylands Na-
 ture Trail: 210–211
Palo Alto Baylands Pre-
 serve: 210
Panorama Trail: 268–270
Panum Crater: 274
Parker Lake Trail:
 275–276
Patrick's Point: 34–35
Patrick's Point State
 Park: **16,** 34
Pebble Beach: 163
Pelican Lake: 164
Pescadero Marsh Natural
 Preserve: 223

Peter's Creek Trail:
 216–218
Peterson Trail: 18–19
Petroglyph Rock: 183
Phillips Gulch Trail:
 91–93
Phoenix Lake: 172
Phyllis Ellman Trail:
 181–183
Picher Canyon: 168
Pilot Pinnacle: 70
Pine Mountain Trail:
 176–178
Pine Tree Trail: 198
Pinnacles National Monu-
 ment: **234,** 242
Pit River: **44,** 58
Plumas National Forest:
 44, 122; Fern Falls Trail
 131–132; Frazier Falls
 Trail 132–134, Grass
 Lake Trail 124–125;
 Halsey Falls Trail
 127–129; Lily Lake Trail
 131–132; Smith Lake
 Trail 129
Plumas-Eureka State
 Park: **122,** Grass Lake
 Trail 124–125; Madora
 Lake Trail 126–127
Point Pinole Regional
 Shoreline: 193
Point Reyes Bird Observa-
 tory: 164
Point Reyes National
 Seashore: **152,** Kehoe
 Beach Trail 156–158;
 Marshall Beach Trail
 160–162; Tomales Bay
 Trail 158–160; Tomales
 Point Trail 154–156
poison oak: 6–7
Pony Gate Trail: 102
Prairie Creek Redwoods
 State Park: **16,** Brown
 Creek Trail 26–28; Fern
 Canyon Trail 24;

Rhododendron Trail
 26–28; South Fork
 Loop 26–28
Prospectors Gap:
 200–203
Purisima Creek Red-
 woods Open Space Pre-
 serve: 207
Pyramid Creek Loop
 Trail: 147–148

QR

Rainbow Falls: 277–279
Rat Rock Cove Trail: 180
Redwood Creek: 32–33,
 188–190
Redwood Empire: 13–39,
 16
Redwood National Park:
 16, Coastal Trail 22–23,
 28–30; Enderts Beach
 Trail 20–21; Lady Bird
 Johnson Grove 30–31;
 Skunk Cabbage Trail
 28–30; Tall Trees Grove
 31–33; Yurok Loop
 22–23
Redwood Trail: 99
Rhododendron Trail:
 26–28
Ridge Trail: 213, 215
Ridge Trail Loop:
 220–222
Rim Trail: 34–35
Ring Mountain Preserve:
 181
Ritchey Canyon Trail:
 97–99
Ritchey Creek: 99
Rock Lake: 125
Rockefeller Loop Trail: 38
Rocky Point: 34–35
Rodeo Beach: 192
Rodeo Lagoon: 191
Root Creek Trail: 54–56
Rubicon Trail: 141–143
Rush Creek Falls: 116–117

Russian Gulch Falls: 89
Russian Gulch State
  Park: Devil's Punch-
  bowl Trail 86–87; Falls
  Loop Trail 88–89; Fern
  Canyon Trail 88–89;
  Headlands Trail 86–87
Russian Ridge Loop:
  212–214
Russian Ridge Open
  Space Preserve: 212

S

Sacramento area:
  105–117, **108**
Sacramento National
  Wildlife Refuge: 110
Sacramento River: **44,**
  46–47, **108**
Salmon Creek: 134
Salt Point State Park: **76,**
  93
Samuel P. Taylor State
  Park: 169
San Anselmo Creek: 174
Sanborn-Skyline County
  Park: 218
Sand Plant Beach:
  239–240
Sand Pond Interpretive
  Trail: 134–136
San Francisco Bay Area:
  149–229, **152**
San Joaquin River: **152,**
  277
San Pablo Bay: **152,**
  178–179, 194–195
San Pedro Valley County
  Park: Brooks Creek
  Trail 203; Montara
  Mountain Trail
  203–205; Valley View
  Trail 205–207
Santa Cruz area:
  231–246, **234**
Saratoga Gap Trail:
  220–222

Sardine Lakes Trail: 135,
  136–137
Sempervirens Falls: 225
Sentinel Dome Trail:
  264–266
Sentinel Rock: 94
Sequoia Audubon Trail:
  223–225
Sequoia Trail: 225–227
Shadow Lake: 67–69
Shadowbrook Trail: 226
Shasta-Hat Creek County
  Park: 58
Shasta-Trinity National
  Forest: **44,** Cantara
  Loop Trail 46–47; Cas-
  tle Lake Trail 48–49;
  Lake Shasta Overlook
  Trail 60–61; McCloud
  Falls Trail 50–52
Shingle Falls: 111
Shorebird Loop Trail: 37
Shoreline Trail: 178–181
Sierra Buttes: 135, 136,
  138
Sifford Lakes: 66–67
Simpson-Reed Trail:
  18–19
Skunk Cabbage Trail:
  28–30
Sky Meadows: 279–281
Skyline Ridge Open
  Space Preserve: 214
Skyline Trail: 218–220
Smith Lake Trail: 129–131
Sonoma Creek: 101
Sonoma Creek Falls: 102
South Cove: 94
South Fork Loop Trail:
  26–28
South Fork Trail: 99
South Yuba Indepen-
  dence Trail: 116–117
South Yuba River State
  Park: 116
Spenceville Wildlife Area:
  111–113

Stairstep Falls Trail:
  169–171
Stevens Creek Trail:
  114–115
Stinson Beach: 168
Strawberry Beach: 240
streamside hikes: 11
Sugarloaf Ridge State
  Park: **76,** 101
Sulphur Works: 69
Summit Meadows Trail:
  222
Summit Rock: 218–220
sunscreen: 4
Swanson Creek: 227
Sweetbriar Falls: 53

T

Tafoni Trail: 208–210
Taft Point Trail: 266–268
Tahoe National Forest:
  122, Fuller Lake Trail
  139–140; Sand Pond In-
  terpretive Trail 134–136;
  Sardine Lakes Trail 135,
  136–137; Wild Plum
  Loop Trail 138–139
Tall Trees Grove: 31–33
Ten Mile Coastal Trail: 79
Ten-Mile Beach: 157
Tenaya Lake Trail:
  256–257
Terminal Geyser: 69
Terrace Lake: 67–69
Three Mile Beach: 240
ticks: 6–7
tips for hiking: 3–8
Tomales Bay: **152,**
  162–163
Tomales Bay State Park:
  162–164
Tomales Bay Trail:
  158–160
Tomales Point Trail:
  154–156
Toyon Canyon Trail: 198
trail maps: 3

Triple Falls: 227, 228
Turtle Back Nature Trail: 179
Turtle Rock: 182

UV

Upper Falls: 228
Uvas Canyon County Park: 227
Valley View Trail: 205–207
vistas, trails with: author's top five 10; Bear Gulch Caves & Overlook 242–244; Brooks Creek Trail 203–205; Bumpass Hell Trail 69–71; Castle Lake Trail 48–49; Chaos Crags 63–65; Coastal Trail 186–188; Coyote Peak Trail 97–99; Crags Lake 63–65; Ecological Staircase Nature Trail 84–86; Griffin Trail 166–169; Kent Trail 166–169; Lagoon Trail Loop 196–198; Lake Shasta Overlook Trail 60–61; Lembert Dome Trail 260–262; Long Ridge Road & Trail 216–218; Matt Davis Trail 186–188; Montara Mountain Trail 203–205; North Loop Trail 166–169; North Peak Trail 200–203; Old Briones Road 196–198; Panorama Trail 268–270; Peter's Creek Trail 216–218; Phyllis Ellman Trail 181–183; Ridge Trail Loop 220–222; Rim Trail 34–35; Ritchey Canyon Trail 97–99; Root Creek

Trail 54–56; Rubicon Trail 141–143; Russian Ridge Loop 212–214; Saratoga Gap Trail 220–222; Sentinel Dome Trail 264–266; Skyline Trail 218–220; South Yuba Independence Trail 116–117; Summit Rock 218–220; Tafoni Trail 208–210; Taft Point Trail 266–268; Tomales Point Trail 154–156; Valley View Trail 205–207; Whittemore Gulch Trail 207–208; Wild Plum Loop Trail 138–139

W

Wades Lake: 125
water: 3
Waterfall Loop Trail: 227–229
waterfalls, trails with: author's top five 9; Brooks Creek Trail 203–205; Canyon Trail 101–103; Carson Falls Trail 176–178; Cascade Falls Trail (Lake Tahoe Basin Management Unit) 143–145; Cascade Falls Trail (Marin County Open Space District) 174–175; Chamberlain Creek Falls 82–83; Devils Postpile 277–279; Dry Creek Falls 111–113; Falls Loop Trail 88–89; Fern Canyon Trail 88–89; Fern Falls Trail 131–132; Frazier Falls Trail 132–134; Grass Lake Trail 124–125; Halsey Falls Trail

127–129; Headwaters Trail 56–58; Hedge Creek Falls Trail 52–53; Horsetail Falls Trail 147–148; Kings Creek Falls 65–67; Lily Lake Trail 131–132; Limekiln Trail 244–246; McCloud Falls Trail 50–52; Montara Mountain Trail 203–205; Pacific Crest Trail 56–58; Panorama Trail 268–270; Pine Mountain Trail 176–178; Rainbow Falls 277–279; Ridge Trail Loop 220–222; Saratoga Gap Trail 220–222; Sequoia Trail 225–227, South Yuba Independence Trail 116–117; Stairstep Falls Trail 169–171; Stevens Creek Trail 114–115; Waterfall Loop Trail 227–229
Waters Gulch Trail: 61
Wedding Rock: 34–35
Wetlands Walk: 110–111
wheelchair-accessible trails: Big Hendy Grove 90–91; Frazier Falls Trail 132–134; Headlands Trail 80–81; Hermit Hut Trail 90–91; Horseshoe Lake Loop 214–216; La Laguna Trail 78–80; Rim Trail 34–35; South Yuba Independence Trail 116–117; Valley View Trail 205–207
Whiskeytown National Recreation Area: 61
White Cloud Falls: 144
Whittemore Gulch Trail: 207–208

Wild Plum Loop Trail: 138–139
Wilder Ranch State Park: 238
wildflowers, trails with: Bear Gulch Caves & Overlook 242–244; Bluff Trail 93–95; Bon Tempe Lake Loop 171–173; Brooks Creek Trail 203–205; Brown Creek Trail 26–28; Cantara Loop Trail 46–47; Cascade Falls Trail 143–145; Chinese Gulch Trail 91–93; Coastal Trail 186–188; Coyote Peak Trail 97–99; Davenport Beach Walk 236–237; Devils Postpile 277–279; Dog Lake Trail 258–260; Dry Creek Falls 111–113; Ecological Staircase Nature Trail 84–86; Emerald Lake Trail 279–281; Fort Ross Cove Trail 96–97; Hat Creek Trail 58–60; Headwaters Trail 56–58; History Trail 100–101; Horseshoe Lake Loop 214–216; Kehoe Beach Trail 156–158; Lagoon Trail Loop 196–198; Long Ridge Road & Trail 216–218; Lukens Lake Trail 254–255; Macdonald Trail 198–200; Matt Davis Trail 186–188; McGurk Meadow Trail 262–263; Montara Mountain Trail 203–205; North Peak Trail 200–203; Old Briones Road 196–198; Old Landing Cove Trail 238–240; Pacific Crest Trail 56–58; Parker Lake Trail 275–276; Peter's Creek Trail 216–218; Phillips Gulch Trail 91–93; Phyllis Ellman Trail 181–183; Rainbow Falls 277–279; Rhododendron Trail 26–28; Ridge Trail Loop 220–222; Rim Trail 34–35; Ritchey Canyon Trail 97–99; Russian Ridge Loop 212–214; Saratoga Gap Trail 220–222; Sky Meadows 279–281; South Fork Loop Trail 26–28; South Yuba Independence Trail 116–117; Stairstep Falls Trail 169–171; Stevens Creek Trail 114–115; Tafoni Trail 208–210; Tall Trees Grove 31–33; Tenaya Lake Trail 256–257; Tomales Point Trail 154–156; Valley View Trail 205–207; Whittemore Gulch Trail 207–208
wildlife-viewing trails: author's top five 10; basic tips 5–6; Bay View Loop 193–196; Bear Gulch Caves & Overlook 242–244; Benstein Trail 184–186; Bon Tempe Lake Loop 171–173; Cataract Loop Trail 184–186; Coastal Trail 186–188; Devil's Punchbowl Trail 86–87; Dry Creek Falls 111–113; Fern Canyon Nature Trail 164–166; Fern Canyon Trail 24–26; Fern Creek Loop 188–191; Griffin Trail 166–169; Hat Creek Trail 58–60; Headlands Trail (MacKerricher State Park) 80–81; Headlands Trail (Russian Gulch State Park) 86–87; Headwaters Trail 56–58; Hookton Slough Trail 36–37; Indian Nature Trail 162–164; Johnstone Trail 162–164; Kehoe Beach Trail 156–158; Kent Trail 166–169; La Laguna Trail 78–80; Lagoon Trail 191–193; Lost Trail 188–191; Madora Lake Trail 126–127; Mark Twain Scenic Tufa Trail 272–274; Marshall Beach Trail 160–162; Matt Davis Trail 186–188; Mickey O'Brien Trail 184–186; North Loop Trail 166–169; North Peak Trail 200–203; Ocean View Trail 188–191; Old Landing Cove Trail 238–240; Pacific Crest Trail 56–58; Palo Alto Baylands Nature Trail 210–211; Sand Pond Interpretive Trail 134–136; Sequoia Audubon Trail 223–225; Shoreline Trail 178–181; Tomales Bay Trail 158–160; Tomales Point Trail 154–156; Valley View Trail 205–207; Wetlands Walk 110–111
Wine Country: 73–103, **76**

XYZ

Yosemite Falls: 265
Yosemite National Park: **234,** Dog Lake Trail 258–260; Lembert Dome Trail 260–262; Lukens Lake Trail 254–255; Mariposa Grove of Big Trees 270–272; McGurk Meadow Trail 262–263; Merced Grove 252–253; Panorama Trail 268–270; Sentinel Dome Trail 264–266; Taft Point Trail 266–268; Tenaya Lake Trail 256–257
Yurok Loop: 22–23

Notes

Notes

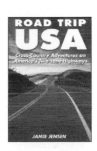